To Dom, my close
friend and goju Black
Belt. Train hard
always, it is the fountain
of youth.
(NANA KAROBII YA OKII !)

ALL THE BEST!

BUDO

and the
BADGE

Exploits of a Jersey Cop

道

Patrick J. Ciser

abbott press®

A DIVISION OF WRITER'S DIGEST

Budo and the Badge
Exploits of a Jersey Cop

All comments and opinions herein are solely that of the author and are not that of the Clifton Police Department or anyone else named in this book. All stories are true with some names changed or omitted, to protect the privacy of those involved.

Abbott Press books may be ordered through booksellers or by contacting:

Abbott Press
1663 Liberty Drive
Bloomington, IN 47403
www.abbottpress.com
Phone: 1-866-697-5310

ISBN: 978-1-4582-0295-6 (sc)
ISBN: 978-1-4582-0297-0 (hc)
ISBN: 978-1-4582-0296-3 (ebk)

Library of Congress Control Number: 2012906279

Printed in the United States of America

Abbott Press rev. date: 04/11/2012

Cover by Nes
Website: www.wickedimagestattoo.com

This book is dedicated to the nearly 19,000 United States Law Enforcement officers, including Clifton's John Samra, who made the ultimate sacrifice, while protecting their communities across America.

Patrolman John Samra
Clifton Police Department
1/8/62 - 11/21/03

Hanshi Edward Kaloudis
Koeikan Karate Pioneer
Thank you for your guidance both in, and out of the dojo.

O'Sensei Brian Frost
1952 – 2009
You were the only one, who truly knew me.

ACKNOWLEDGMENTS

Ms. Miriam Santana, skilled black belt and trusted seito (student).
Thank you for your tireless efforts in making this book a reality.

Stefanie, my wonderful daughter, thank you
for your final editing of this work.

CONTENTS

"It is not the critic who counts, not the man who points out how the strong man stumbled, or where the doers of deeds could have done them better. The credit belongs to the man who is actually in the arena, whose face is marred by the dust and sweat and blood, who strives valiantly, who errs and comes up short again and again, who knows the great enthusiasms, the great devotions and spends himself in a worthy cause... Who at the best knows in the end the triumph of high achievement and who at the worst if he fails at least fails while daring greatly, so that his place shall never be with those cold and timid souls who know neither victory nor defeat."

Theodore Roosevelt

PREFACE

Law enforcement has always peaked interest in the media and entertainment industry; and why not? Crime concerns everyone while entertaining us, as well. From over the top *Die Hard* movies (Willis) to the television reality show *Cops*, crime shows are watched by millions who want to be entertained, with fictional depictions of what police work encompasses. But sometimes people want to be told a true story, while getting a feel for what police officers actually go through while protecting their community. Television sound bites and newspaper headlines only touch the surface, concerning real life and death dramas which take place in cities and towns all across America.

Over the last 40 years of competing in National and International Karate Championships, along with my career in law enforcement, I've been the subject of many local newspaper stories. These stories have caused many family members and friends to ask me about details, as well as what I was feeling, at the time of some of these intense encounters. Taking knives and guns off of people, even shooting a gun out of an actor's (suspect) hand, caused many to say, "Ciser, you could write a book!"

As a result, this work began as a bunch of stories put together at the behest of my Sensei (Teacher), Brian Frost, and others, who believed in me. After reading newspaper accounts that I sent him over the years, Sensei told me that he sometimes lived vicariously through me. Yet if it weren't for his teachings, along with Sensei Ed Kaloudis over the years, I never could have done many of the things depicted in this book.

As I wrote about one event, it caused me to recall similar events that I experienced over the years. That is why the chapters are written with a different theme in mind, rather than a chronological account. This structure actually worked out well, as the reader can skip around and first read chapters that interest them the most.

As far as the Budo ("Martial Way" or martial Arts of Japan) part of the book, I tend to get philosophical in my lessons, whether overt, or implied. Martial artists, more than most, will particularly enjoy the end of chapter quotes throughout, as most of these encompass Eastern thought. The Japanese kanji, or character used throughout the book for spacing thoughts, means "Do" (the Way), which has a deep philosophical meaning. It is used for instance in Budo, Karate-Do, Judo, Aikido, Kendo and also Bushido, "The Way of the Warrior." There are other examples of "Do," including "Dojo," the place where we learn the way.

My approach to law enforcement was only one "way" to handle various situations (There are many paths to the mountain...). I always believed that good people, including police officers who are sworn to protect and serve, should go home safe at the end of the day. As you read each chapter, you'll see that I'm not a big fan of "political correctness," nor do I shed a tear for those that perpetrate crimes upon the weak, or the unarmed. I believe in advanced training for police officers, giving them the skills and confidence to save a life, on either side of the law, when the opportunity presents itself.

Throughout my career people would say things like, "Wow, you're like Chuck Norris!" While I have the deepest respect and admiration for tournament champion and actor Chuck Norris, it is he who plays guys like me in the movies. As I recall, there was no one around to yell "Cut!" when I was confronted with armed adversaries.

While everyone can enjoy reading about these real life events, it is the young police officer who will read and also learn, throughout the book, how they can become better officers as they perform their manifold duties. Veteran officers will be reminded of the many times that they too, stepped up in the defense of others. Martial Artists, whether black belts, or newcomers to the study of Budo, may particularly enjoy the Karate Do chapters interpreted throughout and relate them to their training.

This is my story but there are parallels to what many cops, in many communities, go through in America on a daily basis. After 9/11, many people, especially in the greater New York metropolitan area, including Clifton, New Jersey, showed appreciation for all that we do. That appreciation has slowly waned, as police officers today, are many times, vilified in the press.

So here we go; I'm not a professional writer but I insisted on writing this myself. This, in an attempt to let you share my feelings, through my eyes; the eyes of a street cop!

Lieutenant Patrick J. Ciser, (Ret.)
City of Clifton Police Department

HOPE AVENUE

It was summertime, in the year 1991. I liked summer working the crossover 2000–0400 (8pm-4am) "power" shift. I hated the cold then, as I hate it now. It's funny, but with all the coast-to-coast and world traveling I've done, I still come back to New Jersey to tolerate the winter. I guess that living 20 minutes from New York City and Newark Liberty Airport has its advantages. On this night, like so many others, I was right where I wanted to be, assigned to the east side of Clifton. A couple of post cars (marked patrol units) were dispatched to Hope Avenue, in the city's "Botany Village" section. Dispatch reported that there was an erratic male yelling, screaming and threatening passersby. Car #1, along with a two-man Car, #8, were assigned. Like a lot of good cops in Clifton, I took it upon myself to roll in and stand by, just in case those units needed further assistance. I arrived, finding the officers exiting their radio cars.

"You guys need any help?!" I shouted from my driver's seat.

Officer Robert Little, a rookie then, replied, "No, I think we're okay, Pat."

I really took the old "brothers in blue" concept seriously. Whenever I thought things could get rough, or go bad, I believed it was my responsibility to step up and help. Unfortunately, some guys believed I was overbearing at times. One of our dispatchers, Matt Failla, who was always of great help to me, came up with a nickname for me; "The Colonel." As a patrolman, and not having rank, I guess I came across at times like I was in charge. Some cops thought over the years, I was a natural-born leader, while others at times, probably thought I was an arrogant jerk (okay, maybe the correct word wasn't jerk). The truth of the matter is that I always wanted everyone to be safe.

道

There's an old saying that I picked up from the old *Kung Fu* TV series. A man is but three things: What he thinks he is; what others think he is; and what he really is. Don't ever worry if everyone doesn't like you. Don't be afraid of making the hard choices. Always stand for what you believe in and remember that if everyone likes you, it may be because you're a weak leader.

道

Getting back to Hope Avenue, I had started to drive away toward Highland Avenue when I heard over the radio, "Hey Pat, can you come back here a minute?" Of course, I immediately turned around and pulled up to the scene, where I could hear what seemed to be, a lunatic going berserk. I got out of the car and looked up to the second floor veranda. A shirtless Peruvian man, I believe he was, had two very large butcher knives. He was screaming at the top of his lungs that he was going to kill everyone. I thought, *Hmmm, that can't be good.* The on-scene officers were already calling for a sergeant and additional units to respond. Officers were standing behind their cars with guns drawn. So, I, along with the other officers, monitored his actions and blocked off the area from vehicle and pedestrian traffic while waiting for the sergeant. Sergeant Mike Jupin arrived and was quickly brought up to speed, as was my close friend; Billy Gibson. The sergeant told us that the watch commander was sending our negotiator. Detective George O'Brien arrived a short time later. George was a seasoned veteran with training in interviewing, interrogation and hostage negotiating.

Once all the additional help was on scene, I was feeling a little useless. Finding out the Peruvian's name was Hugo, George attempted to start a dialogue, to no avail. Hugo yelled again, "I'm going to kill everyone, and then I am going to kill myself!" With that, he pressed one of the knives against his neck and drew a little blood.

I now walked up to Gibson, who was in a pretty good position to "cap" him, if necessary. Billy was standing behind his car with his gun drawn pointing it at the suspect. With my hands on my gun belt in a very nonchalant fashion, I stood next to Bill and said, "Hey Bill, you ah, gonna shoot this guy?"

He answered, "If I have to, yeah." Bill was usually very serious and sometimes quite intense.

I asked him, "Do you think he's a threat up there?"

He replied, "Yeah. He can throw those knives."

I said, "Yeah, but then you could duck. Besides, how would it look in the papers tomorrow if you shoot that guy off the veranda? How about we relax a little until they really need us?" Billy then lowered his gun while remaining vigilant.

Hugo now pulled out a cigarette lighter and threatened to burn down the building. The building was a four-family duplex with two apartments side-by-side downstairs and two more upstairs. The upstairs apartments had a veranda, each with a sliding glass door. There were drapes around the double door, which Hugo threatened to ignite. A fire truck was now called to respond and stand by with an ambulance that was already on scene. I was now getting downright bored as I watched the action from across the street. There was a nice lady living across the street, who asked me if I wanted anything, so I accepted some cold water, as I sat on the steps. Sgt. Jupin, a heavy smoker, must have been looking for a second pack by now as he paced past me.

I stood up and said, "Hey Sarge, can I talk to you a minute?" He stepped closer as I continued. "Look, I know we have to be nice guys and try to negotiate with this asshole, but when we're done, and he

3

still wants to kill everyone, I'm gonna go up there and shove those knives up his ass."

Jupin looked at me a little surprised and said, "You can do that?"

I said, "Sure, just let me know when you'll let me kick in that door and go up. In the meantime, I'll just wait here sipping my water." The sergeant then gave me the ole, "Sure Pat, whatever you say "look" and walked away.

I sat down and contemplated, *how should I take this guy out? After all, they're pretty large knives, and he is a highly erratic individual.* I then asked a guy who lived a couple of doors down if he, or anyone else, had an old-fashioned metal garbage can with a cover that had a handle. He replied, "Sure, my neighbor has one."

I said, "Great! Can you ask him if I could borrow the cover?"

He said he would be right back.

My plan was simple, if I didn't have to shoot him. I don't like shooting people unless they're shooting at me. My good friend from California, Sensei Jack Sabat, gave me a nice present that I always kept in my radio car. Jack Sabat (Koeikan Karate 7th Dan) was UFC's Chuck "The Iceman" Liddell's sensei (Teacher) back in the day and the chief Koeikan instructor on the left, or is it west, coast. The present he gave me was a black police baton known as the "Hide-a-Chuck." It was cleverly made with two partially hollowed sticks the thickness of a common night stick. The "sticks" were connected by a steel cable making them "nunchaku." However, you could hide the cable and twist them together so as to look like a single- cylinder night stick or baton. I was told that the weapon could be effective as a baton, without twisting the sticks apart, or nunchaku.

道

In the past, I would arrive with lights and siren to large fights, usually bars spilling out, and jump out with my nunchaku. Whenever I arrived alone with difficult odds, I would do my best Bruce Lee

4

impression, scattering people in every direction. As a brown belt in the early 1970's, I used to do demonstrations with my nunchaku. I would swing two at a time blindfolded which wasn't as hard as it sounds. If you're skilled enough, it doesn't matter if you can see or not. I even performed this demonstration at the Poliedro arena in Caracas, Venezuela.

As a cop, my theatrics broke up a minimum of four large fights. The fights took place at Krackers Nightclub, Joey's Nightclub, a bar down on South Parkway and River Road, but I can't recall the name, and one year at the Clifton City Picnic, off Main Avenue. The only problem at the South Parkway bar; was that after they all fled, they crossed into the City of Passaic; and, unfortunately, continued to brawl, killing one person.

The Clifton detectives, who were working with Passaic, called me at home, waking me up after working midnights, to question me further about Clifton's end of it. I said, "Look, I can only keep the peace in Clifton, and I was alone. Back-up didn't arrive until it was over. Cops can't be omnipresent."

道

Let's get back to Hope Avenue and those knives. I retrieved my baton from my vehicle and then met up with the resident with the tin garbage can cover. Sitting back down across the street, I could tell that Hugo couldn't be reasoned with. I was just hoping that I'd get the "okay" soon since I was getting hungry. You wouldn't like me when I'm hungry!

Suddenly, Hugo went into another rage, screaming at the top of his lungs, and set the drapes on fire. I yelled, "That's it! I'm done!" I ran across the street to the front door while the fire department hit him with their hose. The only problem was that they used a small hose and had it hooked up to the truck and not the hydrant. Hugo now raised his hands and knives over his head screaming, taking whatever water pressure they had on his bare chest. I kicked in the front door, and flew up the steps to the second floor. Clutching my baton in my right hand and my "shield" in my left, I kicked Hugo's apartment door open. He apparently heard the door fly open as he turned into the apartment. There was a couch between the two of us. Without missing a beat, I kept my momentum moving forward as I leaped over the couch. As I landed, we were within reach of one another, with the open sliding glass door just behind Hugo. As my feet hit the ground, I slammed my "shield" down over the knives as he tried to lunge forward. My nightstick simultaneously came down on his front hairline. You could hear a distinctive cracking sound as the top half of my stick flew through the air. I thought, *Shit*, as I looked at this tiny piece of wood still in my hand. Hugo didn't fall, as I thought he might. He didn't even drop his knives. He did, however, look stunned for just a second or two. I quickly dropped my shield and what was left of my baton and grabbed his head. In Aikido, they call this "beautiful violence;" I grabbed and pushed his jaw to his right with my left hand, while grabbing the top of his head for stability. I was now rotating his head so fast that his whole body had to follow. He spun around and crashed to the ground so fast and hard, that he could no longer hold onto the knives. In addition to this, he absolutely looked dazed, making it quite easy to cuff him. As I cuffed him, more officers came up the stairs behind me, and also the fire escape, to the veranda where Hugo threatened officers. The fire department extinguished the flames as I turned Hugo over to Billy to take down to the street.

Many times, when officers do something like this, there aren't a lot of witnesses. In this case, there were plenty. Everyone, from the cops and the firemen, to the area residents, made me feel great. Billy, after searching the prisoner again for contraband, placed him in my car's cage. We then took Hugo to the hospital for a couple of stitches to his head and Motrin, I'm sure. As I pulled away from Hope Avenue, Billy looked at me and said, "Why do you do such crazy shit!" I looked back and said, "Because someday, this is gonna make a great story." I thought I meant for my grandchildren, certainly not a book.

"One who is well prepared for anything that arises,
will never rashly draw his sword in haste."

Ueshiba Morihei (Founder of Aikido)

ASH STREET

The year was 1990 and I was working a two-man unit on the 2000-0400 (8pm-4am) power shift. Billy Gibson was my partner and a great partner at that. It was pretty early in the shift when the dispatcher, Donna Atkinson, asked us and the eastside sergeant to give her a phone call.

Whenever there was a lot of detail available and needed for safety purposes, the dispatcher didn't want to tie up the air (radio). Dispatcher Atkinson explained that a doctor called in about a male patient, who he had been treating, was in a bad car accident and was depressed. The man was in bed in his apartment and needed to talk with someone since he felt suicidal. The man told the doctor that he would leave his apartment door ajar but the doctor suspected that the man *might* have a weapon so he didn't want to go there. Billy and I met the sergeant on scene in front of the EDP's (Emotionally Disturbed Person) home.

It was agreed that the sergeant and I would go inside to speak to this individual as Billy checked for a fire escape outside his second floor window. The sergeant, who let's say wasn't one of the toughest cops in Clifton, accompanied me upstairs. Sure enough, we found the apartment door ajar, as we cautiously entered. As we called out "Police!" we heard a man say that he was in the bedroom. We approached the bedroom and peeked in as the door was half open. The sergeant was positioned in front of me to my right. He pushed the door open and stood in the doorway as I stayed halfway behind the door jam and wall. The alleged suicidal man, "Jim," (not his real name) told us, "Get the fuck out of my house!" The sergeant tried to tell him that we were there to help. Jim didn't want to hear it and told the sergeant that he had a gun under the sheet. With that, the sergeant and I took a step back as I drew my Beretta.

Both of us now stood behind the wall as the sergeant told me that he didn't believe the guy had a gun. "He's BS'ing," said the sergeant, "and I'm going to pull the sheet down and prove it." You see, when the actor (actor, Title 2C for suspect) told the sergeant that he had a gun, he, while lying in bed with a sheet over him, raised his hand under the sheet. Until the sheet was removed, you couldn't tell if there was a gun in his hand or not. The position of the bed put the actor's feet closest to us, while his head, resting on a couple of pillows, was furthest away.

When the sergeant further stated that he was going to enter the room and pull the sheet off of his hand, I strongly told him, "Don't!" I explained to him that we knew nothing about this guy; he might really be nuts, or at least severely depressed. I said, "Let's talk to him while taking cover; we're in no hurry." The sergeant, wanting to show me that *he* was in charge, turned and brazenly entered the door and approached the foot of the bed. Even worse was the fact that he didn't first draw his weapon, and stood right between the actor and me, blocking my line of fire. Still having my Beretta ready to go, I remained in a cover position in back of the left side door jam attempting to take aim. Unfortunately for the sergeant, I would have to wait for his body to drop to return fire. The sergeant grabbed the sheet near the actor's feet and pulled it off his raised hand. This action immediately revealed a small caliber handgun, now pointing at the sergeant's face. It wasn't until the sergeant turned and quickly exited the bedroom that I could identify the presence of a gun and not some other object. The sergeant grabbed the door handle and closed the door about three quarters behind him. He looked like he saw a ghost! The sergeant was now as white as the sheet that covered the gun. I looked at him and said, "Bad idea, Sarge." While this was going on, Officer Gibson entered the apartment. Billy took a position near the door, to monitor the actor with his gun drawn and at a ready position.

I pulled the sergeant aside and told him, "Get me the body bunker." The body bunker was a bullet proof, Plexiglas shield that you hold in front of yourself as you approach a dangerous person or situation.

If you're not a cop, you've probably seen them on television. All of the SWAT units have them. Get me the body bunker and I'll walk up to him and take that gun out of his hand, I explained!

The sergeant said, "You can do that?"

I replied, "Get me the shield!"

The sergeant then asked headquarters for a couple of additional officers and to have someone stop at the headquarters armory to pick up the body bunker.

Clifton's Tactical Response Team, which was our name for our SWAT guys, didn't really like how I handled this situation. You see, because I had a reputation of being a cowboy, or a lone wolf, I could never be assigned to the TRT. I think because of cliques and politics, they may have missed out. I could have taught them a few things.

道

I remember once in Paterson, when I was assigned to the Passaic County Narcotics Task Force, we were having a meeting about a fortified drug dealer's apartment. The CI (Confidential Informant) told us that his door had many dead bolts and it was a very heavy door. So when it was discussed if we should use a ram or a hydraulic door opener, I said, "I'll kick through the wall next to the door. I'll bet I get in before you." I was familiar with the construction and knew it was only sheet rock. I worked construction with my father and brother, Mike, who were carpenters, and kicked in many walls during demolitions. Hell, Mike, who is also a black belt, and I, kicked through lath and plaster walls. The two-by-fours, if you hit them on an angle, were no match for a good yoko geri (side kick). I sometimes like to think outside the box.

道

The Tactical Response Team had to make a big production out of everything. It wasn't exactly "Columbine." They would have had Billy and I back out, giving up a great position, while they surround the building and start over. Last time I checked, I took an oath to do my job too.

Billy engaged Jim in conversation as he stood guard at the door. Jim didn't want to hear it. The sergeant, who looked like he needed a break, volunteered to wait downstairs for the body bunker. I asked Billy to step away so that I could talk to the actor. I pushed the door open to the left, as I maintained a cover position holstering my Beretta. I explained that we were there to help and no one needed to get hurt. I stuck my hands in the doorway while peeking inside. "Look," I said, "I have no gun out. Why don't you lower yours?" I told him that my first name is Pat and asked for his. The actor, Jim, started talking over me and told me to "Get Out" of his apartment or he was going to start shooting. I was in back of the left side door jam, and by pushing the door open behind the wall, I now hoped that the door and the sheet rock wall would be cover enough against his small caliber handgun. It might have been wishful thinking.

I wasn't wearing a bullet proof vest that night; I rarely wore one. They were so heavy and hot and they always slowed me down in a foot chase or bar fight. I couldn't help but think on this night, *what an asshole you are Ciser!* So, vest or not, I always thought that I could reason with most people, so I kept talking.

He, on the other hand, started a countdown. "10, 9, 8, 7, 6..."

I thought, *hmmm, this can't be good.* Sure enough, when he said one, I pulled my hands back and heard pow! the gun went off. Billy and I agreed that the nice guy stuff was over. At least that was my original plan. Jim then yelled out, "The shotgun's next!"

Jim's doctor told us that Jim was mostly confined to his bed. It came as a surprise when he started yelling and began to slowly get out of bed. Billy and I agreed not to retreat. Billy, the great cop and friend that he is, told me, "I'm wearing a vest. I'll go first (to confront him)." I could only imagine the chaos if we retreated out of the apartment and awaited back-up. Jim, apparently able to get out of bed, could use the shotgun, go to the window and fire down at the street.

I told Bill that it was my decision not to use a vest and we would confront this guy together. I was convinced that someone wasn't going to leave that apartment alive. Jim was now holding onto his bed using it as a brace as he called out to us to engage. Billy and I agreed to take him on, on our terms. I told Bill, "You take high, I'll take low," as we appeared in the doorway, guns trained on the actor. We both felt that there might be hope for this guy. Hell, he wasn't a criminal, who just robbed a bank. He was depressed and I started to believe that he wanted to commit suicide by cop. I was kneeling on my right knee as Billy stood next to me.

The actor pointed his gun at Bill and then at me. He started babbling, "We're all going to die!" But something was wrong; he wasn't firing.

He wants to die, I thought. *So you know what? I'm not going to kill him.* I knew that Billy was an excellent shot. I also knew that Billy was aiming center mass. With this, I thought, *Ciser, you ain't got a hair on your ass if you can't shoot that gun out of his hand. What's the point of being a distinguished pistol expert, if you can't prove it once in a while?*

I wanted to share my plan with Bill, who I'm sure had some plans of his own. When does a cop decide to fire? What is someone else's perception of events? I knew Billy was a no-nonsense cop who always tried to help people during his career. He certainly was not the kind of guy who wanted to end someone's life. But I also knew that he would do what he had to do. I couldn't think of anyone I'd rather have there with me, than Bill.

All of these thoughts transpired in seconds as Bill ordered him to "Drop the gun!"

I told Bill, "Keep talking to him," as I pulled back the hammer on my 9mm to single action and carefully followed the actor's gun. He aimed toward Bill's head, then toward me, as he dared us to fire. *I'll take the shot when his aim is shifting away from Bill and toward me. What the hell; it was my idea.* I took aim and double tapped (fired two shots). The gun flew out of his hand as his thumb ripped from his hand and stuck to the wall behind him.

We quickly pulled him out of the bedroom and onto the floor, where his hand was bleeding profusely. The sergeant and back-up officers, hearing the shots, ran up the stairs to assist. I turned the suspect over to them as Billy retrieved a towel to wrap his hand. I apologized to Billy for not warning him, but he understood that if we spoke, it never would have worked. Billy looked right at me and said, "Pat, you saved this guy's life. In about two seconds, I was probably gonna put a couple through his chest."

The ambulance took him away to St. Mary's hospital, in Passaic, where he underwent surgery. A fragment of one of my bullets ricochet off of his handgun and collapsed one of his lungs. The doctors said that it wasn't a serious problem. Bill, the sergeant and I, went to headquarters to file our reports. Guys were calling me "Wyatt Earp" and "Shane" for my trick shooting.

Billy said, "If that's not a medal job, I don't know what is!" with a pat on my back.

The only people not happy with my performance were the Tactical Response Team and Chief Frank LoGioco. There would be no medal or congratulations. But two days later, I received a plaque from Jim, who lay in a hospital bed, thankful to be alive. The plaque read, "Thank you for saving my life, and myself!" My friend, Officer Tommy Lanzalotto (RIP) was guarding Jim at the hospital. Tommy told him,

"You're lucky that it was Ciser. Anyone else would have put a couple of holes in your chest."

Clifton detectives and the Passaic County Prosecutor's Office responded to the scene that night and recovered a black "starter pistol" and a loaded shotgun. My hunch was right. He didn't want to kill anyone.

道

When I first came on the job in 1977, we had the shotgun in the car in a vertical position, with the stock on the passenger floor. The barrel faced up toward the roof with the arm and locking mechanism protruded horizontally from the dash board area. We were encouraged to get out with the shotgun on bank robberies in progress, burglaries and other similar calls. The problem was that few suspects would freeze in their tracks just because you had a shotgun.

It didn't take long for me to realize that the shotgun got in the way, more than it helped. This opinion is coming from someone who was pretty good with a shotgun. My father always used to take my brothers and me hunting. The person that really taught me how to use a shotgun effectively though, was my older brother, Hal. Not only was he fast when a rabbit popped up, but accurate, as well. When we tallied up our take, he was the winner time and time again. Hal, as of the writing of this book, is a captain with the Rutherford Police Department, in Bergen County, New Jersey.

How many times does a suspect call your bluff and run? It's not like TV; we don't rack the shotgun just as we are confronting the suspect. You better be ready to go before that. I love the cop shows that depict the cop exiting his vehicle just to pull out his 9mm, and then pull back the slide. You mean you've been driving around with an unloaded weapon? PALEEZE! You can never run or jump fences with a shotgun in your hands. They can also be temperamental. Like the one that went off in one of our officer's radio car, as he was checking to see if it was loaded. He blew a hole right through the roof and experienced temporary hearing loss. Or the shotgun that went off on another officer when he tripped while chasing a fleeing suspect. I believe that when you jump out of the car to confront a felon, you should choose the weapon that you feel most comfortable using. Some officers are experts with a 9mm, like Clifton's range Officer Glover, then later Officer Broncato, who I heard rumors, used to sleep with his Beretta. Or was it his Smith? Just kiddin. Semi-automatics are sometimes the cause of many accidents, as the State Police reported, when switching from revolvers years ago. A female Wallington cop put a bullet through our range cleaning table. That must have been a surprise to the cops next to her as they cleaned their weapons. Many ex-military men are particularly good with firearms, like Officers Joseph Tuzzolino, Pete Turano, Wayne Stine and David Pereda, just to name a few.

Another lesson is to remain calm, whenever possible. I've been shot at three times and I've shot two suspects over the course of my career. Some big city cops are shot at even more, I'm sure. My point is, however, that for some reason I always remained calm.

道

One day, years ago, I remember I was down at the range. Incidentally, it's the same range that Johnny Depp used in <u>Donnie Brasco</u>, which we thought was pretty cool. The range officer, Bobby Glover, used to get pretty creative when he thought that we were getting bored. Along with our state mandated qualification course, Bobby set up what looked like two balance beams, with five bowling pins spread out across each. Two cops, at a time, would get in their stalls and prepare to fire. At the signal, given by Bob, they would draw their pistols and see who could knock down their pins first. It was a lot of fun as guys would challenge each other. Seven shooters that day left me last, with no partner to challenge. So I asked Bobby, who was a competition shooter and on Clifton's team, if he wanted to verse me. I must have been nuts since Bobby was one of our best, hands down. Even though I was a distinguished pistol expert, Bobby shot bulls eye targets at yardage I had never even attempted.

We both agreed to, a best out of three competition. The pins were set up, as we waited for the signal. "Bam! Bam! Bam!" Five shots were heard from each of us. There were no misses.

"Well Pat," Bobby said, "I guess you got me," as it was clear my pins fell over first. "Second round, set em' up!"

This round would go to Bobby, resulting in a tie. Bobby exclaimed as our adrenaline was pumping, "Well, let's get em' set up again!"

I now thought, *Hey, maybe I have a shot after all.*

We both entered our stalls awaiting the signal. Gun powder created a mist, as anticipation and our competitive spirit was in the air. Taking a deep breath, I told myself to relax. I used the same breathing techniques as when I do my sword demonstrations; blindfolded. "Bam! Bam! Bam!" resonated within the walls like before and now there clearly was a winner. To my surprise, as well as Bobby's, I'm sure, I emerged the victor.

Why though, I thought. Glover was absolutely a better shot than I. The short answer, I conquered my nerves. I remained calm as I meticulously knocked down those pins one at a time. It's even harder if you're going to shoot a gun out of someone's hand. Conquer your fears my friends and fight the good fight.

There's an old story from the samurai era. A great bushi (warrior) was asked, "How will you defeat your enemy?"

The bushi replied, "I know not how to defeat my enemy. But I do know how to defeat myself!"

"Integrity - Doing what is right, even when no one is around to see it."

Taken from; "The Art of Kiai"
Kumashiro Hikotaro (circa 1870)

PURSUITS

The City of Clifton is crisscrossed by five highways, giving car thieves and other felon's quick access in and out. These include Routes 3, 46, 19, 21, and the Garden State Parkway. Interstate 80 runs through our neighbor to the north, Paterson. When I came on the job in 1977, I soon found out that Clifton officers, in general, didn't shy away from high speed chases. Back then, there were no Attorney General Guidelines to follow. You just had to "wing it." We chased cars for anything from a suspended license to a major felony. But one thing they all had in common was that we didn't give up. One of our guys, just before I came on, chased a stolen car through the Lincoln Tunnel. That car ultimately crashed on Eighth Avenue in Manhattan. The chase wasn't all that long, considering that at 100 mph, you could make New York City in about 10 minutes. The late 70's and 80's saw some great pursuits. But it wasn't until the 90's that we saw so many.

In 1990, the Clifton Police Department created the power shift. This small squad of men, including Bill Gibson, Sam Skidmore, Warren Lee, Ricky Klein and me, worked from 2000- 0400 hours (8pm-4am). This squad was to beef up patrols during peak hours and would also become a street crime unit. I still remember my first night working with Sam "Kuma" Skidmore. I gave him that nickname, which means "Bear" in Japanese. Sam is built pretty large and was strong like a bear. I once witnessed him give a perpetrator a "Kumanote," bear hand strike. Of course, he didn't know what it was at the time but it surely was affective. Sam, not wanting to hurt the guy too bad, slapped him

17

upside the head, as they say. The guy not only went down, but was knocked out. Now *that* was a serious Kumanote and I think it's a good bet that guy will never swing at a cop again.

I was driving our marked radio car and we were in full uniform, just the way I liked it. This would only add to our success. Route 21 was a highway that was built from the City of Newark along the Passaic River running north to south. The only problem was that the funds ran out. So instead of going all the way to Paterson, New Jersey's third largest city and Clifton's neighbor, the highway stopped and started in the City of Passaic. Clifton is like a giant horseshoe surrounding much of Passaic. Route 21 passed through Clifton by Route 3 but never reached our Route 46 side or Paterson. I planned on using its shortcomings to my advantage.

We parked our car on Randolph Avenue, which I coined the "Route 21 extension" by virtue of the fact that cars would drive along Randolph Avenue when Route 21 North came to an end, and then continue their trek to Paterson. I liked to do this after 2300 hours (11pm), as traffic, especially on a weeknight, would be light. Also the ratio of stolen and unregistered cars, compared to the proletariat, would improve as hard working people would be turning in for the night. This ratio would continue to improve as the night went on.

The 1990's saw a jump in stolen cars like no other time period that I'm aware of. The most stolen car at the time was older models of the Toyota Camry, as they were plentiful and so easy to steal. If grandma wasn't driving the Camry, run the plate. And what city was the stolen car capital of the world? You guessed it! Beautiful Newark, a city only a couple of minutes away at warp 5 and New Jersey's largest.

My partner, Sam, that night, only had about three years on the job in 1990, so I did the driving and most of the talking. I backed into a parking lot on Randolph Avenue, partially obscured by a building on my right and a house and hedges to my left. My high beams would shine across the street toward the Passaic River. There were a couple of things we were looking for. One was the five top stolen cars in the North Jersey area at that time. But the big thing was . . . their faces. When someone looks at a cop, and they know their driving a stolen car, they always make that big mistake. We called it the look and turn. The curiosity of the bright lights makes the driver, and sometimes the passenger(s), look over at the marked radio car. But once they realize that it's a cop, and they know that they're up to something, they quickly turn their heads back forward, usually with that, "uh oh" expression. And, that, my friend, causes me to pull out and run the plate.

Even after the Attorney General guidelines on vehicular pursuits came out, the case law on running plates confirmed that we needed no reason to run license plates. As we pulled out of the lot, three things usually happened. One, we'd run the plate and it came back SCIC/ NCIC negative (not stolen) so we would peel off and return to our "fishing hole," two, the perps (perpetrators) would start the pursuit by immediately taking off as we exited the lot, or three, the plate was negative but I still had a gut feeling that it was stolen, but not yet reported. In that case, I would follow the car for a few minutes and then activate my overhead lights. If the car pulled over, I drove around it, turned off that street, and shut down my lights. This was a good test, as it was extremely rare for a stolen car to pull right over and we couldn't get accused of stopping cars with no reasonable suspicion, or a motor vehicle violation.

I guess when my brain gets congested enough, an idea pops out. Not only did I increase my stolen car arrests, but the rest of the squad did as well. By the way, that three year "rookie" that I mentioned, Sam, wound up with more stolen cars than anyone. In 1991, I personally chased some 36 stolen cars. I was the primary chase car in about 18 and the secondary car in the others, mostly Skidmore's. Many of these chases would mushroom, where the actors were involved in other crimes, as well, such as drug dealing and street robberies.

道

One such chase was initiated by Paterson Police. They entered Clifton on Hazel Street, heading for the Garden State Parkway South. We had one Paterson car, Bill Gibson, Chris Vassoler and me, all solo in our vehicles. As we pursed the vehicle toward East Orange and Irvington, we learned that the car contained three or four black males that were also wanted for street robberies earlier that day. To my surprise, the Paterson car broke off the pursuit and got off the highway at the next exit. The three of us realizing that it was a felony vehicle, continued the pursuit further south, now traveling under Route 3. We were in the left lane reaching speeds of 100 mph. After a few miles the suspect vehicle started to slow down and move into the center lane, of which there were three.

Why are they slowing down? I wondered silently. *Are they going to give up? Bail out and start a foot pursuit? Start shooting?* To my surprise they decelerated to about 50 mph, only to throw one of their own out of the rear passenger door. As soon as the guy hit the pavement everyone on the parkway, including us, hit the brakes. It was amazing, but not one vehicle crashed as a result. Chris Vassoler and I were the lead cars and were able to whip around the perp in the road and Billy Gibson was able to stop his car in a way to protect our potential road kill. To Bill's amazement, this guy jumped up and started to run. Gibson, being in great shape, ran him down, in a backyard, off the Parkway. A New Jersey State Trooper pulled up and assisted Bill after the tackle.

Meanwhile, the suspect vehicle definitely took advantage of the temporary chaos by speeding up and putting some distance between himself and the two Clifton units. After he blew through the Essex toll plaza, we temporarily lost him. Vassoler later located the vehicle, abandoned in East Orange, with a handgun under the front seat. This was one we lost, but we wouldn't let it happen often.

道

Getting back to our Route 21 extension on the power shift, we were sometimes picking up two at a time. One night, as I watched for the "look and turn," I seemed to get a double hit back-to-back. Both drivers immediately looked away after what seemed like eye contact with me, although I knew that they couldn't see me that well. After they passed me traveling north toward Route 20 and Paterson, I slowly pulled out and cautiously closed the gap. I was only able to run the second vehicles plate, which came back as a hit in seconds. The actor in the stolen vehicle kept tabs on me in his rear view mirror but he made a mistake. Both vehicles got onto Route 46 West, I'm sure in error, rather than 46 East toward 20 North and Paterson. Following both cars onto 46 west, we only drove deeper into Clifton, where I knew I could get plenty of help. Not engaging my overhead lights or siren, I proceeded at the speed limit. I was then able to give dispatch the plate on the first vehicle as they drove in tandem. That car also came back stolen, as several Clifton radio cars positioned themselves along the highway about a half mile up the road. As they spotted the black and whites ahead they had no choice but to drive through the gauntlet. I then activated my lights and siren. The three of us hit 90 mph within seconds and it was off to the races. It didn't take long to enter Little Falls, where their officers are always in for a good chase, so we picked up one or two of their units adding to our four. Zipping quickly through Totowa and into Wayne, we were approaching the Rt. 46/Rt. 23 split. The first car then became involved in a contact action with a Little Falls unit, wiping out at the split. Billy Gibson, Billy Stark, and the Little Falls cop, Patrolman Zon, I believe, arrested the occupants of that car. I, along with Clifton Officer Vito Collucci, continued to pursue the second stolen car. It wasn't long before that car lost control on Route 23, trying to negotiate a curve across from Fuddrucker's restaurant. He slammed into a telephone poll ending his fugacious flight.

Many of our chases ended up in Newark or Paterson. But when they drove west, we could always count on Little Falls, Wayne and Fairfield PD's. I think I hold the record for the longest chase and the shortest. Once I chased a car through the Pathmark lot after the perp's car struck one of our detectives, when I headed the narcotics division. After 15-20 seconds through the lot, he turned right back to the starting point and into the arms of three detectives, who drew down on him. Fortunately, for him, he stopped, as his accomplice threw the crack out the window.

道

My longest chase occurred when I was a patrol sergeant in 2001. It was the midnight shift and I was on the Westside of Clifton near Rt. 3. Patrolman Salvatore Saggio had pulled over a vehicle for a motor vehicle violation on Route 46 West, near the Little Falls border. The suspect vehicle pulled into the Exxon station there. After Sal exited his vehicle to check out this unregistered vehicle, the driver put the car in gear and peeled out of the station. Saggio quickly jumped back into his marked unit, taking off after him. Sal radioed to headquarters that the suspect vehicle was being driven in a reckless manner and was a danger to the motoring public. Headquarters got on SPEN (State Police Emergency Network) and notified jurisdictions west of Clifton; that we were in pursuit of a fleeing vehicle.

It wasn't long before they reached the Riverview Drive exit, about two miles up. Little Falls PD already had a unit on Route 46, so they jumped in rather quickly. The suspect vehicle got off the highway, worked his way over to Main Street, Little Falls and came back toward Clifton. This guy was either very confused or on drugs. As I was responding to Route 46 to assist, I was quite surprised to see the perpetrator, who was wanted for second degree eluding at this point, reenter Route 46 West near the Clifton border. At this time, I entered the pursuit. As we accelerated, Saggio must have thought it was the movie, Groundhog Day, as we again sped toward the Riverview Drive exit. This time the suspect vehicle started to exit as before, only to quickly reenter the highway and run into Patrolman Saggio's marked unit. Saggio's vehicle suffered a blowout and front fender damage leaving him out of the chase. I sped up and assumed primary vehicle status. As the charges mounted against this individual, including aggravated assault on a police officer, we increased our speed on Rt. 46 through Fairfield, towards the Pinebrook section of Montville. Along the way, there were several other marked units who attempted to assist but either couldn't keep up or were called off by their supervisors. Another Clifton unit also joined in, attempting to fill in for Saggio, but eventually couldn't keep up either.

The suspect vehicle exited Route 46 West onto Route 287 North as the suspect took advantage of the open highway. There were few cars on the highway that night as we passed only tractor trailers. I was the only radio car still in pursuit as we cruised at 120 mph. Switching my radio over to SPEN, I was able to request assistance from other departments as well as the NJ State Police. We continued north for about 15-20 minutes as I became unsure as to what town I was in. The suspect vehicle suddenly, as if to shake me, decelerated and jumped off the highway. Seeing this, I laid back slightly remembering what he did to Sal on Route 46. It wasn't long before he reentered the highway, however, this time, going south. Again our speed increased as we continued our trek to who knows where. After about ten minutes, two marked units arrived to assist. The first was a State Police car, the other, a Pompton Lakes unit. The Pompton Lakes car, to my disbelief, pulled up next to me and tried to take primary status. This is where the arriving vehicle attempts to merge, in between myself and the suspect car. This guy was apparently so pumped up that he almost, without realizing it, I'm sure, tore off my front fender.

Allow me to digress just for a moment. For all of you rookie cops out there, hey, I used to be one, and any other officers who don't chase a lot of cars. Pa-leease, put yourself in a position to help, not in a position to interfere. How many of us, while driving about 90 mph, had another cop pull out onto the highway right between you and the bad guy? And what happens as a result? You lock up your brakes and begin to fish tail, while cursing out some "helpful officer" who apparently has his head up his ass! Then, this assisting officer can't get his speed up from a dead stop allowing the perp to, at times, get away. If you are going to assist in a chase, please slide in at the rear and wait for the crash. After the crash, there will be either a foot chase, or a shootout, where you, then, may be needed to assist.

While I'm at it, let me give some advice to supervisors.

First, let me say that this is only theoretical! The Belleville Police Department has always been a big help to us when we fly through their jurisdiction.

Let's imagine that a Clifton officer is chasing a car south on Route 21 towards the beautiful City of Newark. We usually go through Nutley before their officers can make it over to the highway. Belleville PD, however, which borders Newark, usually hears our radio transmission and has time to intercept. Now, let's say that one Clifton unit, followed by one Belleville unit, enters Newark. Let us also add that there are three occupants in the fleeing rocket ship.

Let us imagine that a Belleville supervisor orders his unit to break off and return to their jurisdiction. The Clifton unit usually, a one man car, is now totally alone. The fleeing vehicle either crashes or decides to abandon their car, now fleeing on foot once they hit their neighborhood or projects. Then there is only one cop, possibly up against three actors all alone.

I wonder how that supervisor would feel if the Clifton officer was killed? What if the Clifton officer crashed and needed first aid? Consider asking your officer if the next town sent a unit or two to assist, before you call off your unit! Remember, we're all in this together, don't leave the quarterback without protection.

Note: Again, I'd like to thank the Belleville Police Department for all their continuing support.

道

I'll get back to my longest chase, which lasted, 45 minutes; by the way, while I burned three-quarters of a tank of gas, as we tore down 287 South. I actually had to get on SPEN and ask the assisting officer to back off. Not only did he back off, but he also apparently broke off. The perpetrator, continuing to flee at warp speed, suddenly got off 287 at Route 80 East.

At first, I thought, *hey, this is great, I'll chase him right back toward Clifton and get plenty of help.* The grin on my face was short lived, however, as he exited the highway and drove around who knows where. The State Police car I mentioned earlier was still behind me, and seemed prepared to stay.

Then it happened, it always does, the pursued vehicle decided last minute to turn right. And there he crashed, into a traffic signal/ light pole. We were somewhere in East Hanover. As the smoke cleared and I jumped out of my cruiser to make the collar, I counted five police units, including myself, surrounding the accident scene to render assistance. There were two NJ State Police vehicles, and one each from Pompton Lakes and East Hanover. I know what you're thinking. No, it was a different Pompton Lakes unit than the one that cut me off before.

After pulling the sole occupant from the vehicle, and cuffing him, I discovered a fair amount of CDS in his vehicle. The shocker on this one was yet to come. This guy, turned out to be a retired Essex County Police Lieutenant. He went off the job early for "personal problems." He later told me that he thought if he drove in excess of 100 mph, I would break off the chase.

I told him, "Fat chance, I'm from Clifton." That morning the Watch Commander filled in the patrol captain as to the prior night's events.

The lieutenant said, "That guy Ciser chased last night was a maniac!" The Captain replied, "Yeah, he just didn't realize that *our* maniac was chasing him!"

In each car chase that takes place across the country, the officer never really knows why this individual has decided to flee. Sure, sometimes it's obvious. Sometimes your MDC (Mobile Data Computer) shows a stolen car or a felony vehicle. Sometimes it's a hot pursuit from a crime in progress. But so many times, when you light up (lights and siren) the guy in front of you, there are just so many variables. You are not aware that he's a wanted party or has drugs or a gun in the car. Maybe he's just a drunk going down for the third time and wants to avoid mandatory jail time.

道

My first pursuit came in '77 or '78. It is difficult to remember the year, but the chase was memorable. I was working Car #3 downtown Clifton driving south on Main Avenue. I just passed the Koeikan Karate dojo at Main and Washington Avenues, and was now stopped at the traffic light at Union Avenue. A car with two guys in it pulled out of Union, making a left onto Main right in front of me. The driver seemed to lock eyes with me for a moment, and then suddenly turned away with an "uh oh" look. This, of course, caused me to think, *now that was a look of guilt if I ever saw one.* Officer Jeff Reilly later coined the phrase, "The Look and Turn," or the L and T, which I mentioned previously, that always gives them away.

So I made a U-turn and drove up behind these guys, just close enough to read the plate. They made a right turn just past the park, went one block to Getty Avenue and turned left onto Getty Avenue, north toward Paterson. The dispatcher told me that it's a stolen car and it's wanted for street robberies in Paterson earlier that day. At that point, the suspect vehicle began to accelerate as he observed me turning with him. I would have liked to just follow him for a while until another Clifton or Paterson unit showed up, but these guys weren't waiting around for that. We started hitting speeds of about 60 mph on Getty Avenue, entering Paterson and then onto Straight Street. They turned onto a dead end street which turned out to be unfortunate for them. Three or four radio cars, including me, had them totally boxed in. The men were charged with motor vehicle theft, as well as numerous street robberies, and we recovered gold chains and wallets from inside the car. A handgun was located under the seat.

道

Back in the late 60's and early 70's, a friend of mine, Danny Rocco (RIP), was Clifton's stolen car king. Danny was a great cop and helped break me in when I was a rookie. Danny was a great teacher and forgiving of any foibles. Danny picked guys off using an old "hot sheet" inside the radio car. No computers needed. He studied the hot sheet and knew his cars. He told me years later, that it was easier back then as there weren't even close to as many makes and models as there are today. Well, regardless, I feel that I have to pay homage to my old teacher, Danny, who had so many stolen car arrests that even Scotland Yard (England) contacted him to ask how he did it.

道

Clifton was, and still is, the pursuit PD of Northern New Jersey. Even to this day, Clifton interprets the attorney General guidelines on chases, as giving us permission to chase for various crimes. Many departments run scared, worrying about litigation. Just being a cop, there is going to be litigation! If you wanted to play it safe, become an accountant! I wouldn't want to bore you with too many of the couple of hundred chases I've had in my career, so I'll just talk about a few of the more interesting ones before I close out this chapter.

道

While chasing a stolen car on Route 46 East, approaching Route 20 in Paterson, the actor made the mistake of sideswiping me. Crashing into him, using the correct angle and technique, I almost knocked him into the river. I apprehended the driver, as my partner, Tim Lyons, grabbed the passenger, who thought about going for a swim. They were wanted for street robberies in Paterson and earlier at a Paramus mall. Again, many times you don't really know why they're running, until you catch them.

道

It was the summer of '92, when Officer Ricky Klein ran the plate of a vehicle that caught his attention on Piaget Avenue. The vehicle appeared to be occupied by the driver only, as Ricky could see only somewhat through the back window. The license plate check revealed that the car was stolen, so Ricky began to follow it until back-up units could get into the area.

As Ricky followed the car, it was difficult to ascertain a description of the driver. It was getting dark and the rear window was slightly tinted. It's always good to give the other cars and dispatch a heads up on the actor's race, approximate age and clothing, in case of a foot chase.

Ricky followed the car a short distance as the suspect vehicle headed toward Passaic. Once a Clifton back-up car took a position behind Ricky, he flipped on his overhead lights and signaled the actor to pull over. The stolen car immediately accelerated.

Working the Eastside of Clifton, I, along with a couple of other radio cars, drove toward Officer Klein's position. Ricky, Officer Gibson,

I believe, and one Passaic unit were actively chasing the fleeing vehicle, through Passaic City streets that bordered Clifton.

Marked police cars from both Clifton and Passaic converged on President Street, with the stolen car stopped in the middle of the street. Ricky and the other officers exited their vehicles and drew their guns covering the suspect.

Ricky was now the closest officer to the actor.

"Turn off the engine and throw the keys out of the window!" Ricky ordered.

It was a summer night with the driver side window already down. At Ricky's further command, the actor kept his hands on the steering wheel and in view of the officers but refused to turn off the engine or throw out the keys. Having a bit of a stalemate, Ricky moved closer to the driver door, while covering the suspect with his Beretta.

The driver, at that point, continued to stare at Ricky with a blank or uncertain look on his face. It was Ricky, while keeping the actor covered, who reached inside the vehicle to turn of the engine himself. As he reached into the vehicle with his left hand, the driver took his foot off the brake and punched it!

Officer Klein, with his arm inside the car was being dragged up President Street toward Lexington Avenue.

My arrival time could not have been better as I approached the scene of the stop to see Ricky lying in the street, assisting officers out of their cars and the suspect vehicle fleeing west.

Hitting my siren to warn officers on foot that I was coming through, I accelerated up President Street easily keeping pace with the stolen car. The suspect turned right onto Lexington Avenue as he reentered the City of Clifton. Just a couple of car lengths behind, I heard over the radio that Billy Gibson picked up Officer Klein.

As I pursued the fleeing suspect, I could only hope that Ricky was ok. When you see an officer down, you're never sure of his condition while hoping for the best. Police officers are trained to assist each other and render first aid when needed. Knowing that Bill Gibson, Sam

Skidmore and a couple of Passaic units were with Rick, it allowed me to concentrate completely on the man that dragged him.

I later find out that Ricky was pretty banged up. His determination and adrenalin, I'm sure, kept him in the chase as he became a passenger now with Gibson. The suspect entered Route 46 East toward Paterson with me on his tail. I remember Ricky getting on the radio, in Bill's car, saying something like, "Pat! Don't let him get away."

Don't worry, Rick, I thought, as the actor was wanted for aggravated assault on an officer, in addition to car theft and eluding.

Stopping him on Route 46 would be a better option than chasing him through Clifton or Paterson City streets.

It's pretty interesting what property damage and personal injury or even death was avoided by putting a stop to this chase here and now. If this guy was willing to drag, or even kill Ricky, what else was he capable of?

道

On 9/11, for example, how much death and destruction did Flight 93 avoid when those courageous passengers forced that plane down in Shanksville, Pennsylvania?

California allows officers, in some cases, to use the "pit" maneuver when they need to end a dangerous pursuit.

Attorney General guidelines in New Jersey do not specifically address the pit maneuver when stopping cars but they did put in some discretion when chasing felony vehicles.

The pit maneuver involves driving up to the side of the fleeing vehicle, then positioning, for instance, your right front fender and bumper alongside the suspect vehicle's rear left quarter panel. The police vehicle then taps the suspect's vehicle in a way as to cause the pursued car to spin out. This maneuver works especially well when the suspect's vehicle enters a turn. This can be done on either side of the suspect vehicle.

I moved into the left lane while the suspect vehicle is traveling east in the center lane. As I tapped his left rear, his car spun out in front of mine, causing him to be in a position facing north with me pushing him like a tank, in an effort to totally disable him.

My front bumper was up against his driver side and rear passenger door as I continued to push him. He, on the other hand, attempted to drive forward. I wasn't sure what he had in mind but he was facing the concrete divider with no place to go. I could see a couple of radio cars in my rear view mirror sealing his fate. The actor now jumped on the gas and surged forward. This action had my front bumper pushing his left rear quarter panel, which spun him west, facing the opposite direction of myself. Driver door to driver door, I now pushed him tighter into the concrete barrier, which was about three feet high.

Back-up cars had both of us surrounded as I drew my Beretta and watched that he didn't pull a gun of his own. Gibson and Skidmore pulled the actor from the car through the right passenger window, allowing Ricky to throw on his cuffs. With the suspect in handcuffs, I could now pull away from the trapped vehicle. Further crisis averted, as far as I was concerned.

道

Once, or should I say a dozen times, I chased a car down Route 20 North, in Paterson. This one took the 10th Avenue split with no other traffic around that night at about four in the morning. He slowed down to about 40 mph, as I saw him slide across the front seat, reaching for the passenger door handle. Sure as shit, he jumped out and allowed the car to continue up the street until it crashed. I thought he'd be limping from his reckless dive but he jumped right up and ran like a rabbit. After a short run he went up a back staircase to a house. I successfully reached out for his ankle as he made it to the top, as he tried reaching for the door handle. Pulling hard on his ankle we both went down the stairs together.

His public defender claimed that I had the wrong man who only ran from the police when he saw another brother running as well. I asked if she could explain the stolen car's ignition that I found in his front pocket. He was found guilty.

道

We were so used to chasing cars to Paterson and Newark that it was kind of nice to wind up in the suburbs once in awhile. Seeing Clifton cars in Ridgewood or Paramus was different, but the cops there were always ready to help. One such chase took me to Wayne, off of Route 46 West. It was almost three in the morning when the car crashed into a guardrail on an elevated section of Route 46 just past the Route 23 exit. The driver jumped out of the car and then leaped over the side of the highway. Looking down, it seemed to be about a 14-foot leap. I was a sergeant on midnights at the time and thought, *use your head this time Ciser, don't do it!* I asked assisting radio cars to help seal the wooded area around the ramps. We had Clifton, of course, Wayne, Fairfield and a sheriff's car assisting. The sheriff's department dog sniffed him out for me as this guy couldn't wait for me to take him away from that dog. And, don't you know, he had a broken ankle.

道

Quite often I'd inject humor into an intense situation. Hey, I used to do it in school as a kid. Why stop now? I was traveling south on Parker Avenue in a marked unit. Approaching Highland Avenue, which was the border of Passaic, I noticed a car traveling east in front of me. So many years ago, I can't remember the make of the vehicle, but do remember that it was one that was frequently stolen at the time.

The vehicle passed me as I turned left behind it as I normally do at the border street. Behind the vehicle with New York tags, for only a block, the car turned right onto Dayton Avenue, into Passaic. I followed them as headquarters ran the plate. The vehicle with its two occupants made another right onto President Street and parked at the curb. I double-parked next to them in a position to block them in, yet back a little, to have the upper hand, slightly to their rear. Headquarters blurted over the radio, "Car 1, that's an entered vehicle!"

Telling dispatch that I would be out with them on President Street, I exited my car. The occupants also began to exit their car as I made them think that I was looking for an address. Unclipping my holster I got closer to the driver as I pretended to look for a building number. The two actors apparently playing it cool, as I believed they were abandoning the car in a way that would not raise alarm. At this point, I was standing in front of my car in a position to intercept the driver.

Grabbing him by the collar and belt I quickly put him face down over the hood of the stolen car. Keeping my left hand on his upper back, I pressed my 9mm to the back of his neck. "Don't move!" I demanded.

The passenger standing on the sidewalk, on the other side of the hood, gave me the "Oh Shit!" look. The driver, seemingly content to stay quiet on the hood, didn't move a muscle. The passenger, contemplating his next move, took one step away as he thought about running. I pointed my Beretta at his face.

I commanded, "Let me see your hands!" Looking jumpy, he didn't know if he should take the chance. I then said, "Let me see your mutha fuckin hands, or your momma's gonna hate tomorrow's headline!" He looked into my eyes and decided he didn't want to test me, as he put his hands on the hood of the car. Within about 30 seconds, both a Clifton and Passaic radio car pulled up and assisted with the handcuffing.

道

Last one, I promise. One night on the power shift I was in my fishing hole, waiting for a big fish. I had already pulled out a few times to run plates I liked, only to come up empty. It was a Sunday night, I believe, around three in the morning. An old, pink Lincoln Continental goes by traveling north toward Paterson. There were three or four occupants in this beat up vehicle and I didn't like how they looked. I put my car in drive as I began to pull up in an effort to get their plate. I couldn't pull out right away since there were a couple of cars driving behind them testing my patience.

So, I said to myself, *Ah, Pat, it didn't look that good. And besides, who would want to steal that piece of shit!* So I put the car in reverse and eased back into my spot.

Two minutes later, my radio blared, "All cars, special attention on the Eastside. Passaic just had a shooting. They fled toward Clifton in an old, pink Cadillac. A sawed-off shotgun was used on the victim."

Shit! I thought. I threw my car into drive as I peeled rubber out of the lot. "Headquarters," I called out, "the car isn't a Cadillac, but a Lincoln; it passed me two minutes ago." I raced toward Route 46 East to Route 20 North. Continuing on the exit ramp to Market Street, I drove toward the Alabama projects in Paterson. No sign of the vehicle, as I realized I blew it!

After about 15 minutes I returned to Clifton. A couple of things could have happened, had I pulled them over. One, they pull over when I light them up and as I walk up to the vehicle, not realizing they're wanted, they blast me with the shotgun; Or two, when I light them up they run, knowing full well what they just did in Passaic; which would have been the best scenario, because during the chase, Passaic PD would have broadcast the BOLO (Be On the Look Out).

Things worked out well in the end though. I found out that a friend of mine, Sergeant Joe Patti of Passaic PD, arrested the actors a few days later. Joe was absolutely one of the best of the best! Now there's a guy that could write a book!

Newark reported 15,674 cars stolen in 1989, arguably making it the stolen car capital of the world at that time. Twenty years later, it's a fraction of that number.

It's no wonder we were chasing so many cars back then; Clifton officers, I mean. Many departments had, and still do have, orders not to chase stolen cars. Car thieves were actually burning up their tires while doing "donuts" in front of Newark cops, coaxing them into a chase. Clearance rates were in the single digits for stolen cars as a <u>Fast and Furious</u> mentality took hold. Most car thieves, over 95% in fact, got away with it! Gee, I wonder why this "no chase policy" encouraged auto theft. Hey, they even made a game about it, *Grand Theft Auto*. Specifically, the clearance rate in New Jersey was 4.7% in 1999. In 2009, it went up to a measly 6.1%.

High speed chases are both exhilarating and unpredictable. If you're a cop, be careful out there, don't cut primary police cars off, leave space between you and the suspect, and please, especially if you're married with kids, use your seatbelt.

> *Good people sleep peacefully*
> *In their beds at night;*
> *Only because rough men stand*
> *Ready to do violence on their behalf.*

George Orwell

BECOMING PAT CISER

1975 was definitely my "break out" year when it came to making it, or breaking it, as a Karate-Do competitor. After graduating from Clifton high school in 1974, I was a Koeikan (Japanese system of Karate) brown belt who never won a competition. But it was my entry into the 1975 AAU New Jersey State Karate Championships that gave me new hope and confidence to train harder and excel. There were approximately forty competitors in my division that day. Competitors from all over the state, representing various disciplines including Japanese, Korean, Chinese and Okinawan systems, filled the room. In the traditional Kata division, I performed "Chinto" and won a first place gold medal. To say I was completely ecstatic would be an understatement. This win also qualified me to represent the State of New Jersey at the AAU National Championships in Cleveland, Ohio. In the states, I won my first two matches in kumite, which put me in the top 10, but lost my next match leaving me out of the finals. So, I drove out to Ohio with two other Koeikan seito (students). Mr. Peter Bonsma and Mr. Al Vacca also qualified in the black belt division. Finding myself among a large field of talented competitors from across the country, I was very happy to place 3rd in the kata competition, and win my first bronze medal at a National AAU Tai Kai (tournament). I was listed in black belt magazine's November issue, as winning along with Tae Bo's Billy Blanks. Billy was a phenomenal fighter with a great flying sidekick, as I recall.

After two big wins it was time for a reality check, and unfortunately, a major let down. I received a letter inviting me to the third WUKO

(World Union Karate Organization) Karate Championships to be held at Long Beach, California. I, because of my placing in the nationals, would be part of the U.S. team. Talk about a feeling of rapture and disappointment at the same time. The reality was, like my father used to say, I didn't have a pot to piss in or a window to throw it out. There was no way a guy like me, just turning twenty, bouncing at a night club part time, and living home with my folks, could afford airline tickets and lodging for a trip to the West Coast. My parents certainly couldn't afford it with six kids; my mom didn't work and only had a dearth of money in the savings account for a rainy day. So, ultimately, to my chagrin, I destroyed the letter and hoped for better days.

If you asked me a couple of years earlier what I wanted to do after high school, I would have told you that I would be joining the Marines and going to Vietnam. My brother, Hal, back then, was in Saigon and my first cousin, Gregory McFadden, from Jersey City, was killed in the jungle there.

So, I thought, *where do modern day warriors go? The Military of course.*

Although Vietnam was over, I took the written exam for the marines and scored pretty high. After telling my parents that I was going to report down to Newark, NJ in about a week and ship off to Parris Island after that; I heard no objections. So that night, I went down to the dojo (Karate school) to train and tell Sensei Kaloudis that I would soon be leaving. It was he, who had high hopes for me and asked me to sit with him and tell him my reasons for going. At the time, my father thought that the service was just the right thing for me. He didn't quite understand my love for Karate-Do, or Japanese culture. After all, he was stationed in Okinawa and Japan during the war. It was Sensei Kaloudis who convinced me that I had a future in Martial Arts, and maybe, on the U.S. team. He could be very persuasive, so I called back my recruiter the next day. Lucky for me, I didn't sign anything yet and was able to opt out.

Sensei Kaloudis always looked out for his seito (students) as if we were family. In 1975, allow me to digress, he, along with other renowned martial artists, were invited to demonstrate his art (Koeikan Karate-Do) at Aaron Banks "Oriental World of Self Defense," to be held at Madison Square Garden in New York City. Sensei Kaloudis asked me, and a couple of other Karate students, to assist him. I, of course, eagerly accepted such an honor. Yet again, this man lifted my spirits by entrusting me and only three others, from eight Koeikan Dojo (schools) in New Jersey, to assist in such a monumental event that would be broadcast on ABC's *Wide World of Sports.*

When we arrived at the Garden, it was a who's who of Martial Artists. Sensei performed an incredible demonstration of "ki" (inner strength). Later, as I recall, Sensei Frost who lived and trained in Japan for quite some time, told me that Sensei Kaloudis had more ki than most Nihonjin (Japanese) that he had ever known. Sensei Kaloudis had us hit him with everything, while seemingly immune to our assault. He was struck with full power tsuki (punches) to the solar plexus and throat, Tegatana uchi (hand sword strike) to the throat and rib cage and mae geri (front kicks) to the groin, that actually picked him up off of the ground! As if that weren't enough, we then broke two-by-three's and bricks over various parts of his body. The most punishing blows were the red common house bricks over his head. The bricks struck his skull at the hairline and the back of his head on a 45 degree angle. Sensei then smashed through three house bricks that were stacked one on top of the other, with no spacers, suspended between two cinder blocks with his head. The crowd went wild! Sensei Kaloudis was then asked if he could be interviewed by an ABC commentator. What an incredible day!

This year continued to be full of opportunities for me, and as fate would have it, some successful wins in Karate-Do shiai (contests). I entered the 1975 All Koeikan International Karate Championships, still competing in the brown belt division. I would later test for shodan (1st degree black belt) in the fall of 1976. The elimination matches went very well during the late morning and early afternoon, as I did ippon kumite (point sparring) with five different individuals, successfully defeating them all. Pretty good trick too; since I was a bouncer at a Hackensack disco (nightclub for all you young people), and had to work the night before until 4:00 am The Kata (form) competition didn't go too well though, as it was the first thing out of the box in the a.m. I must have slept through part of it. I seem to always wake up, however, when they yell, "HAJIME!"(begin) in the kumite (sparring) rounds.

At around 3:00 pm, when the eliminations were over, I was told that I wouldn't fight for 1st place until about six o'clock. That was death! Anyone who's competed knows that when you're warmed up and "hot" in the ring, the time is *now*. Once you cool down and feel how tired you are, it is sooo hard to get it back. So my best friend, Dennis Buongiorno, who worked with me in the club the previous night, and I, retired up to the top bleachers and tried to take a long nap.

At about 6:30 pm, someone woke me up and said, "Pat, what the hell are you doing up here! You're supposed to be down in that ring!" As I looked down, I could see Kenny Jackson, another Koeikan brown belt from Detroit, Michigan, ready to take me on. Kenny was a great guy who I was very familiar with, as he also trained in New Jersey and Pennsylvania. Kenny, like I, had won all of his matches that day. So I hustled down the bleachers and did a two minute stretch, just before hearing the "hajime!"(begin) wake up call.

So, I lost that 1st place match to Kenny Jackson on points. But I'm not going to tell you that I lost because I was tired. Hell, I'm sure Kenny was fatigued himself from the long arduous event. I lost, plain and simple, because Kenny was apparently faster than I, and he deserved to win.

In 1975, the Venezuelan government, in conjunction with Marcelo Planchart, invited several U.S. black belts instructors and a team from the United States to compete in the International Championships in Caracas. A team was put together and I earned a spot. All expenses were to be paid by the Venezuelan government. Kenny Jackson and I couldn't believe our good fortune. I was elated that I wouldn't suffer the same financial difficulties as I did, at the WUKO Championships out in California.

The American contingent was a *Who's Who* in martial arts. My Sensei(s), Edward Kaloudis and Brian Frost, from Michigan, Aaron Banks, Gary Alexander, Thomas La Puppet, Andrew Linick, Alex Sternberg and Ki Chung Kim rounded out the martial arts stars there. Chuck Norris was originally slated to go but couldn't make it in the end. He was to start production on his first movie in which he had the lead role, Good Guys Wear Black, I believe it was.

Teammates and I arrived in Venezuela to find out that we were staying at the Hilton. *Holy shit!* I thought, *these guys don't fool around.* Those were the good ole days (no Hugo Chavez hanging around).

The competition went on for two days. On the first day, some of the karate masters would perform demonstrations. The "Poliedro" in Caracus, was huge sports venue that was packed with spectators. Even the Vice President of Venezuela was there with his numerous bodyguards. The military, armed with their rifles, were everywhere. You could see them at the airport, in the Hilton Hotel and on the streets.

Sensei Aaron Banks performed first. He was tall, thin and had very large knuckles. *Must have done a lot of makiwara* (striking post) *training*, I thought. For his demonstration he broke 30-40 one inch boards in half, one at a time. The first one didn't break as he dropped it to the floor. His assistant handed the boards to him one at a time. Sensei Banks held it in his left hand, as he snap punched the board with his right. You'd have to quickly snap your punch since the board was only supported on one side. The demo was greeted by polite applause, as I thought, *even I could do that!*

Sensei Kaloudis performed his demonstration next. It was the same one he did on ABC Channel 7, at the MSG Oriental World of Self Defense. He punched through five stacked house bricks with one blow. He then snap punched three other house bricks, breaking them in half, like Aaron Banks punched the boards. Three more bricks were then broken over his head. For the finale, he stacked three red bricks across two support bricks, and then cracked them open using his head! Sensei Kaloudis did this, amazingly enough, without using spacers between the bricks. The bricks were so tight against each other that they all cracked in half, but didn't fall. The crowd started to jeer! My friend, George Scordilis, who is Kaloudis' cousin, became so upset that he started giving the middle finger to the crowd. Vacca and Bonsma had to restrain him as Kaloudis put his index finger under the bricks and lifted them up, just enough, to watch them all fall apart. The crowd then cheered as all was forgiven. We then reminded George about the guns.

The kumite (sparring) events started along with the kata competition. In my division, they took the six highest scores in kata, which included me, and we were told that we would be in the finals the next day. After winning my first two matches in kumite, I was getting pretty fired up. My third match was getting ready to start as I went up against a competitor from Aruba. I had a devastating right side kick in those days that could break a two-by-four in half. Hajime (begin) was heard as I viciously attacked with my trademark kick. Down went the Aruban fighter as the kick found its mark. Clearly in pain, holding his left ribs, the doctor was called over. It appeared that they might have been broken or at the very least, badly bruised. Apparently, a pretty tough fighter, he told his coach that he wanted to continue. His coach told him that he could continue if he fought on his left side.

Karate is not like boxing. Most good fighters can fight in either a left or right side stance. He entered the ring with his injured ribs away from me. The referee shouted, "Hajime" and bam! I threw the right side kick. This time he got his right arm in the way to block his ribs. Crack! was heard, as my kick broke his arm. He went down screaming in pain as I jumped up and down, exclaiming, "Get up! Get up!" (Told you I was fired up). Not something I would do later in my career, but hell, I was only 19. The crowd got angry when I was declared the victor. I would rei (bow) out of the ring and exit proudly with large U.S.A. letters on my back.

It was a "no contact" event, meaning no contact to the head. Body shots were fine. The next day, the injured Aruban came to the tournament with a bandage around his ribs and a cast on his broken right arm. We spoke awhile and he asked me to autograph his cast! Although Saturday went pretty well for me, Sunday did not. I lost my first fight, which took me out of medal contention, and I placed 5th or 6th in kata. I returned to Venezuela in 1976, however, to win my first International gold medal. I didn't make the team again until 1979 as a black belt. I had a fair showing in 1979, but not enough to come out on top. I did get a good taste of the full-contact fighting, however, as they added a "round robin" kick-boxing event that year. A long day with many fighters had me fighting at midnight. Not doing so well, I lost my second match on a decision.

Caracas was a fun place, if you knew where to go. Seeing that we had friends down there in the martial arts world, they hooked us up. The only thing I regret was that I didn't speak Spanish. In 1975 and 1976, I was a free man and the girls down there were smoking hot! We used to go to a disco (yeah, that's what we called them), called City Hall. It was nice and as upscale as any Manhattan club. It was my <u>Saturday Night Fever</u> days and man, could I dance. The girls down there wanted me to teach them the hustle, so, of course, I did. Unfortunately, that's all I did because of my limited communication skills.

Sensei Frost knew some good local bars for us to navigate. One time, someone brought up the fact that I could take a bite out of a cocktail glass. Something I used to do in New Jersey working as a bouncer. So, just like back home, I bet a couple of beers that I could do it. This was in 1976. The owner of the bar liked the glass with the bite out of it so much that he still had it on display when we returned in 1979.

One of the black belts on the team, Peter Bonsma, wasn't much of a drinker. When he went into the bathroom, we put the bartender up to playing a practical joke on him. Every time we yelled over to bring shots of vodka to our table, Pete would be the only one to actually get vodka. The rest of us were drinking water. After about six shots, Pete was getting pretty hammered, so we called off the joke so he wouldn't puke in the cab going back to the hotel.

There were quite a few funny stories and one that I didn't find very funny, like in 1975, when someone stole my cowboy boots from the dressing room. Not real funny as I had to walk, and ride, back to the Hilton barefoot.

The years went by as I racked up quite a few wins from State, National and International events. I met my idol, Bill "Superfoot" Wallace, in 1975. My good friend, Charlie Castronovo and I attended a major tournament in Philadelphia. Charlie trained with me at Sensei Kaloudis' dojo, which I own today. He was a green belt and I was a brown belt at the time. Charlie later became a Passaic Police officer and retired, just before I did, at the rank of sergeant. Charlie was always a real character. We would affectionately call him "Tackleberry," as he would always carry two guns and sometimes three. Today, Charlie is one of my san dan's (3rd degree black belt) at my dojo. Charlie always had a dry sense of humor, so people didn't know how to take him.

道

I remember a story when Charlie was on loan to the county narcotics task force.

One day, the squad rounded up a half dozen dealers and look outs on a street corner in Paterson. As they were being booked, the detective removing the handcuffs said, "We have cuffs with no initials here, who owns them?"

Charlie turned around and said, "They're probably mine."

As the cop tossed them over, he told Charlie that he should engrave his initials into them so there's no further confusion.

Charlie said, "What are you, nuts?"

The detective looked confused.

Charlie then said, "What if they find a guy one day at the bottom of the river and he's wearing handcuffs with my initials!"

Nobody knew what to say.

道

Getting back to Philadelphia, there were several martial arts stars in attendance, including Wallace and Jeff Smith, of D.C. Smith was the current Light Heavyweight Kickboxing/Full Contact Karate Champion of the world. Wallace, with his unbelievable left leg, was arguably the fastest kicker in the world and middle weight champ. Joe Corley was also present. As a matter of fact, I think Corley was one of the tournament promoters and a top middleweight himself.

Charlie and I competed that day but didn't do well since we missed the cut for the finals. Late in the afternoon as we became spectators, I spotted Bill Wallace sitting by himself in the stands. He was just relaxing before sparring in an exhibition match, wearing his team stars and stripes gi (karate uniform). Charlie and I approached him and I introduced myself. Charlie took a picture of me sitting with "Superfoot," which to me at the time, was really cool. To my delight, Mr. Wallace, as I called him, came off as a regular guy! He was even kind enough to give me pointers on stretching. After this ten minute meet I remember thinking, *Man! Would I like to train with him one day!*

It wasn't until about 1987, the same year that I won 1st place kumite (sparring) in Athens, Greece, that I saw him again. I, along with a couple of my students, attended a Bill Wallace seminar held in Rutherford, NJ, at Rick Ricetti's dojo. The seminar was great, but it got even better. The next day, two other black belts and I joined Bill to play golf. Now, I gotta tell ya, I hate golf. I always thought golf was for two types of people: Professionals who make their living at it, and retired guys that lack the testosterone to do something a bit more challenging. But if Bill Wallace wanted to golf, I suddenly thought it was a great idea. Four of us played the first nine holes, and to my surprise, I didn't do too badly, for a non-golfer, I mean. By the time we did finish nine holes, however, the boredom started to really sink in. When I suggested, perhaps, we could call it a day, I was glad to hear Bill agree. "Superfoot" then suggested that we go for ice-cream. It seemed that he liked Carvel as much as I did. I could usually say no to most junk foods, but soft ice-cream? That was tough. We all had a great time hanging with the former world champ that day, as well as the entire weekend. My kicks could only improve as a result.

Over the years, I've had the pleasure of meeting many top martial artists in the country and even a few in Japan. Sensei Gary Alexander was one pioneer of American karate that helped me in my early years. My Sensei and Sensei Alexander were very close. We would attend his tournaments on a regular basis. Ed Kaloudis was actually vice president of Alexander's Martial Arts Institute back in the day, so Sensei Alexander would even visit our dojo in Clifton. Alexander was, and is, an imposing figure and a strong fighter! I always looked up to him. In the 1970's, he started his full contact kick fighting league, which allowed black belts only to participate.

One day, as a brown belt, I approached him with a rei (bow). "Sensei Alexander," I said, "I think I'm ready to fight the black belts. I really want to get involved in full contact as quickly as possible." I wanted so badly to be like Wallace, Joe Lewis, Jeff Smith and others on the full contact circuit. I always knew I started karate training a little late at age 16, compared to other fighters and I wanted to make up for lost time. My parents couldn't afford karate lessons for my brother Mike and me, so we had to wait until we had decent jobs to be able to pay for our lessons ourselves.

Sensei Alexander hearing my plea and believing that I was a good, respectful kid, said, "Yes Pat, you can fight. I think you have what it takes."

Not only did I fight all black belts that day, full contact, but I won third place. For me, it seemed like first! My picture even appeared in "Fighting Champions" magazine. *Now*, I thought, *it's time to pull out all the stops. Ciser, you gotta train like a maniac.* Only problem is, where do I go for training? Most instructors in the 70's were teaching traditional point sparring known as ippon kumite. So I ran five miles a day and on Saturday, I ran 10 miles. On Sunday I took off. Training at the karate dojo three or four times a week, I also started boxing at Lou Costello's Gym, in Paterson.

In 1976 I was promoted to 1st degree black belt at the age of 21. It was a big day indeed, as I went out to get a tattoo in celebration.

I continued to compete in Koeikan, AAU and outside tournaments for years to come. I also got a spot on the New Jersey All Star Team, which was organized by Sensei Jerry Thomson.

One of my strongest and most imposing opponents in the late 70's and early 80's was a black belt from Michigan by the name of Dave Spearing. Detroit and the surrounding area was a hub for Koeikan Karate dojo(s). Sensei Brian Frost was, as I've mentioned before, from that area and was responsible for producing some very talented fighters. Sensei Frost's top students opened a satellite dojo in the suburbs. Jack Sabat ran the Drayton Plains dojo before he relocated to California. Jeff Mason opened the Utica dojo and Sensei Frost owned and operated the Hazel Park school. In later years, Sensei Spearing, my old nemesis, opened a dojo in Lake Orion. Nemesis then, close friend and Koeikan brother today, Dave Spearing was tall, athletic and hit like a mule. His punches would make you wish you played golf and his front kick could send you to next Wednesday. By the early 80's, I had bulked-up with weights, to come in at about 207, so I'm sure he remained somewhat cautious himself. If we ever hurt each other in a match, however, we certainly wouldn't let the other one know.

Meeting at Koeikan's annual Tournament over the years, we would battle it out with him the winner one year, while I would win the next. One year, as I recall, Dave came to New Jersey with a group of competitors from Michigan. They attended a special class given by our Sensei, Brian Frost, at the Clifton dojo. There was no rough stuff, as the tournament was held on Sunday, two days later. Sensei taught gaku-te (reverse joint techniques) on this night. The class ended as all of the yudansha (black belts) began to leave the floor, following Sensei's command, "Ikimasho!" (Let's go! Dismissed)

I walked up to Mr. Spearing and said, "Hey Dave, wanna go a round?" I was tired of referee's always yelling "yame" (stop) or "matte" (wait) during a fight. That game of tag they call ippon kumite, (light contact sparring) just didn't cut it for guys like me and Spearing. Dave, a guy that loved to mix it up, happily agreed. Sensei Frost would referee this dojo fight, where punishment could be meted out. "Hajime!" was heard at a pitch that would get your adrenalin pumping as we attacked.

My yoko geri (side kick) immediately found its mark to his rib cage. This, my signature technique, would introduce him to the wall behind him. Spearing, though, could take punishment, as well as dish it out. He would hit me with a reverse punch that made me wonder if this was such a good idea after all.

Kicking and punching, we tested each other's breaking point as neither of us would give an inch. I narrowly deflected a front kick that looked like it could cave in a man's chest. My foot sweep was effective as the big man hit the floor. After he got up, bam! bam! a back fist to my skull and another reverse punch made me wince. Sensei, wanting us to be injury-free on Sunday, yelled "Yame!"(Stop) as we took a position to rei (bow) out.

This was dojo kumite at its finest. Banging each other off the walls gave us each a deep respect for the other. In 1990, we would take our Godan (5th degree black belt) test together, engaging in further combat.

道

Back in 1983, we faced each other, creating a story that would be told for years to come. It was the 1983 All Koeikan National Karate Championships held at Fairleigh Dickinson University, in Rutherford, New Jersey. Competitors from coast-to-coast were in attendance. There were some hard fought battles in the black belt division, with Dave and me making it to the finals. It was looked upon as the puncher versus the kicker. Known over years for my kicking demonstrations, including a seven and a half foot high mae tobi geri (front jump kick). With Spearing known for his punching power, including punching through several patio blocks, the stage was set.

Back and forth we battled as we matched each other point-for-point. "Time!" was called out by ring support as the referee jumped between us. "Sudden death" overtime would have to decide the match. First fighter to score a point would be declared the winner. Kamae, or guard position, would be held for a long few seconds as both of us cautiously waited. We waited for that perceived opening, that tacit body language or look of an eye. Who would attack first, looking for some weakness in our opponent's guard?

Suddenly, with focus and control, my forward right leg launched from a left straddle stance. A hook kick was my weapon of choice because I had not thrown one up until this point. The bottom of my right foot rose up, hooked in, and made contact with his right cheek, barely rocking his head back; a textbook hook kick for this particular tournament's rules. The rules were full contact to the body, light (touch only) contact to the head, for a quick point. Only problem was that as soon as I made light contact, I pulled back my leg, so as not to hit him too hard and get disqualified. You see, a successful full contact kick could not be answered as the person getting hit would be somewhat dazed, as a result. In this case, however, Dave lunged forward as my foot re-tracked and punched me in the back of the head, as I turned away. "Ippon!" yelled Sensei Frost, who was the center ref, raising his left hand in the direction of Dave Spearing. So there you have it, Dave won, and I lost. Fortunately though, I had a video of the match clearly showing my foot making contact first. Maybe I lost because of a bad call, but inside I knew that I had won. As it turned out, Dave broke his hand or knuckle on the back of my head, leaving some of my students wondering why he wasn't disqualified. I told them not to worry, these things happen.

Afterwards, Spearing was sitting on the bleachers with some ice on his knuckles. I walked up to him and said, "Hey Dave, you broke your hand huh? Gee, that's tough! I guess now I'll have to win bogu." Spearing loved bogu (full contact fighting with protective gear) and was very good at it!

Sure enough, I won match-after-match and ultimately took the first place trophy. I can remember to this day standing on the winner's platform with Sensei Kaloudis shouting over to me, "You did it Patrick! You really did it! You said that you would and you did! Congratulations!" He was always proud of his Jersey Boys. Anyone who has ever fought in point competition will tell you nothing is 100%. When you deal with human error, sometimes you get screwed. Just make sure you get it on video.

道

Another tournament I recall getting a bad call was when I fought Wayne Police Sergeant Ron Gaeta. Ronnie, like Dave, was a great compete-tor, and we became fast friends. But on this day at an AAU NJ State Championships, things went wrong again. Ronnie and I were tied with that sudden death scenario same as before. Ronnie knew that I was good with a front right leg yoko geri (side kick) since I threw a few of them during our match. *Now, a little trickery*, I thought. I threw a technique called "Kani Basami" (flying crab scissors). The beauty of it would be that Ronnie will think that I'm throwing another side kick that actually misses as my foot glides past the front of his chest. What he didn't realize is that my left foot was also moving forward, hooking behind his left calf. In mid-air, I now squeezed my legs, hitting him high with my right and low with my left leg, taking him down to the ground. I threw a back fist to his face believing it would be the point to win the match. I got up, as did Ronnie, with a surprised look on his face. Every judge just looked at me with a blank stare. Not one flag went up out of the four corner judges. I think their excuse was that they don't call that technique. Ronnie scored the next point to win the match with a perfectly executed reverse punch. And what a standup guy Gaeta proved to be as he told me, "Nice point, Pat. You had me."

It's funny, but after he said that, I didn't even mind losing to him.

道

Not to beat it up, but it happened to me in Venezuela in 1992. Two-to-two, sudden death would decide the match. As I sized up my opponent, I thought of chess. *Make him believe he has figured out my strategy, only to attack from another angle.* Throwing more kicks than punches during our match, I thought he might be ready for another kick. Lifting my left front leg to fake a front kick, I dropped it quickly as he went for the lower block. A smack was heard as my left ridge hand strike made contact with the Venezuelan's right temple. Yame was called as I could see myself advancing to the finals. Standing at attention on my starting line, I saw only one flag (the American judge) calling a point for me. Still in disbelief as the ref then yelled Hajime! I got caught with a reverse punch. Those South American judges liked that one okay, as three flags went up. "Ippon!" yelled the referee, awarding a point, and match to my opponent. After the match was over, I inquired why I didn't get a point for my textbook ridge hand. I was then told, "Oh, we don't call that technique down here." Man, if that wasn't a WTF moment.

These are some of my biggest title wins:

1975 New Jersey State AAU Karate Championships
1976 International Karate Championships, Caracas,
      Venezuela

1981 National Koeikan Kumite (sparring) Champion, USA
1983 National Koeikan Karate Full Contact Champion, USA
1987 International Karate Championships, Athens, Greece
1992 Triple Medal Winner, USNKF New Jersey State Karate
      Championships (kata, kumite, weapons kata)

1995 International Open Karate Championships, Athens, Greece

There was a time there in 1976 that I thought that I'd one day turn pro and get a paycheck for fighting rather than a trophy. But then I became a cop. On May 10, 1977, I discovered my calling when I was sworn in to the Clifton Police Department. It was then I realized that I would stay an amateur while training and fighting simply for the love of it!

> **"Karate is like boiling water,**
> **Take away the heat,**
> **And it gets cold."**
>
> **Gichin Funakoshi**

NEW YEAR'S EVE

Some cops want off on New Year's Eve. Hell, some cops want off every holiday. If you're celebrating Christmas with relatives you like, you tell your wife that you can get off. However, if December 25th means dinner with the ones you don't like, it's pretty easy to tell the Mrs. that the schedule read NTO (No Time Off). Some holidays, like Christmas Day or Easter, are boring at work, so having off was okay. But sometimes, working New Year's Eve was pretty entertaining. Cars #1 and #3 on midnights, which I worked quite often, was 2300–0700 and a non-stop shift. The only calm time on this night was 2345–0015. At midnight, Clifton looked like 4:00 am on a weeknight. Everyone apparently had arrived at their party destination for the Big Ball Drop and midnight celebration. Then, like clockwork, cars would start moving about to get to another bar or relative's house. The disputes that erupted between inebriated individuals ranged from shouting matches to stabbings. Gunshots, of which we had few, were more common in the larger cities of Paterson and Newark.

One such New Year, I believe it was in the late 80's, was particularly entertaining. My first call was a loud party, with too many people, in a small apartment. It was on the second floor of a three-story building on Main Avenue, a couple of blocks up from the Passaic (city) border. Arriving in my one-man Car #1, I called on scene and entered the building. As I walked up the approximately sixteen steps, I observed about a half dozen males at the top of the stairs engaging in horseplay. As my head approached the landing, one of these individuals spun around and kicked at my head. Spontaneously, I blocked the kick, trapped his leg and kept his forward momentum rush past my left shoulder, causing him to career down the flight of stairs. Four of his friends rushed past me down the stairs to check on his condition as I descended in a cautious manner. They found him bruised and shaken up, but otherwise okay. His friends became very apologetic while one even asked if they could bail him out tonight (a simple assault, on a police officer, in New Jersey becomes an aggravated assault and a 4th degree crime). After they realized this, they were surprised when I told them to take him home for the night and watch him. They could also take him to the hospital as a result of his fall. Taking him out of the building, one of his friends lagged behind to thank me again for not arresting his friend.

I then said, "Look, Pal. It's New Years and my shift just started. We're a little short-handed, as usual, and I don't, quite frankly, have time for your friend. I'm sure he'll be paying the price for a few days." All of this took place in just a few minutes as my back-up arrived. We called 10-7 detail complete and listened for our next call.

Some of my friends used to think I was nuts for not waiting for back-up on most calls. I did try to coordinate with other units giving an ETA (estimated time of arrival), on serious brawls or gang fights. Family disputes, where a woman is being victimized, were the ones I rushed into. Minutes, if not seconds, would matter to a female being pummeled. I guess I was either brave enough or stupid enough to see myself as a "white knight."

We didn't deal with a lot of crime per se on New Year's, just a lot of people acting stupid, including men and their "Beer Muscles" and the never-ending "I can still drive" mentality. Like my friend, Ricky Klein, used to say, "you can always find someone doin' somethin' stupid!" Bar fights, car accidents, including fatalities and domestic violence, filled the night. I always taught the rookies that police work is a little like fishing. Sometimes, you throw back the little fish, hoping for a big one.

道

We had countless stacked calls this night, as I went from call-to-call- to- call until the early hours of the morning. Then, just as I was ready to head down to the Lexington Diner, another Eastside call came in.

The radio crackled, "Cars 1 and 3. Come in." Car #3 was manned by a good cop, who actually came on the job with me in the spring of 1977. Richie Lekston was a tough son-of-a-bitch who never backed out of a fight. He was always a good back-up in a bar fight where anything can happen. Richie and I pulled up pretty much together, due to our proximity to the call on Third Street and Barkley Avenue. It seemed that a male guest, who had been drinking most of the night, was no longer wanted at the apartment by his female friend. He refused several pleas to leave and was becoming agitated.

Richie and I entered the dwelling and agreed to physically remove the now hostile New Year's guest. As we exited the dwelling, he didn't like the fact that I was pulling his arm at the shoulder. He expressed himself by cursing at me and telling me I was a "punk." He threw a right haymaker at my face. This action, of course, was no match for a duck and left hook to the side of his head. He fell to the sidewalk, as I was in no mood to take any shit after a non-stop shift. Richie and I helped him up as Richie went for his cuffs. Richie seemed a little surprised when I told the man to beat it and not come back.

As he walked north on Third Street, seemingly happy just to leave, Richie asked, "Are you sure you don't want to lock him up?"

I said, "Rich, how can you compare locking him up with six eggs over easy at the Lexington (Diner)."

道

Bar fights in the Botany were sometimes memorable; sometimes for the violence (i.e. aggravated assaults, homicides) and sometimes for the humor. One night I was working Car #1, Botany village, when I was dispatched to the Cozy Corner Tavern on Lake and Hope Avenues. It seemed there was an unruly patron throwing beer bottles and bar stools and everyone was afraid to confront him. I pulled up to the front of the bar angling the corner on the wrong side of the street. This way, I could jump out of my cruiser and slip inside the front door, avoiding any wasted time.

It was a summer day, so the heavy wooden door was left open to the inside while the screen door remained closed. As soon as I entered, I saw the owner of the tavern, who I came to know, crouched behind the bar. To my right, near the pool table, was a white male with a beard, dressed like a member of a motorcycle gang. He appeared grumpy and was definitely in a bad mood. He was a pretty good size and someone who could do some serious damage, even if you won the fight.

By the way, I never carried mace or endorsed its use, as it bothered me and the other cops just as much as the guy who is being sprayed. I used to have a little joke with the guys, "I never knocked out or swept the wrong guy."

I always had a knack for sizing people up. They say that you can't judge a book by its cover but that's bullshit! Sometimes, it's easy to tell. When a punk has a knife or an ex-military man wields one, you'll know the difference immediately. Sometimes, you see fear in the eyes of a big mouth, while noting rage and a determined spirit in another. If he's a punk and unarmed, sweep his legs out from under him. It may be necessary to help him up and then do it again, so he realized that he is outclassed and comes to appreciate a break when he sees one. In some cases, truly dangerous individuals need to be rendered unconscious.

This violent adversary had all the markings and behavior of a real threat. This was a time I thought to use the proper heiho (strategy). As I sized him up looking around the bar, I felt that I needed to close the gap between us without appearing as a threat. I started talking while walking closer on a slight angle, holding him near my right shoulder.

This allowed me to keep a non-aggressive stance while maintaining balance and the ability to use tenshin waza (dodging techniques).

Ostensibly showing no interest in the actor, I started babbling, "Wow! As I scanned the damage to the bar, "this place looks like one of those old John Wayne movies! Is everybody okay?" (I was implying everyone, including the actor). This was even better than two years ago at Nick and Steve's bar. I knew this was a bunch of BS, but I could tell that he was dropping his guard as I seemed friendly. My BS continued as I found myself within reach. "Hey Rich!" I called out to the owner behind the bar. "Are you sure okay?" I could see every move that the actor (suspect) could make with my peripheral vision.

Suddenly, without warning, my right hand shot toward his chin, palm up; snatching his beard with a grip that said, "I mean business," I yanked him forward, ran him toward the front door about 15 feet away, and flung him past me, right through the screen door. He tripped on the step outside and landed on the concrete sidewalk. The screen door slammed shut with its heavy springs. I told Richie, "I'll be right back." Stepping outside to confront this individual again, he was on all fours about to stand. Before he could stand, I grabbed him by the back of his collar and belt buckle and rammed his head into the fender of my cruiser.

Richie came outside and told me that he was usually a really good customer. By now, I was putting the cuffs on him and doing a search of his person. My back-up arrived and assisted me placing him in the back of my radio car. With my back-up watching the prisoner, Richie pulled me aside and said, "Hey Pat, do you really have to lock him up?"

I looked at him incredulously, "Lock him up? Are you serious, Rich? He just trashed your bar and terrorized your customers!"

He looked at me, sighed and explained, "Well Pat, here's the deal. A couple of hours ago, he found his girlfriend giving oral sex to some black guy that he never saw before. He's devastated. Look, nobody really got hurt and he'll be sorry tomorrow. Let me talk to him."

"All right Richie," I replied, as I opened the door to the back seat of my cruiser where the guy sat dejected.

He said he'd had enough and just wanted to go home and sleep. So, because Richie used to give me tips on drug dealers in the area, I relented. "All right, Rich, you owe me one." I then removed the actor from the rear of my cruiser and "unarrested" him. There's really no such term in NJ law enforcement, but it sounded good.

This was a case where I used deception in order to raise the odds of a favorable outcome. Police officers should try to avoid rolling around the ground with someone, thereby giving them the chance of rendering you unconscious, taking your firearm and causing additional mayhem. Always remember, in a civilized society, the police have to win. We are in the vanguard; we take all the risks when doing the job. Just use and listen to your instincts. Cops can't testify to having a gut feeling, but we know it's there. Ensure that you go home to your loved ones at the end of the day. We are not the ones who woke up in the morning intent on committing a crime. We wake up with a daily intention of stopping one.

Bar fights are so unpredictable. The actors (suspects) might be half in the bag or on drugs. They may have a weapon or just use what's available like a beer bottle or pool stick. Many times they have friends waiting on the sidelines to assist them. Even girlfriends will sometimes jump on your back as you try to handcuff an actor.

道

As I previously stated, some are punks while others can be a tough son-of-a-bitches who will remain branded in your memory. One such guy was "Hitler." Over the years, the Botany Village section of Clifton had some pretty tough bars. One of the toughest was a Yugoslavian bar called the Atlantic Inn. We used to moonlight there on weekends. A frequent flyer, or should I say fighter, there and throughout the Botany was known as Hitler. He was a really strong, determined individual, who after having a few drinks, loved to fight. I think he liked to test himself and enjoyed smashing anyone who challenged him. Back then, it was the Yugoslavian community who called him Hitler.

One Saturday night, two of my friends were working at the Atlantic Inn when I received a radio call of a fight at that establishment. Working midnights in Car #1, I quickly arrived on scene. I entered the bar and was greeted by the two off duty officers. They immediately told me, "Pat, it's Hitler and he's out of control." I then took a couple of steps deeper into the lobby as Hitler emerged from the bar. We confronted each other as my friends took a few steps back. I used to tell the cops I worked with that if it looked like things were "about to heat up," step back. I work better with no one in my way.

At this point, I told Hitler that he had to leave the bar and if he did, he could probably return tomorrow. I had no idea yet if I was locking him up, or if he would ever be let back in the bar, I just knew that I wanted him outside. Hitler replied, "We fight!"

I then stated, "Hitler, you don't want to fight me. 1) You'll lose and 2) you're gonna go to jail."

He then replied, "You have badge? You take off badge. We fight!" He swung off his jacket and flung it to the floor as he took up a pugilistic stance.

At this time, I could only remember and respond with what's known as "Sen, no Sen", which is Japanese for, "attack the attack."

My right hand launched. With little thought, I threw a crushing blow to the bridge of his nose sending him reeling backward. His approximately 240 pound frame, struck the closed coat check room door, as he crashed through the bottom half. I followed him into the coat room as he seemed half out of it, yet still making a very determined effort to stand back-up. I looked down at him and said, "Sorry Hitler, but you're too dangerous for me to let you get back-up." I then delivered a second blow, knocking him out. When he woke up, he found himself wearing my handcuffs.

That morning after working midnights, I was in municipal court on a couple of cases. Hitler got arraigned and was now sitting in his cell waiting for transport to the county jail. He refused any treatment and signed off on a ride to the hospital. He was certainly a tough SOB. He did request one thing from the jailer, however. He wanted to talk to me. I agreed and went to the cell block area.

Hitler looked me over from behind his cell bars with a look that was harder than the steel that now encased him. He said, "You won! I fuck up. You very strong, I respect!" and grunted. Shit, I now had some respect for him. He knew he was wrong, accepted responsibility and pleaded guilty. After this episode, whenever I saw Hitler on the street, he would wave to me and even stand by on the street if he thought I might need help with someone I was confronting. That's the way it should always be. You screw up, you pay and you move on.

道

It's funny, but I used to get an occasional vandal or drug dealer that would ask me if I could just take them in the alley and "tune them up" instead of arresting them. Some thought a quick beating would be swifter and they'd recover in a few days. I refused, of course, as the handcuffs went on.

There were so many altercations with various actors over the years this book would be twice as long if I spoke about all of them. I'll try to narrow them down to the most entertaining, or if I think there could be a lesson to be learned. Here's a lesson I learned from a good municipal judge.

In the late 70's, I was working Car #3, and still considered a rookie, when the radio crackled, "Cars 1 and 3, come in. Respond to Spring Street off Clifton Avenue on a disturbance in the street." Spring Street was only a block long so it wasn't hard to find the unruly male yelling and screaming in the middle of the road. I arrived easily before Car #1, who was down in Botany Village at the time of the call. I drove up and exited my car confronting this irrational individual. He was possibly on CDS, and having trouble with a neighbor. The neighbor retreated into his home as the actor's brother witnessed me confront him. It became apparent almost immediately that this unruly actor could not be reasoned with. The actor, not happy with my intolerant attitude, swung wildly at my head! I reacted swiftly and spun him in a half circle, putting him over the hood of my car. I wrenched his arm behind his back and got one cuff on him as he struggled to spring off the hood while continuing to resist. I continued to keep his arm locked behind his back and grabbed the back of his neck with my other hand. I felt a POW!! His brother punched me in the back of the head from over my right shoulder blade. What worked well for me is that he punched me at about 45 degrees from center. This was one of the exact spots on my skull that I have had wood broken over me during sanchin (deep breathing exercises). Boards can strike your hairline in the front and the rear on both sides approximately 45 degree angle. Sensei Edward Kaloudis taught me this when I assisted him doing a demonstration at Madison Square Garden's Felt Forum in 1975. Sensei Kaloudis had us break red 'common' house bricks over his head just before breaking 3 stacked bricks with his head. Surely, one of the most incredible feats I've ever witnessed. Sensei Kaloudis had more "Ki" in his finger than I had in my entire body.

So, as the punch had little effect on me, this ill-advised assailant shook his hand in pain. He then received from me a side kick to his ribcage. The first actor now broke free and charged at me, only to be rendered unconscious with an overhand right and left hook combination. I then swept his brother's feet out from under him as back-up Officer Bobby Bais arrived in Car #1, to assist me. We handcuffed both actors and placed one each in our radio cars for a trip to headquarters. Upon making bail, these two brothers hired a lawyer and charged me with assault. Their attorney apparently did all his homework and found out a lot about me personally before the trial in municipal court. Presiding in Clifton was the Honorable Harry Fengya.

Harry was a no-nonsense judge who had some foibles but had a good sense of right and wrong. There, of course, were counter claims filed, including simple assault against me (two counts) and simple assault against a police officer on both men and resisting arrest and interfering with a law enforcement officer. In New Jersey, a simple assault against a police officer automatically became a 4th degree aggravated assault. In the late 70's, however, we were still using Title 2A rather than 2C, so a simple assault (I was not injured regardless of the punch to the head) remained a simple assault.

I testified to the facts, as I knew them, as did other witnesses and back-up Officer Bais. The defendants then testified putting forward their spin on events with their specious story explaining that they were in fear of me.

道

In most cases, I couldn't truthfully testify that I was in fear, as I blocked and punched, sometimes in a perfunctory manner. Later, I learned more about "fear" being an important component in proving various crimes had even taken place. Robbery, for instance, is one such crime. I remember stories of a detective, Robert Challice, who was extremely effective on the streets of Paterson, testifying that he was not even slightly fearful of two perpetrator's that he confronted one night. As the story went (but I did not verify), Challice lost the case rather than fabricate stories of fear. Challice had a "Clint Eastwood" tough guy image that many cops admired. A true bushi (warrior) doesn't fear death, but this is a difficult concept for most people.

道

Getting back to their testimony and their attorney's preparation, I thought, *Shit. This guy should be my agent!* Their attorney regaled the judge with a story that depicted me to be the next Chuck Norris!

"Your Honor, Officer Ciser owns and operates a karate school. He is a former member of the United States karate team (Now hold on, this is where it gets really good). "His hands and feet are weapons and he used them on my clients (I couldn't help but envision images of Billy Jack). "My clients were in fear and were helpless against him." The judge, leaning back in his chair, appeared to absorb his entire BS story and allowed the attorney to finish his diatribe.

It was now time for Judge Fengya to render his decision. He leaned forward, in his robe, peered over his glasses, and said, "Mr. Prosecutor, Mr. (their attorney), it is my decision that not only could Officer Ciser defend himself against two assailants using his hands and feet; if he had a nightstick on him, he could have also used that. Your clients have the gall to attack a police officer in full uniform, during the performance of his duties and then *claim* that *they* were the victims? I find Officer Ciser not guilty and I commend him for his actions. On the other hand, I find the defendants guilty on all counts. You are both very lucky that Officer Ciser received no injuries during this altercation."

It was then that I realized that as long as I, or a third party, was in danger or under attack, I could take appropriate action as needed. Judge Harry Fengya did the right thing that day, but it wouldn't always be so with other Judges.

道

One evening, on the midnight shift, I brought a guy in for stealing a car in the Botany section of Clifton. All the way into headquarters, while sitting in my back seat, he had his face up against the cage telling me that I was a punk. "You hide behind that badge," he said. "One-on-one, I'd beat your face in," he continued.

I, of course, tried to explain to him that it was the **badge** that was actually saving him.

He just kept rambling on as the insults mounted. These guys could get very abusive, especially when they bring your wife and kids into it.

道

Another guy I locked up, for instance, said that he was glad I worked midnights, so he could find out where I live and visit my wife one night. He explained in vivid detail what he would do to my wife while tying her up. "And before I leave, I'm gonna set your house on fire," he boasted.

It was then, that I decided to make him fear me, more than I would ever fear him. I'd rather not discuss the approach I took with this sadistic low-life; I can only say that he urinated all over himself as a result of our little talk.

道

Getting back to the guy in my back seat; he began to tell me that my wife sucked him off last night. Rather than becoming angry, I started to laugh. "Who the "F__" are you kiddin', you're such a punk! My wife would kick the shit out of you!" My laughter only pissed him off more. Sometimes you just can't win.

道

Pulling into the car port, the desk officer came out to assist me. I locked up my firearm as the desk officer took him out of my back seat. This loud mouth was handcuffed behind his back and could do little more than scream and kick. As he continued to call me out, the desk officer said, "Hey, Pat, what do you wanna do? I know, I know, we're supposed to strap him in a chair or put him in a cell, until he calms down. But I wanted to process him including fingerprints, and get back on the road."

"Take his cuffs off," I replied.

"Are you sure, Pat?" asked the desk officer.

"Yeah, he'll be alright, he's just blowin' smoke."

The officer removed his cuffs, while standing behind the actor, while I took a position in front of him.

The right-hand haymaker came at me the second the cuffs were off. Not surprised, I blocked and countered with a punch of my own. He fell backward with a surprised look on his face. He lunged forward, so as to tackle me, receiving a left hook to the side of his head for his efforts. I turned slightly to walk away, in a tacit way to let him know we're done. Beaten, but not yet defeated, he lunged forward to jump on my back. He was then met with a back kick (ushiro geri). This kick lifted him off the ground as gravity quickly pulled him back down. Lying on the floor, he apparently decided that he had enough.

The desk officer put him in a cell and told dispatch to have the ambulance crew take a look at him. The sergeant, seeing me a short time later, asked me what happened. I explained that I tried to process the prisoner for car theft, when he jumped me. The sergeant, not happy with the outcome, asked me why I took the cuffs off, if I knew the guy was that violent.

Always quick with a retort I asked, "He had to take a piss; did you want me to hold his dick for him?" The sergeant walked away speechless.

道

There were a lot of violent guys that wanted to test themselves over the years. I remember one that I sent to the hospital. The same sergeant as before grabbed me in the hall and asked, "Hey Pat, the doctor at the hospital said that you broke a guy's nose in three places! How do you break a nose in three places?"

I looked at him and said, "Good technique, I guess."

道

As a fighter, whether it's Karate-Do, Boxing or MMA, there's nothing better than throwing the perfect technique that is devastating to your opponent. As they say in Aikido, "We create beautiful violence." Sometimes, after executing that perfect technique, there is a bad feeling, however, like an incident in 2004.

At the time, I was a detective sergeant in charge of Clifton's Narcotics/Street Crime Unit. I was cruising through the Botany village section in my unmarked Dodge when I spotted a large adult male pulling the hair of a female. It appeared that she didn't want to cross the street so she was being dragged.

Once they crossed the street, I pulled over and exited my vehicle while telling dispatch to start a back-up officer. As I walked toward the couple, I pulled out my shield from under my tee shirt (on a neck chain), displaying it as I announced that I was a Clifton police officer. Inquiring what the problem was and asking if the female knew, and felt safe with, this male. I heard a strong Polish accent, "You police? You no police!" He reached for my badge as I blocked his arm away. He appeared irritated and took an aggressive posture. Now, remember how I said that I could size most guys up? Well, this guy was and looked stronger than "Hitler." He looked to be about 6'2", 250-260 lbs. He also looked like he wasn't used to taking any shit from anybody.

I thought, *if I knock his teeth out, he'll probably smile and then rip my head off. I don't want to break his knee unless he attacks violently and I have no recourse.* So, I chose my favorite technique. I decided to levitate him. That is what I call a perfectly delivered foot sweep. It's not a sweep of his front leg, however; it is a beautifully timed sweep of the back leg. I perfected this sweep in the ring years ago. Sensei Brian Frost told me in the early 90's, that I had one of the best sweeps he had ever seen; a great compliment from my mentor. In the beginning, I watched my opponents start to lift their front leg in order to kick. At that split second of their attack, I would use sen, no sen, attack the attack, and swept their back leg with such force that they seemed to come up off the ground, like floating, only to crash down. I performed this technique on one of my opponents in Greece, in 1987. He crashed to the ground so hard on the marble surface, that I was later relieved to learn that he was okay. As my sweep improved, I realized that I didn't need to wait for an attempted kick. Whenever my opponent shifted his weight from his front foot to his back foot, I could aggressively attack. I blitzed, or suddenly lunged in, causing my opponent to shift his weight, thereby setting him up.

Getting back to this "strong-like bull" Polish guy, I read his body language like a page in a book. I knew if I allowed him to grab me or draw first blood, he would not only beat my brains in, but also be in a position to take my Beretta. It quickly became apparent after exchanging a few words to calm him down, that my efforts were futile. Just when I needed beautiful violence, my levitation technique was superb. His feet flew up into the air, as I guided him back to earth. But we had a problem, so I thought.

He hit the back of his head so hard on the concrete sidewalk that you could actually hear, "Thump!" I thought, *Holy shit! I swept him too hard.* Well, as it so happened, in another second or two, I was never so happy to see a guy try to stand and fight some more! He pushed himself up to a seated position as I grabbed his throat, not his neck, with my left hand.

I told him, "Don't even try to get up or I'll rip your throat out." Still confused on how he hit the ground so fast, he didn't seem to want to challenge me on this one. Two radio cars pulled up, at this point, and two uniformed officers assisted me getting the actor to his feet. As the officers spoke with him and called me "Sergeant," it seemed that he realized his mistake and visibly calmed down, as I saw him relax his shoulders.

The three of us were now surrounding him, as I couldn't wait to check the back of his head. Man! Was I relieved that I didn't see any blood. This guy had a hard head. He could probably do sanchin better than me! I took his girlfriend aside, as back-up officers stayed with the actor. She explained to me that they lived together in Passaic and he didn't mean to pull her hair. He had a couple of drinks and had a bad day. She begged me not to arrest him. I knew that if I charged him with domestic violence against her, she would be a hostile witness later. I decided to go back to looking for street sales. Hell, he got the worst of our confrontation and it helps me keep in practice. I, of course, made him promise not to ever hurt her or I'd come after him. He promised, apologized and was allowed to leave.

道

On average, from 2000 to 2009, over 59,000 law enforcement officers were assaulted each year in America. Never get complacent; always be prepared for battle, both mentally and physically.

There is discretion built into all areas of law enforcement. The cop has discretion to arrest, the judge has discretion at sentencing, and the parole board has discretion to release.

Sen Sen No Sen: Pre-Emptive Initiative.
To attack the instant prior to the opponents attack. This is the most advanced form of "sen" (attack), and comes from a highly developed sense of perception and anticipation of the opponents attack intention. This by reading subtle things which may be termed "tells," such as slight movements of foot, hand, head, or a minor shift in weight distribution, etc.

Taken from the book "Maze Koze"
By Brian Frost

UNINTENDED CONSEQUENCES

While working the 2000–0400 (8pm-4am), power shift, in the early 90's, I became very interested in locating a Clifton fugitive, who we'll call "Kyle Logan." He was wanted on a couple of minor warrants from out of town, and a Clifton warrant for aggravated assault on a police officer. One of our guys attempted to arrest him one night on Lake Avenue, but he got away by striking the officer in the face, before fleeing on foot. I thought, *how nice would it be for him to take a swing at me?* I proceeded to ask the folks in the neighborhood if they had seen him, or knew where he was staying, but no one was "snitchin."

About three or four days later, we heard that Kyle, snatched his baby from the mother, who had sole custody, and fled to an unknown location. I was working Car #402 on this evening and was patrolling through the Village Square, when a young woman flagged me down. I recognized her from the neighborhood and she told me, "Pat, I'm not one for snitchin, but that boy, Kyle Logan, has gone too far. He took my friend's baby and I know where he's stayin. He be with his friend on Barbour Avenue in Passaic." She added that the baby was with him and that she was concerned the infant was not being properly cared for.

With this information, I asked headquarters to call Passaic (City) PD and ask if they had two plain clothed officers that could meet me in Clifton's Village Square. The Square was right on the Passaic border and Barbour Avenue was just around the corner in Passaic. I then got on the air and asked Officer Richard Klein for a favor. "Hey, Rick," I said, "stop by San Remo's Pizza (which was on Main Avenue), and ask Jimmy for an empty pizza box. I'll meet you in the square." A short time later, two street-crime Detectives Juan Gonzalez and Joseph Rios, showed up, along with Ricky. I briefed them on my plan and gave them a photo from the BOLO (be on the look-out) inside my cruiser. Kyle was a black male in his mid-twenties, average build, with short cropped hair. I knew him from the neighborhood but never locked him up before.

One of the Passaic detectives was to pretend that he was delivering a pizza, but apparently had the wrong apartment. The other detective would serve as his back-up or cover officer. Ricky would take the back of the building, while I would take the front. We all drove over to Barbour Avenue and parked outside the three-story building. We took our positions as the Passaic detective with the "pizza" climbed the stairs. As it turned out, Kyle Logan opened the third floor apartment door, just as the detective approached. Kyle saw the cop and ran back into the apartment with both detectives a few steps behind. Kyle ran through the apartment and dove right through the front apartment window facing the street, glass and all. I was standing out front, and witnessed him land on the fire escape. Glass flew out raining down to the sidewalk. Drawing my 9mm, I pointed it at him and yelled, "Logan, give it up!" With that, he looked at me with the old, "Oh Shit" look, turned around, and started to climb the steel cable for the fire escape to the roof. Both, the Passaic detective and I, called for back-up as Passaic police took custody of the infant found in the apartment.

Back-up officers, from both cities, surrounded the building as four of us climbed the interior stairs to the roof. As we ascended the stairs with caution, one of the officers wondered if he'd still be on the roof. I remember commenting that unless Scotty beamed him up, he's up there. Ricky and I came through the door to the roof together, as we lit it up with our flashlights, guns drawn. The roof was empty.

Ricky said, "Shit! Where did he go?"

I replied, "Maybe Scotty beamed him up after all."

We spread out and walked across the roof only to discover a large opening in the center of the building. It was a giant air shaft for kitchen or bathroom windows all the way down. I shined my light down on the concrete floor, and there, at the basement level, lie Kyle Logan. I turned off my light for a moment and realized that you couldn't see a thing. When he made it to the roof, he must have tried to run across, only to fall four stories, including the basement, to the cement ground floor. Once downstairs, we found him barely alive. We rushed him to Passaic General Hospital, where they put him in ICU (Intensive Care Unit). I was assigned to guard my prisoner. Stationed outside his room, I witnessed him "code," as he breathed his last breath. A couple of days later, I ran into the female who "snitched" on Kyle. She broke down in tears saying that she never expected that he would die. But in her next breath, she thanked me for getting the baby back to its mother, safe and sound.

道

Another incident while on the power shift, I was working a two-man car with Warren Lee. Lee was always fun to work with, as he had a lot of good stories, mostly from his days in the Navy. We spotted a car in the Botany section of Clifton, on Parker Avenue that raised our suspicion. Three occupants of the car, all gave us the look and turn. I was driving as Warren ran the plate. The vehicle turned to cross the Ackerman Avenue Bridge to Garfield (City) as I continued to tail them. Over the bridge they turned left onto River Road, now in Garfield. Having a Clifton cruiser follow you into Bergen County probably didn't make them feel well, as I could see the driver's eyes watching me in his rear view mirror.

Dispatch called to us, "That's an entered vehicle, 402! (stolen car).

"Okay headquarters," Warren acknowledged. "We're gonna light em up," (engage lights and siren) notifying dispatch.

Heading toward Elmwood Park, I flipped the switch and Bam! It was off to the races. Every time they accelerated I used to think, *when are they going to realize that running only makes it worse?* Then of course I wonder, *what else do they have to hide?* Hitting speeds of about 60 mph, the chase didn't last long. We approached train tracks which are always raised, supplying a serious speed bump you might say. While I lay back a little, touching my brakes, the stolen car never touched his. And as you could imagine; the car went airborne and landed hard just over the double yellow line. The car's front left corner, hit head on, into the vehicle coming toward us. The surprised and innocent driver coming the other way wound up with a broken ankle. The driver of the stolen car wouldn't be so lucky. He wound up dead.

This chase had a tragic end for this reckless felon, as he decided to "up the anty" and run. There are good arguments on both sides of the aisle relating to car chases. As far as I'm concerned, the bottom line is that the criminals purposely prey on the citizenry to get what their voracious appetites desire. They choose to break the law. They choose to run and start a pursuit. Police officers take a sworn oath to protect people and property and are what is good in our society. If Clifton didn't chase stolen cars, we would see a dramatic increase in stolen cars. Let's examine a scenario and consider what you would think, if this were you.

You just bought the car of your dreams, a BMW, Mercedes, or a Corvette, for instance. It's a cold morning and the car isn't quite warmed up enough as you pulled into the Dunkin Donuts. You figure, *I'll be out in a minute or two*, as you leave your car running with the heat on. As you exit the store with your cup of "joe," you're in disbelief as someone is driving away with your brand new ride. What good luck, however, as a police car is just arriving for a coffee of his own.

"Officer! Officer!" you scream, "Please chase my car, it was just stolen! I can see it a half a block away!"

But instead of screeching out of the parking lot in hot pursuit, he tells you, "Sorry, we're not allowed to chase stolen cars."

You stare, or scream at him in disbelief. It's your car! Now is it okay for cops to chase? I can't tell you how many stolen cars we chased over the years that were involved in other crimes as well; which is another reason why we need to stay proactive.

END OF WATCH

November 21, 2003: Clifton officers have come to know this date all too well.

It was the day shift when Clifton motorcycle Officer John Samra, pulled over a van on Third Street facing south. It was a routine traffic stop like so many others. But like they teach us in the police academy, nothing is routine.

Officer Samra, a dedicated cop that kept himself in top physical condition, was a "Lakeview" kid like me. I grew up on East Second Street with five siblings. John grew up around the corner on East Third Street with four. We all went to St. Brendan's Grammar School, with many of us graduating with each other. I was older than John and graduated with his sister Michelle. When I was a rookie, I recall John asking me what it was like to be a Clifton cop. "It's a great job, kid," I would say, as I encouraged him to come on the force.

And so, John Samra, a fifteen year veteran and former marine, dismounted his motorcycle after making the stop. With heroin still in his system from the night before, the driver of the van waited nervously as he watched "Johnny," as we called him, start to walk up to the driver window. Suddenly, the van's driver decides it's better to take off, rather than get caught driving while suspended again. The van pulled out as Officer Samra quickly ran back to his motorcycle, while calling out his situation to Clifton dispatch. As John got back on his bike, he could see the van that was traveling south turn left onto Union Avenue, ostensibly heading east to Main Avenue. Samra, apparently realizing that if he tried to follow along the same route he would never catch up in time, to see which way the van turns when he gets to Main Avenue, about three blocks down from Third Street. So, John turns left down Washington Avenue, paralleling the van, also heading toward Main, in an effort to get an eyeball on the fleeing van's direction. Once the van hits Main Avenue, he could turn right and drive further south toward the City of Passaic. If he's from Paterson, he could turn left when he hits Main and then drive right past Samra who would have already arrived at Main and Washington.

Officer Samra was now heading east on Washington, as the van he was after made two left turns, now heading toward Washington Avenue on Maple. The timing and route they both took could not have been worse for John. The van ran the stop sign and plowed into the right side of Samra's motorcycle, at the Washington Avenue and Maple Place intersection. This would be John's last ride.

The van's driver then attempted to flee on foot as Officer Samra, one of Clifton's absolute finest, lie dying in the street. Two passersby, Michael Rabel and Anthony Di Martino, ran after the suspect and held him for the police. They were later commended for their brave actions.

A couple of days later, the entire department would line up in front of Quinlan's Funeral Home, on Van Houten Avenue for John's wake. Missing was a detective captain, who thought it was more important to attend a Jets football game at the Meadowlands. His aspirations to be named chief one day would now become a chimera, as word would spread of his political suicide. Living in his sheltered bubble on the second floor of the detective bureau, he didn't have a clue, or apparently, a heart.

This, the same detective captain due to his ignorance of the law, would make John look foolish in his prepared press release. Too high and mighty to ask for someone else's opinion or help, he erroneously wrote the following; "In an apparent attempt to 'cut off' the fleeing vehicle." We, as a department, had two very big problems with his statement! Firstly, the Attorney General's guideline in NJ, regarding motor vehicle pursuits are very specific. The police will not 'cut off' a fleeing vehicle. Secondly, if you're sitting home reading your morning newspaper, you might think the following. Motorcycle cop 'cuts off' fleeing van! Duh; why did a motorcycle cut off a van? Didn't he know any better?"

So anyone living in Clifton, and especially anyone who knew Johnny, let me make myself clear! Officer John Samra did not cut anyone off! John was "street paralleling" in an effort to "head off" the van only. John was an excellent police officer who knew the law and was a good friend to many of us. May he rest in peace!

道

It's sad, all of the death that we witness. I remember a teenager who hung himself in a garage. Cutting him down as a rookie, I wasn't much older than him.

The pretty young girl that died in my arms, after a terrible car accident, the left side of her mouth and cheek lacerated to her ear. Blood would gush out this wound, with each dying beat of her heart. Her eyes locked with mine, tacitly asking me to save her.

The little kid, that was run over while riding his bicycle.

The suicides; there are too many to count.

The human "road kill" on the highways. "He was struck here," said Little Falls Sergeant Brian LaPooh, as we discussed if the accident was in his jurisdiction or mine.

"Yeah," I said, "he was struck there by the first car, over there by the second car, and there where his intestines lie, by yet another vehicle."

The vicious homicide of that poor pregnant girl in her own bed, lying in her blood soaked sheets.

The bizarre case of the guy who put a drill in a vise, then proceeded to drill a hole through his forehead, and into his brain.

The "Hail Mary" murder next to school 15.

The autoerotic asphyxiation guy we found hanging from his closet door; masturbating for that ultimate climax. Hope it was worth it.

The guy that blew his brains out with a high powered rifle, I can still see them dripping from the ceiling.

Passaic(s) little Devina; kidnapped, raped and murdered; we still remember you.

The Third Street Church shooting; Why?

Opening the door on Harrison Street to discover an entire family was murdered; the surviving toddler, trying to warm up to her cold dead mother.

Unless you were there, you don't know how it feels. People want to help you by offering advice. You sometimes just want to scream, "Were you there?!!" You have to find a way to work this out in your mind so you can respond to your next call. You're on an emotional roller coaster, while you try to be many things to many different people. Big city cops have it even worse.

There are countless cases that end in tragedy in the career of a cop. You start to become numb and jaded. People don't understand, your own wife doesn't understand. You come home from a traumatic event thankful you made it, while she's nagging that you didn't cut the grass. If you're a cop, talk to your brothers, brother. They're the only ones who can relate.

I never dreamed it would be me
My name for all eternity
Recorded here at this hallowed place
Alas, my name, no more my face.

"In the Line of Duty" I hear them say
My family now the price will pay
My folded flag stained with their tears
We only had those few short years.

The badge no longer on my chest
I sleep now in eternal rest
My sword I pass to those behind
And pray they keep this thought in mind.

I never dreamed it would be me
And with heavy heart and bended knee
I ask for all here in the past
Dear God, let my name be the last.

--Sgt. George Hann, LAPD (ret.)

LAKE AVENUE

It was February of 1988, when I was working Car #1. It was in the early evening when I met up with Billy Gibson, who was assigned to the Clifton Tactical squad. I was driving a marked radio car, assigned to the patrol division, while Billy was in plain clothes driving an unmarked car. We were parked car-to-car, taking a short respite, as it was not a very busy night. Well, that was all about to change. Dispatch called out, "Cars 1, 3 and 18, come in." Robert Luciano was in Car #3 and the Eastside sergeant was in Car #18. "Respond to Lake Avenue on a man with a high powered rifle," dispatch continued. His wife called and said he pointed the gun at her, so she ran out of the house. The husband was down in the basement. Luciano, the sergeant and I, all acknowledged the call by stating our locations and giving the other cars an idea how far away from the call we were. Since Bill was with me in Clifton's Village Square, he knew immediately that 1) we were both two blocks from the call and 2) the other cars would take a few minutes to arrive. Billy got on the air as he followed me down Lake Avenue.

Gibson said, "502, I'm responding with Car #1 from the square."

The dispatcher replied, "502. K." Billy was the perfect back-up. Not only was he a good cop, but he trained with me for a number of years at my dojo (karate school) and had excellent speed and reflexes. And on these calls, we sometimes had to move fast!

Billy and I rolled up as the complainant, on her neighbor's porch, flagged us down. Exiting our cars with our guns drawn, we cautiously approached the house. The man's wife met us between the houses to fill us in further. "My husband," she said while trembling "is in the basement. He's in a chair holding his hunting rifle. He can't really walk too well and he would need assistance to come upstairs." She further explained that he was 72 years old and very depressed, as of late. His quality of life had certainly diminished the last few years, not being able to walk and all. She informed us that he called out to her when she was in the kitchen. She went to the basement stairs and started to descend. Not wanting to go down all the way because she was busy, she leaned over and poked her head below the basement ceiling to ask her husband what he wanted. To her shock and amazement, he pointed his rifle, taking aim right at her. She quickly jumped back and screamed. That's when she bolted from the house, ran to her neighbor's porch and frantically rang her doorbell.

Billy and I entered the house as I thought to myself, *Ciser, you're such an asshole for not wearing a vest.* This was not the first time, nor the last, I would think this. As I walked closer to the basement door off of the kitchen, I recalled a story about a New York City cop. The cop got shot with a high-powered rifle while wearing a bullet proof vest. Unfortunately, the vest only slowed the bullet down just enough to lodge it into his chest. Most vests will only stop a handgun. It is said that if you get shot with a rifle, you might be better off without a vest. If the bullet misses any vital organs and passes through you, chances are, you'll live.

Well, either way, I believed in attacking the job. The vest thing was my decision. Being in full uniform, I thought that I should be the one to open a dialogue with this individual, rather than Bill. Plus, I always felt confident in my ability to communicate with people. The actor, in his state of mind also might not recognize Bill as a cop. I originally had my gun in my right hand as I called out to the man. He didn't seem particularly hostile to us, but did say that he was going to blow his brains out. I wouldn't see a guy blow his brains out with a high powered rifle for years to come, but it didn't sound good to me anyway. I asked the actor if I could sit at the top of the stairs so that we could talk. He didn't seem to object. I stepped down about three steps where I could see him. He was seated in a chair, on the other side of a coffee table, which was to the right of the stairs' banister. The stock/butt of the rifle was planted to his right side on the floor. He held the barrel to the right side of his head with his left hand, about six inches from the top. His right thumb was inside the trigger guard. One jerk of his thumb would blow half of his head apart, leaving little room for error.

I holstered my weapon and spoke to him like a friend. Billy, just behind me, stayed out of the man's sight while keeping his firearm at the ready. I talked about family, telling him I had children. With some coercing, I got him to talk about his kids, who were grown up. He had tears in his eyes as he spoke of them. He sniffled as he exchanged hands on the barrel of the rifle. He reached for a handkerchief with his left hand, which he had in his shirt pocket over his heart. I couldn't help but feel better when he took his thumb out of the trigger guard to perform that maneuver. He wiped the tears from his eyes and put the handkerchief back into his pocket. I felt disappointment when he resumed his threatening position. The one thing I did accomplish, when he wiped his tears, was that I slid down one step closer without him realizing it. Thankfully, he was in the mood to talk as I asked him about his grandchildren. I asked him if he sees them often and if he played with them on occasion. He started to cry as he told me how much fun they had together whenever they would visit. He wiped the tears as I slipped down one more stair. I now found myself sitting halfway down the flight of stairs. I thought, *If only he takes his thumb out of that trigger guard again, I might be fast enough to jump him. Or, he might be fast enough to shoot me.*

道

Having recently won 1st place in the black belt division of kumite (sparring) at the 1987 International Karate Championship in Athens,

I thought, *maybe I can blitz this guy*. The term "blitz" was used in my karate dojo when you, suddenly and successfully, jumped the opponent without telegraphing your move. My heiho (strategy) in this case would pay off, as he talked more about his grandchildren. I asked him how his grandchildren would feel about their grandfather, if he took his own life. I said, "You know, they're going to miss you terribly." With that, he started to bawl in earnest. Tears were flowing, his nose was running and I thought, *this might be it; it's not going to get any better than this*. He removed his right hand from the trigger guard, stood the rifle straight up from the floor and blew his nose into the handkerchief using his left hand. As he blew his nose, his head would momentarily nod downward, losing sight of me for a split second. As he looked down, I leaped over the banister and landed next to the coffee table. He looked up with his eyes opened wide, startled, he dropped the handkerchief.

道

I jumped over the coffee table as I watched his left hand grab the rifles barrel and pressed it to his head. I landed on his side of the coffee table with my forward momentum pushing me closer. His right hand was now traveling down the length of the barrel, about to enter the trigger guard. It was then, that my right hand reached out and grabbed the rifle's barrel with such a grip, that I ripped the rifle completely out of his grasp. So much energy and momentum was built up in that maneuver, that I not only ripped the rifle away before his thumb hit the trigger, but I spun with it to my left completing a full revolution. He looked up at me, both annoyed and amazed as I said, "Whew... what a time we had with *that!*"

Billy rushed downstairs and took custody of the distraught actor while Bob Luciano took possession of the rifle. Luciano would unload the firearm to find just two shells loaded. The actor then told us that he wanted him and his wife to go together. However, after his wife escaped the basement, he decided to go out alone. The actor was taken to St. Mary's psychiatric ward, where experts there determined that he meant it. He absolutely was going through with it. My Captain, Robert Kelly, would later call the newspaper telling them what had happened.

I received a life-saving medal from the awards committee for my actions that evening. In Clifton, you have to risk your own life to save another, to receive such an award. Saving someone using CPR for instance, would not amount to a commendation. In Clifton, giving CPR is merely your job.

> **"What we have done for ourselves alone dies with us.**
> **What we have done for others and the world remains immortal."**

> **Albert Pine**

TO CATCH A CRIMINAL

It was summer in the late 80's or early 90's; I can't remember the exact year. Like so many jobs over the years, you don't keep notes on them; you file your report and move on. I was planning a week-long vacation with my family as we took reports of a "cat burglar," hitting the Botany Village/Randolph Avenue area of the city, known as Post 1. Not overly eventful, as Clifton suffered many burglaries on a monthly basis. We were never short on burglaries and stolen cars. I, like most city cops, have several arrests of burglary suspects. You pull them out of attics and crawl spaces or find them out front, under parked cars. However, cat burglars are different. Most burglars go through an unlocked window, push in an air conditioner, or kick in the back door during the day when no one is home. These low lives, however, enter your home when the family is sleeping. They occur with more frequency during the warm weather, as people leave their windows open overnight. The cat burglar can become extremely violent when a home owner confronts him or he sees something he wants while observing a sleeping female. When you think about it, a cat burglar must have a big set of balls, considering the chances he takes, while displaying such brazen audacity. I've always despised cat burglars and had to resist the temptation to teach them a lesson.

I went on vacation after hearing of two burglaries that detectives were investigating. After spending a week down Seaside, I returned to work raring to go. The A-9 bulletins in the squad room listed additional burglaries since I left, as well as a few that were originally unreported. In any case, he was hitting the same neighborhood with frequency. Seeing a pattern from a criminal was a beautiful thing for a cop. I never knew if some burglars were just plain stupid or just didn't give a rat's ass.

The watch commander, Lt. Richard Less, who I always looked up to and admired, was the boss on this particular night. Richie had always noticed how effective I'd been in the past, and would usually go along with my proactive approach to catching criminals. Richie Less, without a doubt, was one of Clifton's most highly decorated officers. I asked him for three officers to help me set up a stakeout. He agreed. I asked the officers to meet me at Lee's Hawaiian Islander on Lexington Avenue.

In Lee's parking lot, I retrieved my Clifton map and spread it on the hood of my car. I theorized, like some others working the case, the actor might be walking into the neighborhood from Randolph Avenue, which parallels the Passaic River. I concluded that if we posted an officer on the next north-to-south street, up from Randolph Avenue, we might just get lucky and observe him crossing over into the victimized neighborhood. The street I chose was Fleischer Place, which ran five short blocks from Clifton Avenue to East Clifton Avenue. The blocks were short as most of the houses faced out on the avenues that crossed Fleischer. I asked one officer to sit on a porch near Mahar Avenue looking up to Knapp Avenue and down to Clifton Avenue. Another would be near Van Riper Avenue, while I would be near Seger Avenue, basically looking up and down Fleischer. A fourth officer, Bob Luciano, was stationed on East Clifton Avenue, as we thought there was a chance that he could also come in from the north. We set up at around 0100 hours (1am), getting dropped off by other units, as we wanted no black and whites (marked police cars) parked in the area.

Two hours had elapsed and we were still sitting in the shadows as we remained both patient and committed. Suddenly, as I sat on the fourth and top step to a porch on Fleischer Place, I was pleasantly surprised. My hunch was right. A Hispanic male was slowly creeping south on

Fleischer Place, right in the middle of the street. When I spotted him, he was only two doors down to my right. I felt that I couldn't move or talk on the radio as he stepped slowly, continuously scanning the homes to the right, then left. I remained frozen, hoping that he would not detect my presence until he was much closer. I wondered if I would be quick enough to leap from the top step and sprint after him successfully, after sitting motionless for two hours. I would soon get my chance to find out, as he moved closer to my position.

I was conflicted about breaking radio silence while calling for back-up or remaining still and silent. There was a brief moment when he was almost in front of me and actually looked my way, while continuing to scan the area. His eyes seemed, though intent, to gaze past me rather than stare at me, identifying a threat. I, along with the other officers that night, picked houses that had no street light out front, keeping us cloaked in dark shadows. *"BAM!!"* I heard in my head, like a sprinter that just heard the starter pistol fire, as I leapt from the porch directly to the sidewalk. I tried to time it as he looked slightly to his right. His peripheral vision, however, and my feet hitting the ground, caused him to jolt in surprise. It seemed to take a second for his brain to tell his feet to run, as I sprinted into the middle of the street. My right hand brushed his clothing as he jerked away in a panic. He fled south on Fleischer, now turning right up Segar Avenue. As I pursued him only a couple of steps behind, I yelled out into my hand set (radio), "Seger Ave! Seger Ave!" as I attempted to get immediate back-up.

After a few more steps, he made a sharp turn toward the rear yards which backed up to East Clifton Avenue. Now jumping over fences, shrubs and occasional backyard debris, we worked our way across adjoining yards. After a couple of minutes, I encountered a problem. My foot got caught on some debris lying in a pile that we ran through, causing my heel to pull out of my shoe. Not feeling confident that I could continue jumping over fences without a shoe, I was forced to stop and put it back on. To make matters worse, I used to double knot my patent leathers so, ironically enough; they wouldn't come off during a chase! All I could do now was to tell my back-up to set up a perimeter, as I lost him in those dark yards. Although I was able to get my shoe back on fairly quickly, seconds mean a lot in a chase, never mind close to a minute. There was no sign of him, as I tried in vain to search him out.

Luckily for me, with the three back-up officers already there and a couple of post cars (radio cars) nearby, we set up a sound perimeter fairly quick. The watch commander knew exactly how much we wanted this guy and called in our tactical/street crime unit to assist sealing the area. There was no way we wanted this guy to slip through. The Passaic County Sheriff's Department sent an officer with a K9. Once everyone was in place, the German shepherd and his handler started right where I left off. After about 30 minutes of checking each yard between Seger and East Clifton Avenue, the dog hit pay dirt. Clamoring under a pick up truck's camper type cover that lay on the ground, he sniffed out a nervous and sweaty Hispanic male. I quickly identified him as the man I chased about an hour ago. The sheriff officer and K9 turned the actor over to me as I slapped the cuffs on him. Man, I was so happy that I felt like buying that dog a steak! I later received the same "Letter of Merit" in my personnel file that the officers woken up at home received, for their contribution. Detectives got a search warrant for his apartment in Passaic, discovering evidence and contraband, connecting him with over a dozen burglaries. Case closed.

道

Running the statistics some 20 years later, it became apparent that burglaries will always remain a thorn in our sides. In 2009, for instance, there was a burglary in New Jersey every 14 minutes. Our feckless politicians continue to be soft on punishment for such a crime. Burglary to a dwelling in New Jersey is a third degree crime. Juxtapose that with our neighbor, New York, who categorizes it as a second degree.

Sentencing and our parole system is completely mind-boggling and difficult to understand; not only to the victims of these psychological attacks, but to the cops that make the arrests as well. How many people can no longer sleep soundly in their beds while anticipating another break-in? Children may feel the need to climb in bed with their parents as they envision someone standing at the foot of their beds. Burglary can be quite traumatic as you feel completely violated with the thoughts of a criminal walking around your home.

The newspapers always report that a burglar "faces" a five-year prison term for this third degree crime leading people to believe that we're tough on these perpetrators. In my experience, I've seen burglars do 180 days before we let them out to do it all over again. Many burglaries are downgraded to criminal trespass leading to even lighter sentences of three months. The career criminals that we eventually nab, can do three months standing on their heads. It's merely an inconvenience. If we catch you breaking into a home, how many did you do where we didn't catch you?

Politicians unfortunately will only feel the psychological effects on their families if it happens to them. We need to write tougher laws that discourage this repetitive behavior, so fewer felons consider it a worthwhile risk. But I digress. Let us get back to "To catch a criminal."

道

If you try to "think" like a criminal and have good instincts, you can sometimes make, as my friend, Chief Bob Ferreri, used to say, "The double play."

Another quick story comes to mind using this concept. It was a relatively quiet evening in October of 2003, when I was cruising through the city in my Dodge Stratus. I was running Clifton's narcotics/vice unit at the time. The dispatcher informed all cars that the Passaic County Sheriff's Department was involved in a pursuit of a stolen Camry on the Garden State Parkway Northbound. He was somewhere between Route 3 and Route 46 in Clifton. Major highways crisscross Clifton, so we wind up assisting many agencies as they pursue through our city. In this case, it was a local agency in which we interact with on a regular basis. The New Jersey State Police, who patrol the Garden State Parkway, already had a unit assisting the county unit. At that time I was out on the Westside, as I monitored the situation. Driving toward the Eastside, I heard that the car crashed on the Parkway North ramp to Route 46 East/Route 20. The county officer now began chasing the suspect to a grassy, wooded area, between highway ramps. The county officer, Anthony Abate, would lose the actor in that area. Back-up officers would now arrive from Clifton and the Passaic County Sheriff's Department, as well as the State Police. It had been raining quite a bit beforehand, so the wooded area was saturated. After monitoring the situation for a short time, it became apparent that there were more than enough back-up officers in the area. Hell, the state police even sent a helicopter that they had close by. I was on the Eastside of town and thought, *let me go down to the Botany*, which had only a dearth of coverage while all of this was going on. Maybe with the black and whites gone, somebody will do something stupid.

From what I understood, the state police helicopter lit up that area pretty well as the officers and K9 did their work. Unfortunately for the dog, it was difficult to get a scent with the rain and poor conditions. They seemed to have a solid perimeter and, as I said, plenty of help, but no luck on coming up with the elusive actor. About 45 minutes later, the county would call off the search. Having a good description of the actor, a tall black male in his early 20's, along with a clothing description, I thought I'd play the area. Most marked units and the helicopter resumed patrol as a couple of unmarked county cars remained in Clifton.

There are cops that just drive around hoping to get lucky. Even worse, some black and whites actually drive down side streets at night with their high beams and white alley lights on. I used to laugh out loud when I saw a lot of old guys doing it. I wasn't sure if they were lazy or just plain dumb. Did they expect the suspect to stand there and wave to them? If you're "fleeing" the police, I think you might duck down out of sight when you see the cops coming a block away!

道

Getting back to the story, I surmised the actor was apparently getting off that particular exit because he was heading to Paterson. The two most efficient routes were 1) Route 46 East to Route 20 North, which was less than a mile away or 2) walk up Lakeview Avenue straight into Paterson. I decided to drive a loop from the area where he was last seen. I got on Route 46 East off Lexington Avenue, near the Hot Grill. This way, if I got hungry, I could stop (Just kiddin).

I drove north on Route 20, got off on Market Street and took Lakeview Avenue back to Clifton, only to do it again. After two or three loops, I spotted a black male, somewhat fitting the description, walking on Lakeview Avenue north in Paterson. Pulling over, I exited my car and identified myself as a police sergeant. Looking at my shield now displayed from my neck chain, he reluctantly answered a few questions. It didn't take long to disregard him as a suspect, as he didn't strike me as a man on the run. Continuing my "loop," it wasn't long before I spotted a likely suspect walking on the shoulder on Route 46 East. He looked soaking wet and totally spent.

Knowing he was a runner and didn't want to go through all that again, I decided to bring him to me. I was in a good position to do this, with my unmarked car and shabby look. Passing him by about 150 feet, I asked headquarters for back-up as I pulled over on the right shoulder.

After putting on my flashers, I popped the hood and feigned car trouble. I got out of my car, totally ignoring the suspect, as I took up a concealed position in front of the car and raised the hood. At this point, I updated my back-up officers of my situation. I asked the narcotics detectives, Chris Vassoler and Tommy Burrows, to come in quietly. My holster was now unclipped as I peered through the opening under the hood. As he got closer, I could see that he had nothing in his hands, enabling me to keep my Beretta holstered. Some cops might draw down on him, but this affords him an opportunity to run. You'd be surprised when you draw down on someone just how many times they call your bluff. Most "players" know that you can't shoot an unarmed man. So as he reaches my rear bumper, I slammed the hood and met him next to my front left tire.

He immediately said, "Hey Bro, can you give me a ride?"

Asking him where he was going, I moved to his left, appearing to move toward the driver door. But once I took two steps, my left hand grabbed his collar as my right grabbed his belt. He quickly found himself over the car's left fender and hood. Maintaining control and pressure on the back of his neck, I shifted my right hand to his right arm and wrenched it behind his back. "CLIFTON POLICE," I announced, "You have the right to remain silent..." At first, he remonstrated that he did nothing wrong and I must have the wrong guy. As I pointed out that he was soaked to the bone and had mud on his clothes, he got quiet. Detectives Vassoler and Burrows now pulled up and assisted with the handcuffing and search of his person. As he now stood erect with his hands cuffed behind his back, I pressed my ear against his heart. Why would an innocent man's heart be pounding, like he just finished a race, I asked?

The actor then broke down and said, "Man, just take me to a dry cell, I'm freezin'!"

Det. Burrows found some marijuana on his person, and along with Vassoler, transported the prisoner to Clifton headquarters. Both detectives, who were involved in the original search, told me that the county officer found a good amount of CDS, including "crack" cocaine, in the abandoned stolen car. Back at headquarters, we brought this

Newark resident to the narcotics office to get his pedigree. Once he got a little warmer, he started to talk. He told me that he was going to offer me some marijuana to get him out of there. He also told us that he hid under a pile of wet leaves to avoid apprehension. At one point, he stated, a cop actually stepped on the side of his foot as he lie motionless. As we chatted, we found out the Toyota Camry was stolen out of Jersey City and there was also an outstanding warrant for this individual, out of Hudson County. I had dispatch notify the Passaic County Sheriff's Department to come and pick up their prisoner.

Officer Anthony Abate, a fine young man who did a good job that night, arrived at headquarters with a partner to take custody of the actor. He seemed elated that we got the guy for him. In most cases, Clifton officers assisted other departments would give the prisoner back to the initiating agency. Hell, it was their good work that started the whole thing. On the way out the door, the actor turned and looked at me saying, "Man, you didn't look like a cop out there."

I said, "Yeah, trick or treat!" It was October 29th (close enough).

道

Call it intuition, call it a gut feeling, but whatever you call it, there is no denying that many cops get it. Cops notice things that are unnoticed or benign to most people. I knew cops that seemed able to smell drugs, leading to countless arrests. Although I came to learn and work narcotics while assigned to the Passaic County Narcotics Task force in 1997, drugs originally were not my specialty. If you work in an urban area like Paterson, Newark or Camden, you can't help but make drug arrests. Driving through certain neighborhoods in Paterson, it was right in front of you, if you knew what to look for.

I remember one time I was parked on Belmont Avenue, in Haledon, near the Paterson border. I was watching one of our undercover officers make a buy about a half of a block up. A suspected prostitute crossed in front of my car, did a hand-to-hand (exchanged money for drugs) with a black male standing on the sidewalk. She crossed back in front of me again as she tore open the glassine of heroin, snorted it and dropped the bag like a seasoned pro, which I'm sure she was. Knowing my responsibility watching our undercover, I could take no action. Now that guy was one lucky player (dealer). I used concentrate on motor vehicle theft, robberies, burglaries and such. Probably because we had no "open air" drug markets in Clifton.

道

Let's get back to intuition. Sometimes it's the bumper sticker that doesn't match the driver. A Hispanic male who I stopped once, had a "split wood, not atoms" sticker. Looking at this guy, he looked like he didn't have a clue what that liberal "white boy" sticker meant. Sure enough, he bought the car off a white guy. New York's radio station sticker, Q104.3, won't be found on just any car. A damaged rear passenger side window was always suspicious. I once had a black male with ski racks on his car. Be honest, how many brothers do you see on the slopes? We stopped white guys in the projects all the time, especially the ones with the Pennsylvania tags.

道

I recall another instance on a particular evening in 2004. I was working an unmarked car driving around the Westside of Clifton near Route 3. We had a Bradley's department store on Main Avenue near the Nutley border. There was a car with two individuals parked out front of the store at the curb. Not unusual in a large parking lot if they had a friend just running in and out. What did make me curious, however, was the exact positioning of the car. Instead of being right near the three front glass doors, they parked at the curb about 60 or 70 feet back, while watching the front entrance. I had a hunch, at best, but some cops get lucky from a hunch.

In about five minutes, a guy came running out the front door as his friends in the aforementioned vehicle suddenly accelerated to intercept him. The rear right side window, which I couldn't see from the left of them, was apparently left open. The actor, who exited the store with his arms full of merchandise, tossed the items into the vehicle and dove in after them.

The suspect's vehicle now sped toward the parking lot's exit with their friends legs dangling out of the car. As I took off in my unmarked unit, I watched a store security officer run out the front door in an attempt it seemed, to get their license plate number. He never got close enough, but I did. Calling dispatch I gave the make, model and license plate number to headquarters. I also asked them to call the store to get further information on the perceived crime/offense. Were there weapons involved; did anyone get hurt? The vehicle quickly got onto Route 3 East toward Bergen County and New York City. I activated my lights and siren and was now entering Rutherford. As strange as it seemed, these dopes started to throw some of the pilfered items out of the car. Don't ask me how that could help them.

"501 to headquarters," I said, as I gave updates on speed, traffic conditions and location. I also started to describe the individuals, in case there was a bail out.

Many times, when you get behind a stolen car or another wanted vehicle, you can't get a good look at the occupants. But if you know their race, their approximate height and build and their clothing description beforehand, make sure you transmit the info. It is really hard after the crash and/or bail out, to run at full speed while transmitting. If there are three suspects running in different directions, good luck.

Well, as it turned out, they were only wanted for shoplifting. Someone in the car must have come to their senses and talked the others into giving up. The car pulled over in Lyndhurst near Medieval Times. All three were taken into custody without incident, as a Rutherford and a Lyndhurst car backed me up. A Clifton marked unit also responded to help transport.

道

Most of my good times with the department were obviously when I was on the street. Whether working patrol or narcotics, if I was chasing bad guys, I was happy. Later in my career, my last three and a half years actually, I almost felt retired. I used to think being a lieutenant and watch commander would be great. I could be in charge and call the shots. I had a couple of good bosses, who pretty much let me run the show on my shift. Chief Robert Ferreri and Captain Gary Giardina, who would later become Chief Giardina, supported many of my proactive ideas on the midnight shift. One such idea was having three of our best, proactive patrol officers wear plain clothes at night. Narcotics went home at midnight or 0100 hours, leaving us with no one able to do surveillance. Lt. Robert Bielsten and I picked Keith Allmindinger and John Kavakich, who both had experience working for a year with the Passaic County Narcotics Task Force, and Maurice Scardigno, an intelligent, proactive cop who liked to make arrests. They were all in different squads, leaving us with two of them always working, while the third one would be on his days off. As a result, the midnight shifts drug arrests went through the roof. These guys never disappointed me or Bielsten when it came to filling up our cells. Some of the individuals who were arrested would turn into confidential informants for Clifton's narcotics squad.

Another thing the bosses did, or rather didn't do, was stop us from running down criminals. Sure, we had a couple of lieutenants that called off chases, but that didn't happen on my watch. I remember once as a patrol sergeant, my guys lost a stolen car on Route 21 to Newark. The next night in the squad room, I tossed out Butterfinger candy bars.

As a lieutenant, in 2005, I remember telling the line-up that we are a proactive department with a reputation to uphold. Of course, I reminded them that in 1991, I was involved in 36 high-speed chases, and only one got away in the teeming rain! (yeah that's right, I was bragging.) That night, a couple of our marked units, lost a stolen car on Route 21 toward Newark. So the next night, I told them not to lose anyone again. No one gets away from the Clifton PD, I insisted. That night, we got into a chase with a guy in Passaic, who purposely drove into a brick wall, killing himself on impact.

After that happened, I had the line-up at 2300 (11pm) hours the next night. Everyone was waiting to see what I had to say. "Look guys..." I began, "I told you that I didn't want them to get away, but I don't want them dead either. Please get me a live one tonight so I can type up some complaints." They thought I was nuts but morale remained high. A good cop should be proud of himself at the end of the day. No political correctness, no sucking up, just doin' the job.

道

There was an occasion when I was the watch commander and a call came in at about 0400 hours (4 am). A female was petrified. She received a call from her ex-boyfriend, who had been drinking, telling her that he was coming over to kill her. According to her, he belonged to a Paterson street gang and had access to a gun. One of the reasons that she broke up with him was because he wouldn't give up his gang affiliation and she feared for her life. I told Car #8, which was a two-man unit, to drop off one man immediately and get out of the area. The officer being dropped off had instructions to sit in her kitchen and stay on high alert. I had the road sergeant give me a call to tell him that the female lived on Harding Avenue, but not to expect this loser to ring the front doorbell. Watch the street behind hers even more than the front, as he'll probably come in on Union Avenue, jump the back yard fence and kick in her back door. I also had the Sarge tell his men to park their black and whites in the shadows and lay low. You couldn't easily find a parking spot in that part of the city overnight unless you're a cop. Surveillance cars would always park away from street lights, blocking a hydrant or driveway. Sometimes, we'd pull in a driveway between two houses, whatever worked.

Well sure as shit, as if I had a crystal ball, two "dopes" came walking down Union Avenue turning into a yard behind the victim's house. Two of our guys nailed them before they could hit the house, possibly disappointing the officer in the kitchen.

After bringing them into headquarters, one of our newer guys came to me and said, "Lieutenant! How did you know?"

I said, "I didn't. Know for sure that is." Try to think where *you* would hide, where *you* would run. What you would do if *you* were the bad guy. Sometimes, just sometimes, you might get lucky.

> "Intuition and action, must spring forward
> At the same time."
>
> **Taizen Deshimaru**

CENTER STREET

It was 1986 when I was assigned to Car #1 on the midnight shift. It was just a couple of minutes past 2300 hours when we got a call of a man shot on Center Street in Botany Village. Being Car #1, an odd number vehicle, I worked 2300-0700 hours and was still behind police headquarters checking my equipment. The even number cars from the last shift don't get off until 2345 (11:45 pm). The staggered shift change ensures that all city radio cars are not at headquarters at the same time, leaving distant parts of the city unprotected. The even Eastside Car #'s 2, 4 and 8, the last one being a two-man car, responded first to the shooting. Upon their arrival, while I was still doing warp six down Clifton Avenue, Officers reported a few people running out of the Center Street building where the shooting occurred. Witnesses said that some youths were on the stairs and landing, making a lot of noise. A middle-aged white male came out of his apartment with a rifle and opened fire. One young male was struck by the bullet as the man returned to his apartment. The victims' friends, not wanting him to bleed too much waiting for an ambulance, rushed him to Beth Israel Hospital in Passaic, near the Clifton/Botany area border.

As I pulled up to the scene, officers were setting up a perimeter, watching the exits. I entered the building to find the two officers from Car #8, rookie Bob Bielsten and veteran Gerry Kino, outside the shooter's apartment door on the second floor. They briefed me on what they learned. They also said that the alleged shooter yelled through the door, "Go away, I don't want to be bothered." When the officers, with their guns drawn, ordered him to come out, he replied, "Fuck you! And, first cop through that door is gettin shot!"

I said, "What?! He's gonna shoot one of us? Well fuck him!" I was in a bad mood that night and had no patience for his bullshit. I can't really explain why I was so cocky and in a hurry; I just know that I was pissed because he shot that youth. I already had my Beretta out as I was briefed. I then took a position to the right side of the door where the knob and deadbolt were. I whispered, "Get ready boys," and kicked in the door with my left foot. I always stomp the door with a front kick above the doorknob and over the deadbolt. The door flew open as I came face to face with the shooter. The way I saw it, it was either his lucky day or mine. He had placed the rifle down for a moment thinking, according to him, that we were going to negotiate first.

Rushing in closer, I swept his forward leg out from under him, causing him to hit the kitchen floor. I then yelled to my two back-up officers to cuff him while I started a search of the rest of the apartment. As Bielsten cuffed him, I quickly discovered a second suspect, unarmed, in the living room. He said, "Whoa! Whoa! I'm not involved with that lunatic." I ordered him to the ground and began a search of his person.

The road sergeant showed up from the Westside with one or two more officers from outside the building. The rest of the apartment was secured as we began interviewing the second occupant in the living room. The sergeant, to my surprise, ordered the two guys from Car #8 to take in the prisoner and book him. I told the sergeant that it was my arrest and that I'll take him in. The sergeant replied, "No, Car 8 is a two-man car; they'll do it. Ciser, you can go back to work." I stood there, stunned and amazed for a few seconds, and then exited the building using some choice curse words.

It's funny, but taking knives and guns off of people was getting to be a habit. One amusing story comes to mind when I was a Detective Sergeant in the narcotics squad. I always worked the day shift one day a week just to catch up on paperwork. It also gave me a free night to go to my karate school. One Monday, I was downstairs by the front desk, which is close to the cell block, when the watch commander seemed upset. The desk officer, who monitors the prisoners, told the lieutenant that a prisoner who was just brought in was put inside cell #3 with a pocket knife. It seemed that the rookie officer who assisted with the booking missed it somewhere on the prisoner's person. Now, the guy is back there waving it around, acting like an asshole. Lt. Kenny Dal Pos ordered three cops to get ready with the Plexiglas shield and mace. A baton was also in order. The new kid was shaken up as he hoped no one would get hurt as a result of his error.

I then approached the lieutenant, who I worked with for years and was a friend of mine, and said, "Look Kenny, don't make a big deal. Give me a minute; I'll get the knife off of him."

The lieutenant agreed and said, "Okay, Pat. See what you can do."

I left my gun at the front desk and entered the cell block area. The desk officer and two other cops followed me for back-up. I asked the three of them to lie back as I spoke to the prisoner.

I was dressed in plain clothes that day, with jeans and a tee shirt which was appropriate for narcotics. I went up to the bars purposely standing about six inches away. I started to ridicule the prisoner as follows. "So, you're the asshole they told me about? Man, are they gonna kick your ass. I'm just here to watch."

He angrily replied, "Who the fuck are you?"

I said, "It doesn't matter who I am; I'm just here for the entertainment. These guys got night sticks, mace, you should really think about turning over that knife." As I spoke to him, he looked as though he was on something. He certainly didn't seem rational. I continued to push his buttons as I made fun of him and his plight. "You know," I said, "You're probably a real fuckin' punk without that knife.

Yeah, I met guys like you before, you're a real dick!" as I grabbed my junk. Now, getting serious, I looked into his eyes and said, "Yeah, you're just an asshole with no balls!" That did it! He immediately lunged at my chest through the bars with the knife. A quick turn sideways and a hand/sword strike (karate chop) to the inside of his wrist, sent the knife flying to the floor. I moved away from the bars and said, "Remember when I said that you were the asshole with a knife? Well now, you're just an asshole."

He started kicking and screaming as I picked up the knife and gave it to the desk officer. We exited the cell block as I approached the watch commander to tell him what happened. The lieutenant said, "Great job Pat, I'm sure you'll get an 'Atta boy' (Letter of merit) from the awards committee." It was then that I asked the lieutenant to let it go. Any reports written could only hurt the kid in his probation, I said.

"Let the kid charge him with possession of the knife, if you'd like. I was never here." The rookie later thanked me and apologized for missing the knife. I told him, "Hey kid. 'Even monkeys fall out of trees.' That incident will only make you sharper, period. I'll bet you'll never miss a knife again."

道

When I was a rookie, Captain Capuano once told me, "Kid, you're just ink in my pen," when I asked him if I could work Car #1 Botany Village, as I thought that I could make a difference. Fast forward, as I was actually making a difference while supervisors would request my presence on certain assignments. In the 1980's, I can't remember the year, I was working Car #8 on the day shift. I had a motor vehicle stop on Main Avenue near Clifton Avenue when I heard a call crackle over the radio. "Cars 1, 2, 3 and 18 (sergeant), respond to Clinton Avenue on an EDP"(Emotionally Disturbed Person). He was what we called a "Frequent Flyer," who lived at home with his mom. We'll call him

"Jack." If Jack didn't take his medication regularly, he would go off the deep end and flip out. Jack's mom told the dispatcher that she was in fear for her life, as Jack had a large kitchen knife and was cutting up her curtains in the living room.

The sergeant pulled up to the scene and noted that I wasn't there. He asked dispatch what I was doing and what was my location. The dispatcher informed him that I was on a motor vehicle stop on Main Avenue. The sergeant radioed to me to quickly finish issuing a summons or let the driver go, but come over to Clinton Avenue as soon as possible. As it turned out, I was just handing a summons to another satisfied customer and was available to respond in about a minute. I drove over to Clinton Avenue which was only about a half mile away.

Upon my arrival, I saw the sergeant and a few men standing outside the house. I exited my car and asked the sergeant, "What do you need?"

He looked at me and said, "He's inside." Now, I know that the cops standing outside were more than ready to handle the situation. But I guess it was like a compliment that he wanted me. The only thing that bothered me is that this particular sergeant could break your balls for silly shit, like getting out of your car for a coffee without calling it out, or worse, not wearing your hat. Then, when they need you to bail them out of a sticky situation, they wanna be your best friend (Don't you hate that).

I walked into the house as his mother left the front door open. Jack was yelling at his mom, still clenching the large knife. I had my holster unclipped and ready to go as I felt the other officers following behind me. Entering the doorway to the kitchen, I said, "Jack! What the hell are you doing? Throw that knife in the sink and sit down." I sat at the far side of the kitchen table as he stood on the other side near the sink. I again said, "Jack, lose the knife and sit down, will ya'!" Jack looked at me a little puzzled. I guess he didn't expect the "nice guy" treatment and didn't know how to react. "Come on Jack.

Sit down. I'm here to help you." Jack had a couple of minor run-ins with me in the past, and also knew of my reputation as the "karate guy." He tossed the knife into the sink and had a seat across from me. I proceeded to tell him that he could never win an altercation with so many cops so I'm here to protect him. Truth be told, Jack was a big son-of-a-bitch that you wouldn't want to see angry. I explained that I was the one who was going to take him down to St. Mary's psychiatric ward and me alone.

I told him to pay no attention to these other cops saying, "You know you can trust me." After some convincing, I got Jack to agree to my request. I had the other cops back off as I escorted Jack to my radio car. A quick pat down and into the back of the car he went. I'm not sure who I saved that day, Jack, the other cops, or myself. With a guy that strong, sometimes even when you win, you lose.

道

Case in point, there were full-contact kickboxing matches that I had won. As the referee raised my hand indicating that I was the victor, I sometimes didn't feel like one. My nose would be broken again, or I would need a couple of stitches over my eye. In 1978, I remember training for the New Jersey golden gloves at the Dumont Athletic Club. New Jersey's Light Heavyweight Champ, Jerry Palmieri, and owner, Eddie Helbig, helped me get ready. Jerry Palmieri later became a trainer for the New York Giants. In 1978, this guy was fast. I could never beat him to the punch. Well, maybe I'd get lucky once in awhile. If I wanted to beat Jerry, I'd probably have to use my legs. We became good friends, however, so we would never find out the ole, Boxer vs. Karate outcome. In 2011, Jerry invited my son Ryan and me, to the Timex Training Center at the Meadowlands. This was pretty cool, with both of us being Giants fans, and Ryan playing football since he was seven. Now at age 16, he's 6'2", 205 pounds and one of my bogu fighters (full contact).

Boxing was a sport I did in 1977 at Lou Costello's gym in Paterson, followed by my switching to the Dumont A.C. in 1978. Kickboxing was really my love, along with karate-do, and I wanted to improve my hand speed. I could punch through patio blocks but I needed more speed. In 1979, I had a kickboxing match in Caracas, Venezuela and noticed an improvement.

道

It was funny back in those days at the old police station on Main Avenue. Being a pumped-up rookie in the 70's, I never wanted to take a sick day. I guess I was afraid I'd miss something good. Like the night I called in sick, I was scheduled to work Car #1. Ross La Corte took my place, and then delivered a baby in a bar on Parker Avenue. Watching a baby come into the world was a lot better than watching someone go out. The latter was unfortunately the norm.

One Friday night, I was fighting in New Jersey's Golden Gloves down at the Elizabeth (City) Armory. I had made it to the semifinals in the weeks prior, but then lost on this night. So the next morning, I show up at the police line-up (roll call) with a broken nose. As a result of the broken nose, I also wound up with two black eyes. The Watch Commander looked at me and said, "Ciser, you look like shit!"

"Thank you, sir," I replied.

"Don't you know we get sick days? Get outta here! Go home, will ya'!"

"Yes, sir," I exclaimed!

The next day they hid me inside, manning a post called 9A for a few days, until I looked better. I hated 9A.

As I went through my career and was confronted with armed and unarmed adversaries, I always remembered something that I heard years earlier while watching the series *Kung Fu* with David Carradine, on television in the early 70's. There was a Buddhist monk who called Carradine, "Grasshopper." I'll have to paraphrase but it went something like this: Check rather than strike. Injure rather than maim. Maim rather than kill.

It apparently made an impression on me as I used this philosophy for years to come.

> **"Attack when they are unprepared,**
> **Make your move when they don't expect it."**
>
> **Sun Tzu (Sun Wu)**
> **Sonshi (Japanese pronunciation)**

GREECE

Greece, my friends, is a wonderful place. After teaching and competing there on six separate occasions, I've experienced the beauty of Corfu and Hydra and the hospitality of Athens. Whether sightseeing at the Acropolis or shopping in Monastiraki, it was always a pleasant experience. Sensei George Doukas of Athens, who had a large karate dojo downtown, was our host.

It was 1987 and my first visit. We stayed in Athens at the hotel Titania near Omonoia Square. The international championships were held at the "Sporting" arena. I, along with other team members and coaches, stayed for a week, to compete and teach at the local karate schools. We had participants from several states including New Jersey, New York, Pennsylvania and Michigan. Conveniently, Sensei Kaloudis and Sensei George Scordilis both spoke fluent Greek, making the visit and competition go smoothly.

The black belt division was broken into two pools. Throughout the afternoon there were two fighters who couldn't be stopped. Winning pool "A" was Jeff Mason of Utica, Michigan. Mason owned his own dojo and, I believe, was a San Dan (3rd degree black belt) at the time. Pool "B" was mine to dominate. The fights were "round robin" as the winner would advance and the loser would go home. I won four fights before meeting Mason for the 1st place gold medal.

During one of my matches there, I had a moment of fear and apprehension, as I didn't realize for a moment what type of surface we were fighting on. Greece, as you can imagine, has lots of marble. The marble floor, we were sparring on had a thin felt type carpet over it. Out of sight, out of mind, I guess. Frank Gonzol, of Pennsylvania, was my opponent. Over the years, I constantly worked on a back leg foot sweep that usually worked like a charm. This time was no exception. I called the sweep my levitation trick because, when done correctly, both of my opponent's feet would fly up in the air, causing them to crash to the ground. Nice technique on tatami (Japanese mats) not so good on marble. I guess we are creatures of habit as my reflexes kicked in. Gonzol threw a front kick as I took his back leg out. As he hit the floor, the back of his head also hit the marble. The last thing I wanted to do was seriously injure an opponent for a medal or trophy. Plus, he was one of our own.

After about five minutes of talking to him, the coaches had him stand up. When he exited the ring on his own steam, he received applause from the spectators and competitors alike. Except for maybe, a headache, he suffered no ill effects and still trains today.

For the final round, Jeff Mason and I entered the ring. For this final match, Sensei Ed Kaloudis would be the center judge and referee, with four other judges manning the corners. My friend from Michigan and I, would battle for three minutes, resulting in a tie, when time was called. Another round began as a result, as we studied each other intently looking for that tacit body language that could sometimes cause a weakness in a fighter's heiho (strategy).

This round, I swept Mason causing him to break fall, giving me a full point as I punched my downed opponent. You could hear the crowd murmur, "Woowoo," as they could see the fight's intensity escalate. Jeff got up as Kaloudis yelled, "Ippon!" awarding me one point. Not to be outdone, Jeff returned the favor and employed my own text book sweep on me. I gotta tell ya, nobody there was more surprised than me, as I was now looking up. "Ippon!" Sensei said as he motioned to a standing Jeff Mason.

The end of round two also resulted in a tie. Judging from the looks on our faces, we both looked a little spent, as the strain of the days competition became apparent. Sensei Kaloudis called a third round as Jeff and I bowed to each other, showing mutual respect. "Hajime" was shouted as we attacked again and again, giving not an inch to one another. Three rounds, tie score. Kaloudis had the corner judges stand and face away from the ring. On the whistle, they would raise their flags indicating a winner. All four would simultaneously cross their flags overhead voting for a tie. Sensei, looking at us both, also felt that we were locked in a tie. So he announced that first place this year would be shared by two members of the U.S. team. Jeff and I were so exhausted at this point, we happily agreed (not that it would have mattered if we didn't).

道

After our 1987 trip to Greece, we were asked to return to teach and judge at future tournaments. My brother, Mike, and I put on demonstrations a couple of years in a row at the request of the tournament promoter. I remember one day, while walking around Athens, Mike and I came across an alley that had both broken and unbroken wine bottles lying around. So we slipped away from our group and walked a little deeper down the alley. One at a time, we placed a bottle on a kind-of shelf there and try snapping off the neck of the bottles. This particular technique required great hand speed as we would use tegatana uchi, or hand sword strike. It's basically a vertical open hand "karate chop" to the untrained individual, who contacts the bottle at the neck. Performed correctly, the top of the bottle neck snaps off, leaving the rest of the bottle in one place. It's also nice if you don't slice open the back of your hand while following through.

So there we were in our own little world, quite polarized on the wine bottles about to be blasted with a tegatana, when we heard the sound of applause. The group we were with doubled back and were silently watching our impromptu demonstration. So, Mike and

I decided to add a bottle break to our demonstration at the sporting arena. We each broke a bottleneck in quick succession.

At the tournament finals that Sunday, we took turns performing kicking and breaking techniques. My kicking demonstration consisted of putting an empty soda can on two of my students' heads. One can was knocked off with a jumping front crescent kick; the other can with a jumping spinning back kick. Two boards were held by a student sitting on the shoulders of another student. These boards would be held at about seven and a half feet above the ground. With a running jump, I leapt into the air with a double front kick and hit the board dead center, with the ball of my right foot. Four pieces of wood flew through the air, as my assistant couldn't hold on. Another double front kick snapped two boards held head high, in half, by two other assistants.

Mike would now come out and break concrete slabs. Back home, he stacked patio blocks seven or eight high and blasted them with a palm heel technique resulting in a pile of rubble. In Greece, however, he couldn't find patio blocks, so instead used these approximately 30x30 inch slabs that they used for sidewalks. Assistants would hold one each as he punched through one, used a hand sword strike through another and kicked yoko geri (side kick) through a third. He then smashed through a stack of five or six of them with a palm heel strike. After this, he performed sanchin (deep breathing) as I broke wood over various parts of his body. Mike lay on a bed of nails as I, placed more of those concrete slabs on his chest and abdomen. Bam! My sledgehammer crashed down in the center of the slabs. Bam! Was heard again as I destroyed the ones that survived the first punishing blow. Mike rose up to a thunderous applause. Mike and I took turns performing this stunt at each demonstration while the other would wield the sledgehammer.

Back in New Jersey, at the All Koeikan National Championships, I used two nail beds. As I lay on one bed of ten penny nails, another was placed upside down on top of my bare chest. First, I'd have one of the guys stand on top of the bed of nails that was on my chest. Then, he would step off and place five patio blocks on top of the nail bed which was now digging into my chest. After the blows from the sledgehammer hit, they assisted me off of the bed. The trauma suffered was so intense that I blacked out but remained standing while hearing the intense applause. I couldn't see a thing as everything was black. Rather than panic at the prospect of being blind, I decided to calmly bow with a quarter turn four times, buying time to recover. Sure enough, my sight came back slowly as I was relieved to see the crowd.

道

Getting back to Greece, I closed out the demonstration with my sword. Placing my brother between two folding chairs, like a human cutting board, I laid a watermelon on his bare chest. Blindfolded, I would draw my sword and slice the watermelon in half. But before the halves could fall, I would slice the halves in half. Years before, I heard that a guy slipped while performing this demonstration at Madison Square Garden in Manhattan. It was said that his assistant required 50-60 stitches as a result.

My follow-up to the watermelon was a cucumber on Mike's throat. Again, I was blindfolded as I drew my sword. With sure-footed quickness, I sliced the cucumber in half. The crowd went wild as audiences would for years to come. From 1978 to 2011, I used four incredibly brave assistants for the demonstrations, including Dennis Buongiorno, Mike Ciser, who was the first one to agree to the cucumber on his throat, Bill Gibson and Steven Slezak, who I used in the 2011 "YouTube" video (Search "Pat Ciser").

In 1990, Kancho Sensei Eizo Onishi himself brought a team from Japan to Greece, to teach and demonstrate various waza (techniques). I found myself in a privileged position learning kata from the master each morning in his hotel room. The only problem with this type of training is that it takes place when Kancho Sensei demands or requests, depending on your point of view. Like Sensei Kaloudis used to say, karate is a "benevolent dictatorship." I was extremely honored with the invitation and would have stayed up all night if I had too. But it was this year, when I wasn't competing that I felt like enjoying my vacation. This included putting down a few cold Heinekens before bed with friends. Each morning, I would wake up early, put on my gi (karate uniform), knock on Kancho's door at the exact minute requested and try to look alert for my one-on-one lesson. Kancho Sensei, a tenth dan, studied with renowned martial artists, including Yasutsune Itosu and even has samurai blood running through his veins. You can imagine the honor, receiving private lessons from such a man.

In 1995, Sensei Kaloudis, and USNKF (United States National Karate Federation) NJ President Walter O'Neil, organized a tournament called the Kaloudis Peace Cup, to be held in Athens. Many countries were invited to compete by the Greek Federation, including the United States, England, Saudi Arabia, Jordan, Germany, Venezuela, Israel, Syria and Italy. The United States allowed competitors, who won in previous years, a place on the team. This invitation included me, since I won in 1987. This was a goodwill tournament and not a sanctioned event.

Individuals from various styles of Karate-Do made up the U.S. team. Koeikan black belts Carlos Hernandez, Steven Slezak, Mark Skawinski and I, were all on the team. Mark and I were the U.S. heavyweights. So as to not draw out this chapter, I won a 1st place gold medal in the "open" kata division, performing "Chibana Kushanku." Carlos Hernandez took the 2nd place silver medal and an Italian won the bronze.

The heavyweight free sparring division was won by a talented Syrian fighter taking the gold medal. After fighting our way into the finals, he defeated me by just one point, as I now could only fight for 3rd or 4th. Mark Skawinski also won all of his fights in his pool up till this point, putting him in a match with the Syrian, for 1st place gold. The Syrian again was fast and outpointed Mark, who was one of our best, by only one point in overtime. Mark, winning 2nd place, showed good sportsmanship by lifting the Syrian into the air, congratulating him on a hard fought match. I then outpointed a Greek fighter for the 3rd place bronze medal. *Not bad,* I thought, *for an old guy* (I was 40).

When the tournament concluded, the Syrian coach asked me through a translator, if I would be interested in visiting Damascus, to teach karate. He knew from speaking with the Greeks that I was an adroit instructor. I told him, no thanks, I'd probably wind up with a bullet in my head. He assured me, however, that I would have bodyguards who would not let that happen. I still declined his offer and thanked him for the compliment.

This would conclude my over 20 years competing from 1973 – 1995, winning my first International gold medal in 1976 (Venezuela) and my last gold medal in 1995 (Greece).

"Courtesy to all, respect for some,
Admiration to few,
Fear of none."

O'Sensei Brian Frost
1953 – 2009

Sensei Frost and Kancho Sensei Onishi
Clifton Dojo 1974

Caracas, Venezuela 1975
Including Thomas La Puppet, Alex Sternberg, Andrew Linick,
Gary Alexander, Brian Frost, Author, white shirt kneeling

1977 Rookie "Mug" shot

Training at the Botany Village Clifton dojo in 1979
Author shown on right with Bill Gibson pushing his leg up

1979 Caracas, The "Poliedro"
Alvaro Rodriguez, Dennis Buongiorno, Sensei Brian Frost, Ciser (Author)

Author, Sensei Katsumi Nikura, Sensei Frost, D. Buongiorno 1981

Koeikan International Tai Kai 1982
Sensei Kaloudis in foreground

Author, 1984

1984 Bodybuilding Contest (Author on left)

Author breaking flaming boards 1985

Training with Bill "Superfoot" Wallace 1986

Ciser with his boa 1986

1987 Clifton PBA Bench Press Team
L-R Dara, Gibson, Ciser, Sloth, LaCorte

Athens, Greece 1990
Kancho Sensei Onishi, Ciser, Fuduta, Hoshi

Me and My Girls, 1992
Stefanie, Tracy, Nicole, Danielle

Sensei Kaloudis, Ms. Miriam Santana, 1992

Mr. Chuck Liddell and Koeikan Tournament Director Pat Ciser 1993, N.J.

1995 Bushi Shugyo, California
J. Mason, D. Spearing, Sensei Kaloudis, Sensei Frost, J. Sabat, G. Scordilis,
Author kneeling

Ciser accepting a compliment from Sensei Brian Frost as
Sensei Kaloudis looks on. California, 1995

1995 Athens, Greece, performing "Chibana" Kushanku Kata

U.S. team members Pat Ciser and Carlos Hernandez posing with the
Syrian National Team. Athens, 1995

Mom and me 1996

Posing with some new interceptors 1998

Starting my boys out early. Summer, 1999

Koeikan Karate Banquet, 2002
Sensei(s) Al Mendillo, George Scordilis, Brian Frost, Gary Alexander
(guest), Ed Kaloudis, Author

Prosecutor's Ball 2002
Nate Butler, Tony Urena, Ciser, Herman Carter

26 Kilo's of Cocaine 2002
B. Frank, M. McLaughlin, Ciser, G. Passenti, T. Rinaldi

D/Sgt. Pat Ciser 2003
Author with uc (undercover) Lexus

10 Kilo's of Heroin 2003
Burrows, Passenti, Frank, Ciser, Vassoler, McLaughlin, Rinaldi

Stealing a kiss from my Shannon 2003

Kamakura, Japan 2004

The author posing with his many awards 2005

Kancho Sensei Onishi visit to U.S. 2006
Front row includes author, Sensei Yamamoto,
Kancho and Sensei Brian Frost

2007 Koeikan reunion with Chuck "THE ICEMAN" Liddell
and Author. California

Author judging at a MMA Event in California 2007

Sgt. Allmendinger, Author, Sgt. Bienkowski 2007

Dad and Shannon 2007

Farewell party to the L-T (author) in 2008

Author's Retirement Banquet 2008
J. Serafin, (Paterson PD), Author, Bill Gibson, (Clifton), J. Speziale,
(P.C. Sheriff), J. Patti, (Passaic), C. Trucillo, Chief, Port Authority

2010 Author and his wife Lisa, Chris Trucillo and his wife Cidalia

Congratulating The Captain 2010
John Ciser, Captain Harold Ciser, Harold Ciser (Sr.), Author, Mike Ciser

Ryan and me making room at the Giant's "Timex" Center for a
fourth Superbowl Trophy 2011 (lol)

2011 Koeikan National Tournament
Shannon, Author, Kyle, Ryan, wife Lisa

Kelly Graduates FBI National Academy, 2011 Quantico
Author, Chief Gary Giardina, Lt. Chris Kelly, Former Clifton Chief
Robert Ferreri, Lt. Jeff Camp

Son in law Michael Sapena and his Jägermeister.
(Man, could I have used that in some of my pursuits!) 2011

Clifton Dojo 2011 (N.J.)
Esposito, Hernandez, Slezak, Sensei Ikushima (Japan), Author and Sonta

Utica, Michigan Dojo 2011
Standing: M. Brown, D. Spearing, Sensei Ikushima, Author, J. Mason
Kneeling: Fife, Cowan, Ruble, Colo, Okane

Grandpa's 90th, 2011
Nicole, Tracy, Danielle, Stefanie, Author's Dad

Portugal 2011

Stefanie and family at Alex's graduation. Rome N.Y. PD 2011

PASSAIC COUNTY
NARCOTICS TASK FORCE

In January of 1997, I was still a patrolman and working the day shift. Many good years were behind me and I was feeling a little down. We used to rotate shifts prior to 1990; one week of midnights, one week of days followed by one week of the 1600-2400 hour shift. Every three weeks, we'd start all over. It was good and bad, as you would, at least sometimes, get your favorite shift. In 1990, the department started the power shift which you'll read about more than once in this book. Four years on the power shift, which was 2000-0400 was a blast. It was the busiest shift with the most action. You start work when the night starts to heat up and you don't go home until after the bars close at 0300.

After four years, the higher echelons discontinued the shift, which was a bone-head idea, if you asked me. Then again, no one ever asked me. Enjoying overnight high-speed chases so much, I decided to work midnights, because it was the closest thing to the power shift. I couldn't work days; I was bored to death. If I worked 1600-2400, I'd rarely see my kids. Midnights seemed the answer. Besides, I thought, I could see a lot more of my beautiful wife Lisa. Well it didn't take long, about a year, for me to start hating midnights. I was assigned to Car #2, the Lakeview section of the city. Not a bad car and sometimes pretty busy if you were proactive, but the hours sucked, 2345-0745. After 0500 (5am) it really sucked, and I was having a hard time sleeping during the day. I resigned myself to the fact that in 1996, I would work, it's hard to admit, the dreaded day shift. I thought, *Hell, I can see my wife and our little boy, Ryan,* even more. Furthermore, I could get down to the evening classes more at my dojo (karate school).

道

So here I am, the new and boring, Pat Ciser. I have to admit though; I did catch a couple of burglars on this shift. I remember once, I stopped at my favorite deli one morning for a bagel and coffee. While I was waiting on line, an older woman, noticing my bars (medals), stacked up over my badge, and she asked me, "Wow, what are all those for?"

"Well," I told her, "they're for actions I took that were above and beyond the call of duty."

She said, "Oh, I see. Can you give me an example?"

I said, "Sure. One day there was a cat up in the tree. No one could get him down. Not animal control, not even the fire department. But I got him down!" I bragged.

She said, "Really? Oh wow!"

I replied, "Yeah, and it was a pretty good shot too!"

She walked out.

Then it happened! Driving around one day, headquarters called and said, "Car 2, come in. Car 2! Car 2, report to the Chief's office."

Ah shit, I thought, *what did I do now?* Not being able to think of anything recently, I drove to headquarters.

The chief's secretary announced my presence as Chief LoGioco told me to have a seat. Surprise is too mild a word for my reaction to what the chief said. Shock would be a better word. "Patrick, I'm sending you to the county's narcotics task force."

"Now?" I asked. "You wanna send me to the task force? Now? I've been wanting to go for the last 10 years or so Chief! I'm 41 now, enjoying my new bride and son, with another on the way." I even suggested, "Why don't you send that new kid, Billy Frank. He's got a lot of drug arrests; he'd be good!"

The chief looked at me and said, "Are you trying to play chief? I want a seasoned veteran that can work in the City of Paterson, and that's you! And besides, the assignment isn't just nights; you'll work day shift sometimes also."

I asked, "Can you give me one night to talk to Lisa about it?"

He said, "Okay, but I really want you."

I left the office thinking, *did that really just happen?*

My patrol Captain, Robert Kelly, suggested on at least two occasions, once to Chief Edward Kredatus and once to Chief LoGioco, that I should be assigned to Clifton's Narcotics/Tactical Unit, only to be shot down. I couldn't get on our narcotics squad or our tactical response team (TRT is the same as SWAT) to save my life. I never knew if it was politics, cliques within the department, or I just wasn't liked by the powers that be.

After discussing it with Lisa and coming to my senses, I told the chief that I would go. It was one of the best decisions I ever made. Not only did I have a great year at the county, but it would give me the experience needed to run Clifton's narcotics unit in the future.

The offices for the Passaic County Narcotics Task Force were in a nondescript building located in Haledon, New Jersey. My first day on the job there I felt like a rookie again with a lot to learn. Fortunately for me, there were plenty of experienced narcotics detectives there to help me along. The Passaic County Prosecutor's office ran the show and most of the "agents" worked for them. The only thing that I didn't care for much was that we had to listen to attorneys, rather than senior cops. I was never sure if the attorneys had my best interests in mind.

Other officers from departments around Passaic County were also there, including Eric Diaz, Paterson PD, Anthony Fasolas, William Paterson University PD, Laz Carerra and Herman Carter, Passaic County Sheriff's Department. None of us ever worked together before and wondered if we could really count on each other if the shit hit the fan. Another addition, new to the unit was a former NYPD detective, named Jerry Speziale. We would find out as time went on, that this guy was good. Real good!

After one year with the county, I felt much gratitude toward Nathanial Butler, J.R. Cassetta, Antonio Urena and Danny Bachok who taught me everything about the narcotics trade and how to work undercover. In the beginning, I learned that there were 88 known, open air drug markets in Paterson. Man, did they keep us busy. Forget the rest of the county; we will get to that later. Being a fresh face in the squad, I, along with other on loan officers, was given the task of buying drugs on various corners, and the housing projects. The squad bought so many drugs, off of so many players at the CCP, (Christopher Columbus Projects) that we would execute a dozen search warrants at one time. We got help from narcotics units all over the county. Most guys would be from Paterson PD and the Sheriffs' Department, including their SWAT teams. The cities of Paterson, Clifton and Passaic, in addition to the sheriff's department all had teams. We'd have to leave guards in the parking lot to protect the police cars as we raided the buildings. Anything and everything would come out of the windows from six or more stories up. An unsupervised car could even get torched. Ever watch "The Wire" on HBO? Well, there you go. We also executed arrest warrants there, with NYC detectives from the Bronx.

Undercover work became fun. I did a lot of construction work over the years and was a decent carpenter. I worked for my father, who used to build houses and my brother, Mike, who became a master carpenter. I used to play the part of a construction worker that always needed his crack (cocaine) on a regular basis. Early morning was best, as I pretended that I had to get to work soon. I remember one morning I walked down Monroe Street from Main Avenue, in Passaic (City), demanding they hurry up. The dealer told me that it was coming from Paterson and that I would have to wait. I started to yell at him, saying my boss was picking me up on Main Avenue and I needed it NOW! He looked at me like he was a little afraid of me, so I calmed down. Five minutes later, I had my base (crack).

One day I was driving in my undercover pick up when we spotted some action. I pulled up to the corner with D/Sgt. Nate Butler, watching with binoculars. A black male approached the passenger window which was down. I motioned that I wanted two. You didn't even have to say what you wanted as it was known by the addicts which corner sells what. This corner was moving base (crack). He went down the alley, removed a loose brick and grabbed a couple of $10.00 packets. He returned to make the hand-to-hand.

After paying him, I looked at my hand and said, "This is good shit, right?"

He replied, "Maaan, my shit's the best!"

So I looked into his eyes and with my best "Arnold" impression I said, "It better be, or I'll be back." I then drove away, grabbed my handset (radio) from under the seat and confirmed my purchase. Nate ordered the squad to move in, now knowing where he kept his stash.

道

Sometimes you'd find yourself in a position where you feel like telling someone you're a cop, just to allay their fears. One day, I pulled over on 10th Avenue, in Paterson to buy marijuana. It was definitely "Bob Marley" country. As I watched some movement up the street from my Trans-am, a business owner came out of her store. It was summer and my windows were down. You could tell that she was a good person from what she said to me. She started yelling, "WHAT CHEW DOIN HERE! YOU GOTS NO BUSINESS HERE! GET OUTTA HERE!" (Shit! I was being profiled.)

I replied, "Ma'am, I'm just waiting for my friend upstairs."

She continued to yell, "You got no friends around here, you go on and get!" I thought she was going to start kicking the car as she said,

"You're here to buy drugs, get away from my store!" I wanted to tell her to calm down and that I was one of the good guys. I gave her a lot of credit, as she had guts protecting her turf, in a neighborhood where drug dealers could get even if you tried to chase them.

道

Another quick, funny story was also in Paterson. I drove up to a kid on a bicycle asking him for two. He put some loose crack cocaine in my hand as I gave him a $20. I looked at it and decided it was broken off sheet rock. Some dealers, especially in Passaic, would hand you unpackaged crack, this way if you were 5-0 (police), they could destroy the evidence easier. Just to be sure it was sheet rock, I immediately demanded more for my $20.

I said, "Oh, yeah right! That's the white boy price, huh? If I was a brother, I'd get more right?"

He looked at me a little nervous and said, "Oh, oh, okay, here's more, handing me another gram (approximate)."

I thought, *shit, that's absolutely sheet rock. He never would have given me more if it had been real.* Unfortunately, for him, it was still a third degree crime. But fear not, it would almost certainly be downgraded to a DP (disorderly persons charge) at the grand jury. Undercover cops in urban areas risk their lives every day, only to see drug dealers get a slap on the wrist. It's a joke really, how soft we've become as a society. Judges should pretend that the drug dealer standing before them just sold crack or dope (heroin) to their kid, and then you'd see some stiff sentences.

We would buy crack in the morning and then marijuana in the afternoon. Some nights we hit the bars and clubs buying powdered cocaine and ecstasy. Angela, one of our female detectives, did especially well buying in the clubs. Caveats were an operation where we'd pull up in front of an apartment building, where drug dealers could be seen, selling their products. We'd scoop up the dealers and whisk them away. Because it was Paterson and they were black, we would put black undercover officers in their place. The white cops would lie low, inside the building. We would usually find a vacant apartment that we could use for prisoners.

We were ready for business. A customer would walk, drive or ride a bicycle up to our undercover officers. They, of course, had no product on them, so they would direct them inside the hallway to make their purchase. Once they entered the building, we would arrest and handcuff them for loitering/wandering to buy CDS. We used to lock up 60-70 a morning, in a good location. Some of these arrests could become CI's (confidential informants) later. I was always surprised at the cast of characters we would grab; many times people you would never expect.

One caveat we pulled off was on 12th Avenue, in Paterson, that involved some narcotics officers from the Wayne Police Department, as well as a couple others. Because I've lived in Wayne since 1996, I've come to know quite a few of the "boys" there and there are a lot of great guys, I have to say. Jimmy Conforth was already on loan working narcotics and my close friend, Ron Gaeta, assisted on this day.

Ronnie and I go way back in our karate careers. He was always the real deal when it came to tournaments or police work. He's been described as "intense" when he taught self-defense in the police academy. We had a little rivalry going from karate tournaments that matured into a solid friendship and deep respect for one another.

This large "round-up" of addicts would not only produce CI's, as I said, but some pretty funny stories as well. The caveat was over at about 11:00 am and the sheriff's department already removed dozens of disappointed customers, in handcuffs. Nate and I were now sitting outside the building, in our unmarked car with the windows down. Nate was in the driver seat as some strung out female "doper" approached me on the passenger side. She started rambling in a slurred manner something like, "You mutha fuckin 5-0 comin down da hood, harassin' my peeps, shiiit!"

This went on for about two minutes, most of which I couldn't even understand. So when she finally shut up, I looked at Nate, who is African American, hit him on the shoulder, doing my best Ralph Cramden (*Honeymooners*) impression, and said, "You speak Ebonics; what did she say?"

Nate, who had a great sense of humor said, "Well, Pat, she was trying to explain to you that she doesn't think that we, the police, should be in her neighborhood bothering her friends. She also elaborated that we should go back where we came from."

"Oh, I see," I replied. I looked back at her and said, "Have a good day Ma'am," as Nate drove away.

We had so much fun in the squad with a lot of diversity. In certain neighborhoods we had to use the right cop. If I came around on 12th Avenue that day, I was a buyer, a cop or a landlord. Antonio "Tony" Urena, a Dominican, used to buy from individuals who would never sell to me. Tony always had a big pair; not only buying drugs from some very dangerous people, but also guns. I asked once who he just bought from and he said, "Ah, some dumb-minicans." None of us took ourselves too seriously. Tony also held a black belt in Okinawan Karate-Do; the more cops that train, the better, I always say.

道

If I wrote about many of the undercover buys I made or the arrests during my stay at the county, this would be a really long book. Rather than bore you with run-on stories that many cops can relate to, I'll tell a couple of the more entertaining ones.

It was summer of 1997, when we were about to execute a search warrant in a building on the second floor. I kicked in the apartment door announcing, "Police! Search warrant!" as three or four of us entered. Two suspects were sitting on the living room floor at the coffee table. I believe that they were counting money. Being the first one through the door, I went past them, moving quickly into the kitchen. Officers coming in behind me would corral these individuals and secure the rest of the apartment.

Finding a lone male in his 20's, I ordered him to get on the floor. With that, a mean looking pit bull terrier emerged from the back of the kitchen. He was now running full tilt toward me as he barked and growled. I turned slightly toward my left, taking my Beretta's aim away from the suspect and toward the dog. I kicked the dog in his chest, partially lifting him off the ground. The mae geri (front kick) drove him across the room, as I now concentrated on its owner.

I yelled, "Grab that fuckin' dog."

He replied, "Shiiit, I ain't grabbing that mutha' fuckin' dawg, he'll rip my arm off!"

With that, the dog charged at me again! Again, I kicked him in the head and chest area causing him to again sail across the kitchen floor. All of this occurred in seconds, as my attention was drawn to two different threats simultaneously.

The suspect appeared to move closer toward some steak knives on the counter each time I turned my attention to the dog. While giving orders to the suspect and telling him again, to get control of the dog, the pit bull made his move. As the actor (suspect) took one more step toward the knives, the dog charged. With the bigger threat, I thought being the knives; I didn't get a kick off in time. I could feel the dog's teeth biting into my left leg on my calf, as I blasted him. "Bang! Bang! Bang!" three or four shots hit him center mass as his teeth lost their grip. Looking at the suspect, I said, "You're next if you don't get your ass on the ground." Other officers rushed in as they had the rest of the apartment, including the bedrooms, secure. Back-up officers handcuffed the suspect as I yelled at him, "I told you to grab the dog! I like dogs! I shoulda' shot you!"

He insisted, "No way man, that dog crazy!"

I then looked down at the dog that was barely alive, with labored breathing. I told him, "Sorry buddy," as I put one in his head.

Drug dealers commonly breed pit bulls to be killers. The young ones learn to kill squirrels and cats. When they are fully grown, you have to keep a muzzle on them in public. If I didn't shoot that pit bull, he might have torn my calf off of my leg. Try teaching karate without a left calf.

道

There was an occasion in Paterson where another detective and I were chasing a street dealer who ran down an alley. There was a cat in the alley who got startled, so he ran out of the alley in front of us. In his haste, however, he ran past a pit bull that was chained up in the backyard. The pit bull immediately grabbed the cat around the neck, dropping him dead in seconds. Personally, I was glad he was busy with the cat.

道

Getting back to our search warrant, I had to stop what I was doing because blood was now running down my left leg into my boot, and I liked my Carhardts. One of the guys had a first aid kit, so I was able to bandage my leg before getting a ride to Barnett Hospital. After some stitches and tetanus shot, I returned to the office to complete my report. Mace might have been good, but you can't hold your gun on a suspect and mace a dog at the same time. A stun gun, not used in New Jersey yet, would never have worked since the dog was way too fast.

道

We executed so many search warrants that year, I really lost count. The guns, cash and drugs that we confiscated were more than I was used to in Clifton. Then again, I never worked narcotics in Clifton.

And where there is drug trafficking, there are guns. In Passaic County, I saw the most firearms in Paterson, of course. As I said earlier, I learned a lot from the experienced team at the county and the jobs were endless.

I remember one guy who got lucky off Getty Avenue. We had a "no knock" search warrant for the first floor of a two-family house. We hit the door to find the suspect brushing his teeth in the bathroom. It was about 5:30 am and he was getting ready for work. Some mid-level dealers have regular jobs, just to stay under the radar. I discovered a 9mm on his night stand next to the bed, which was fully loaded and ready to go. Sometimes they'll use their guns against us, but in most cases, they have them for rival drug dealers looking to rip them off. I was glad that he wasn't in a position to grab the gun as we entered. Timing may have indeed saved someone's life that morning.

道

Another guy was coming out of the shower one afternoon as I kicked in his door. Dripping wet with a towel around his waist afforded him no time to go for his 9mm. No-knock search warrants are many times the way to go with these dangerous felons, as the surprise factor sometimes saves lives. This, along with the lack of toilet bowls flushing (for drugs) leads to a successful raid.

道

This last story involves my friend, Jerry Speziale, author of, *Without a Badge*. He's the cop that we picked up from New York City. With him, he brought some high tech methods and intel to the squad. Jerry knew more about wire taps and surveillance work than any cop I had met in 20 years. He started a job that involved a team of organized criminals (not to be confused with organized crime) that were involved in various criminal acts. I'm going to remain vague on the details as this was not my investigation to talk about, I only assisted. A Passaic County Superior Court Judge gave us the okay to listen in on the ringleader's conversations which led to the following events.

Jerry and the squad, including myself, were having a meeting concerning tactics that we would use to bring this guy and his posse to justice. Jerry wanted to either bug, or attach a tracking device (GPS) to his SUV. Jerry said that he wanted somebody that was good to watch his back; no teams. He looked straight at me and said, "I want him," as he pointed at me. It was then agreed that Jerry and I would go alone as the squad held back. After a few days, he tweaked the job, telling me that he acquired a duplicate key for the suspects SUV! Jerry wanted me to borrow the car and drive it to an undisclosed location. There, they could install a listening and tracking device. Only tricky thing was for me to "borrow the car" without being detected. We developed information that he would be out of town for a few hours with friends, and he would not be using his vehicle. Then, one evening I was dropped off a block away from his home. Walking toward his house, we had back-up units in place. I nonchalantly walked up his driveway, entered the SUV and backed it out. I drove down the street, picked up Jerry and continued to an undisclosed location.

Speziale, and other back-up detectives, met me as I entered the garage area. Another two-man unit continued to watch the house. The only thing that sucked about the ride was the rap music blaring from the speakers. I hate rap music! Where's Pink Floyd when you need them? Not wanting to touch anything, including the radio station, I turned it down a little. When I returned the car, I turned the volume back-up.

It was time to let Jerry work his magic. All four doors were open, as well as the hatchback, as technicians did their thing. As I intently watched Jerry in action, I suddenly stopped dead in my tracks. *Holy shit!* I thought, *the vehicle's owner had affixed scotch tape to all of the doors and the hatchback!* When the doors were opened, we ripped all of the tape. I guess this guy was paranoid for a reason. It was then that

I asked one of the new guys to find a CVS or something and buy me some tape. I peeled a piece off the car and said, "Make sure that it's the same width." Jerry was glad that I made the discovery and saved the job.

After the car was wired, we closed all the doors except the driver door. I carefully removed the broken tape and took great care to replace it perfectly. The driver door would have to be done after I returned it. Cruising down the target's street, the surveillance car reported that all was quiet. There were lights on in the house and people were home, but no one seemed to notice that the car was gone. Turning right into the driveway, I cut the engine and threw it in neutral. My best guess from my earlier observation would have to be good enough, as to the exact place the vehicle had been parked. After seeing those taped doors, maybe I was getting paranoid. I stepped out of the car, closed the door as quietly as I could and looked up at the house windows. Seeing no one looking out, I replaced the scotch tape on the driver door. As I walked down the street, the neighborhood seemed calm. An unmarked unit followed me before I motioned to him that I was ready for pick up.

Two days later, we had more than enough information for more than one search warrant, which absolutely bore fruit. Case closed.

> *"To have the arts of peace but not the*
> *Arts of war, is to lack courage.*
> *To have the arts of war but not the*
> *Arts of peace, is to lack wisdom."*
>
> *Hayashi Razan*
> **(1583-1657)**

ROBBERIES

I was working on Clifton's Westside, on the 2000-0400 (8pm-4am) "power shift," in 1992. Feeling a little burnt out, I asked my supervisor for a temporary change in scenery. I normally liked the Eastside, including Clifton's downtown area and Botany Village section. The Westside was Van Houten Avenue toward Route 3 and had nice suburban neighborhoods, like Montclair Heights, Richfield, Allwood and Delawanna. It was a nice respite for a while, until I started to get antsy for a good arrest and a little more action.

An armed robbery came in pretty early; I think it was about 2100 hours (9pm) on the Eastside. As it went, this strung-out heroin addict robbed, or attempted to rob, with a handgun three gas stations in a row on Route 46 East. He hit the Exxon, in Little Falls, at the Clifton border, drove about a half of a mile to one of our stations across from the Clifton Plaza, and then a third one further down in Clifton's "middle village." No shots were fired and how much he got from each station was unclear. I thought, *Oh well. He's driving east, even further away from my side of town, but "what the hell" let me head over to the Eastside just in case.* As I drove down Clifton Avenue, a friend of mine, and proactive cop, Sam Skidmore, transmitted that he was in Botany Village and behind a small two door vehicle matching the description of the actor's (suspect's). I think it was a Fiat or something similar. He saw that the driver was a white male also fitting the description of the armed actor (suspect). Throwing on my overhead lights, I accelerated en route to the Botany. Sam chased him in traffic but lost him a couple of minutes later. The Clifton/Passaic border was flooded with marked and unmarked units looking to get lucky. Suddenly, a Passaic officer spotted the suspect vehicle over the line and started a new pursuit back toward Clifton, which seemed to be over in only a couple of minutes. Two Passaic cars and two Clifton cars had him boxed in on Lakeview Avenue down at the lower end. All officers exited their vehicles and held him at gunpoint. I now turned up Lakeview Avenue from Clifton Avenue, as I could observe the standoff. As I closed the gap further, about one block away, I saw the suspect vehicle run into one police car, nudging it up and then reversing, thus slamming into another, creating an avenue of escape.

A couple of the officers who were out with their guns drawn needed to jump out of the way. As the actor broke through, he sped north on Lakeview Avenue toward Paterson. My timing, it was dumb luck, allowed me to then pursue him at high speeds, leaving the other officers scrambling back to their cars. Passaic police, I believe, got orders at that point to return to Passaic and allow Clifton to handle it.

The suspect vehicle drove up Lakeview Avenue, over the double yellow lines, in the center of the road. Closing in nicely, I observed a red light up ahead at the Crooks Avenue intersection (appropriate name, huh?). Two vehicles had already been stopped at the red light side-by-side with maybe, just maybe, enough space between them to squeeze a vehicle through. Well, this desperate individual, without even touching the brake, gunned it and narrowly made it through without making contact. Vehicles driving on Crooks Avenue locked up their brakes and allowed me to pursue. I thought, *Shit! There's no way I'm putting this Caprice through there! I'm sure to sideswipe both vehicles* but *this guy ain't getting away; he's armed.* So, I said to myself, *Self; grab your nuts and floor it.* Okay, okay, I didn't actually grab my nuts. Both of my side view mirrors struck the side view mirrors of these stopped motorists' cars, creating a very loud slapping noise. My next transmission to headquarters was that I crossed into the City of

Paterson, was still in pursuit, and if anyone calls about my car striking theirs, have them stand by for later assistance. No one ever called, so I couldn't help but think about how glad I am that they now make flexible mirrors! On television shows, cops don't have to worry about damage to their vehicles, but in real life, we do.

While, traveling north along the cemetery wall, on Lakeview Avenue in Paterson, the suspect vehicle made a quick right turn onto the ramp, for Route 80 East. Our dispatchers were on SPEN (State Police Emergency Network) at this point, keeping surrounding towns apprised of our situation. Route 80 is considered a "Super Highway," where cars drive faster and use some five lanes at times. As I entered Route 80, I checked my rearview mirror for any back-up officers, but saw none. As I zigzagged through cars, as the suspect vehicle narrowly avoided collision, as he became more desperate, while showing no signs of surrender. He exited in Elmwood Park as a Saddle Brook unit appeared in front of him. The suspect immediately slammed into the driver side front fender, disabling the Saddle Brook car. He backed away and attempted to flee to the right when I bore down on him. I thought, *two can play at that game!* I slammed into the passenger door on the right side of his vehicle and pushed him like a tank. I hit him with such force as I floored it, I pushed him sideways, blowing out his front and rear left side tires, on the curb on the opposite side of the street.

道

Now, crazy as it sounds, especially to me, I almost never wore a seat belt, even at speeds of 120 mph or more. I knew from experience that after the crash, and there's almost always a crash, there would be a foot chase or even shots fired. Since I couldn't stand to see someone get away, I wanted no delay jumping out.

Also, just a tip; after the crash, spin out, or whatever, try to position your car immediately next to the driver door so he can't jump out.

Sometimes, this is difficult or impossible because of the vehicle's position or the speed at which these events unfold. But it especially pays off if you're not a runner.

道

I remember one time I was chasing a stolen car down Route 21 in Passaic heading south. This was usually beautiful because Clifton is like a horseshoe around Passaic. From Botany Village, in Clifton, I would enter Route 21 South in Passaic (City) but then re-enter Clifton on our Route 3 side. Our Westside cars would just lay in wait. On this night, however, it turned out even better. As I got on Route 21 south from Monroe Street (BTW Route 21 in those days came up from Newark and came to a dead-end in Passaic), I turned my radio to SPEN, where I could talk directly to the Passaic dispatcher. A Passaic unit got on the highway just ahead of me from State Street and turned on his overhead lights. He drove in the center lane, of which there were three, and kept his speed at about 50 mph. As the suspect vehicle started to catch up to him and tried to pass, the Passaic officer drifted back and forth, not allowing his passing attempt. I was now alongside the actor (suspect) on his driver side in the left lane. Together, the Passaic officer and I decreased our speed while "pushing" or guiding the stolen car toward the right shoulder. Suddenly, a second Passaic marked unit appeared in my rearview mirror and tucked in behind the actor's vehicle. Now we had a beautiful three-way box and slowed him to a stop. It's amazing that later the Attorney General would frown upon this masterful maneuver. We exited our radio cars and drew down on the suspect. As I walked closer to the driver door and ordered the actor out, he looked at me, and then locked the door. Well, back then, we were still using wheel guns (revolvers) so I had no problem with a slide. I took my Smith & Wesson .357 Magnum and punched it through the driver window. As he reacted to the tempered glass striking him in the face, I holstered my weapon, reached in, grabbed him and pulled him out through the broken window. Once he landed on the hood of the car and felt my handcuffs attach to his wrists, I think he realized that locking the door wasn't a great idea!

道

I digress. On this night after a successful ram, disabling the actor's vehicle, I was wearing (hate to admit it!), a seatbelt. Now try to visualize this…

I T-boned this guy in a way, that has me staring at the perpetrator through my windshield and his front passenger window. He could raise his right hand and start firing through the glass at any moment. Normally, I could duck and slide out my door to take cover. But WTF; I'm trying to watch his hands and feel for my seatbelt release at the same time. Seconds felt way too long for someone who prides himself on efficiency. My right hand found the release as my left hand opened the door. I slid out low affording some cover as I drew my Beretta. My position was now behind his left corner trunk with me ordering, "Throw the gun out the window! Do it now!" The actor, apparently realizing he had no place to go, threw his gun out onto the ground and followed my additional command to show me his hands. Sam Skidmore now pulled up and acted as a cover officer while I holstered my 9mm. I stepped over and kicked the actor's gun further away as I dragged him out of the driver side window. As Sam continued to cover the actor, other units were pulling up as I cuffed him. In addition to the handgun, proceeds from the gas stations were also recovered.

道

Sometimes, or should I say many times, a desperate actor will do the unexpected. One time, Officer Ross La Corte and I, had two suspects stopped on Crooks Avenue and Lee Place. We both drew down on the actors (suspects) with Ross on the passenger side of the car while I was near the left front of the vehicle. We ordered the driver to throw the keys out of the window. He complied as he turned off the engine and threw out the keys. Seconds later, the driver, to our surprise, started the car with a duplicate key and gunned it. I quickly jumped out of the way as they raced off. Ross and I later caught up to these individuals over the Paterson border and took them into custody. The driver was properly levitated with a foot sweep and cuffed.

道

Another surprising ending to a motor vehicle stop happened on the 1500-2300 shift (3-11pm). We had an actor's car boxed in on Lexington Avenue, near Clifton Avenue. We got a call that there was a man at the Grand Union, threatening someone with a gun. We spotted the suspect's car on Lexington Avenue and had him surrounded at gunpoint ordering him to show his hands. He wouldn't show his hands as we now had a bit of a stalemate. Another radio car (marked police unit) or two had pulled up to assist as I'm sure the actor realized, at this point, there was no escape. In a flash, the actor placed his handgun into his mouth and fired. The bullet went clean through the top of his head and the roof of the car. So remember, any rookies out there, expect the unexpected.

道

Gas station and 24-hour convenience store robberies were all too common. Most cops have a few good stories. Even in normally quiet Wayne, NJ, where I live, we had an officer shot in 2010 during a robbery on Route 23 and Packanack Lake Road. It was a gas station/convenience store. The police officer survived his wounds and the perpetrator was caught some time later!

In 2004, when I was running Clifton's Narcotics/Vice Unit, a few North Jersey towns, along with Clifton, were experiencing highway gas station robberies. The description of the lone actor and M. (Modus Operandi/Method of Operation) were the same, or at least very similar. The actor had committed at least seven armed robberies and also shot a gas station attendant during a robbery in Elmwood Park, leaving many North Jersey officers on high alert. Reading our A-9 sheets, BOLO (Be On the Look Out) bulletins, I tried to think a little like the actor and guess what station he might hit next. I focused mainly on a Route 3 West Exxon station, just past the Main Avenue exit. It was only a few blocks away from an Exxon station on the corner of Passaic Avenue and Allwood Road which he hit about a week earlier.

This was my fourth night watching this highway Exxon station and was getting a little antsy. I wondered if lightning could strike twice. The Exxon he hit a week ago might be a good target and was only a short distance away. Partially out of boredom, I decided to set up on the Passaic Avenue station for awhile. After about a half hour on Passaic Avenue, I drove down Allwood Road to Main Avenue, got on Route 3 West, drove through the original Exxon and then checked out the Sunoco near Bloomfield Avenue. Getting off Route 3, at Bloomfield Avenue, I would drive down Allwood Road East, which paralleled Route 3, back to the Passaic Avenue Exxon. I was driving a Dodge Stratus at the time and had my Jimi Hendrix CD on, making it a pleasant circumnavigation. Call it dumb luck or keen insight (I like the latter) but on the third or fourth look, I spotted a car that caught my attention. Traveling East on Allwood Road, there was a car stopped at the red light at Passaic Avenue. The driver, and lone occupant, took a long stare at the Exxon station. The light changed green as he started to move up slowly, and then crossed over Passaic Avenue. *Funny*, I thought, *that he didn't pull in for gas after such a hard look.*

I followed this Hyundai while noting the New Jersey license plate. The actor drove two blocks and then turned right into Hollywood

Avenue, a dead-end. There was a parking lot at the end of the street where people would sometimes ingest CDS. Ironically enough, I lived on Hollywood Avenue, in one of the only three houses, so I knew this guy didn't live there. I passed Hollywood Avenue as he turned in and then I doubled back. The next block over from Hollywood also dead-ends into the same parking lot, so I drove down with my lights out. I could now observe the Hyundai parked in the lot, facing out, with his lights off. As I called in the plate and requested a back-up, I couldn't stop wondering about that long stare. *Imagine...* I thought, *if he was casing the gas station and he was our boy.* Then I thought, *Nah, nobody could be that lucky.* The vehicle came back negative stolen and was ready to be approached. I thought a patrol unit would roll up to assist me, but as it turned out, two of my narcotics detectives were working a two-man unmarked and were very close by. Sometimes it feels good to have guys you work with everyday back you up because we already work well as a team.

Detectives Gary Passenti and Tommy Rinaldi turned right onto Hollywood Avenue and pulled in nose-to-nose with the suspect car. I approached through the parking lot, lighting up the whole left driver side and the suspect, with my high beams. The suspect's right shoulder appeared to dip, as he leaned to his right. Det. Passenti picked up on this movement best as he exited his driver door. Det. Rinaldi and I stepped out of our cars to talk to the driver as Passenti stood on the passenger side illuminating the interior. Passenti, who had some good gun and narcotics arrests himself, called out immediately, "GUN!" With that, Rinaldi and I quickly drew down on the suspect and ordered him out of the car. He was out on the ground in seconds, as we guided him. Passenti pointed out that the gun was lying on the back seat floor behind the front passenger seat. This, of course, was right where he put it as he leaned over just a minute earlier. After searching the suspect for weapons, Rinaldi and I cuffed him as I noted that he was wearing a black leather jacket. Passenti pointed out the handgun to me as I confiscated the same.

While unloading two rounds from the .38 caliber cylinder, I pointed out the uniqueness of the weapon to Gary. I said, "Gary, this is the guy that's been holding up all the gas stations."

Gary looked at me like, "that's a stretch." Thinking that we were checking him out for CDS in a parking lot, Passenti and Rinaldi never saw the long stare at the gas station. I studied the bulletins and remembered what a couple of victims said. They said that when the actor pointed the gun in their face, he had the hammer "cocked back." Well, the gun I was holding was an Iver Johnson and had no hammer, so it looked as though he had it cocked back. I could tell that Gary wasn't totally convinced.

I continued to press my point and said, "Look, he's even wearing the same black leather jacket that he wore the night he shot that gas station attendant in Elmwood Park."

We impounded the Hyundai and had a black and white take in the prisoner. Narcotics Detective Thomas Burrows followed the tower to the Impound to perform a more thorough search of the vehicle. I learned from working with Burrows, nothing gets missed with Tommy. Sure as shit, Burrows found more evidence of the robberies stuffed up in the springs of the passenger front seat. Items included latex gloves and a black nylon ski mask. This individual, a light-skinned Hispanic male was a United States recovery agent, better known as a bounty hunter. The night I grabbed him, he also had a recovery agent shield (badge), mace, a flashlight, handcuffs and a baton in his possession. He ultimately confessed to seven armed robberies. Case closed.

道

The next armed robbery I'd like to highlight, occurred in 2001, when I was a patrol sergeant cruising the Eastside. It was the midnight shift and I just stopped by my Main Avenue Karate dojo to use the bathroom. I don't recall the exact time but believe it was about 0100 hours. The Clifton dispatcher called out using an emergency ringtone, followed by "All Eastside cars, an armed robbery just occurred at the gas station on Main Avenue, corner of Hadley. Two actors, possibly teens, showing a 9mm handgun, robbed the attendant. No shots fired, actors (suspects) fled on foot." I jumped into my radio car and directed our Eastside cars to different streets in order to set up a perimeter. The first car on scene was Car #3 who quickly furnished us with an additional description. The attendant stated that the actors crossed Main Avenue on foot when they fled. The city of Passaic was just about three blocks away to the south. Crossing Main Avenue took them east, toward the railroad tracks. They either had a car parked on one of the streets heading toward Getty Avenue or were heading on foot toward Clifton's Botany Village section. While I knew that a couple of units were already exploring the first option, I thought I'd get on the other side of the tracks fast.

There was an old factory of Central Avenue, on the other side of the tracks, called Royal Silk. It had a really long parking lot adjacent to the tracks and a high fence that they would have to scale in order to get down to the Botany area. *How nice it would be to trap them in that lot*, I thought to myself. So, I followed my hunch and quietly parked my cruiser just off Central Avenue. If they jump the rather high fence, they would have a very long factory building standing in their way. There was one opening between the buildings, however, out to Central Avenue. And that my friend was exactly where I would stand. I peeked around the corner of the building with my Beretta drawn. My instincts didn't fail me. Two young men were walking through the lot and toward my position. I stepped back around the building and radioed my position to headquarters and the other units. I lowered the volume on my radio and emerged from the opening so these youths could see me. I kept my hand on my gun, which was back in my holster. I knew that if I drew down on them, they would either run or open fire, forcing me to kill them. So I yelled to them, "Hey! You guys aren't smoking pot out here are you? Come on, you guys gotta leave." With that, I saw them look at each other as one of them began to walk toward me. The second actor crouched down and left something behind near a tractor trailer, then started to follow his friend. Resting my hand on my 9mm, I started to engage them in conversation. I explained to them that it was getting to be a major problem for me that so many teens were using the parking lot for narcotics and alcohol. I further explained that if they didn't have any drugs on them, they would have to go home and not come back. My conversation and stall tactics were of course trying to buy time for my backup to arrive. I had these fools thinking they were home free after a search for CDS (controlled dangerous substance). I made one sit on his hands, as not to discard any drugs, while I searched his friend. Finding no contraband on the first one, I had them switch. Nothing was discovered on the second one either as I continued to BS them before supposedly kicking them out of the lot. I was glad they bought the ruse because if they ran, I never would have caught them both and keep an eye on whatever they concealed in the parking lot.

Two radio cars finally pulled up as the back-up officers now held the actors at bay. You should have seen the look on their faces when I told the officers that I now had to check what they left behind. I walked over to the tractor trailer to find a fully loaded Sig Saur 9mm handgun and a brown paper bag containing cash from the gas station. Both teens were cuffed and brought back to the gas station for positive I.D. (State vs. Carter).

That was a fun and rewarding arrest because, finally, I was the "Road Boss." It took me about 20 years to get promoted to sergeant and it was nice to call the shots. As I directed my men that night to plug up the area, it reminded me of a job a couple of years earlier.

道

I was working Car #3 on the 1500-2300 hour shift and was parked on Main Avenue near the White Castle. There was a shooting in neighboring Passaic as a description and BOLO were broadcast. We had an Eastside sergeant working who will remain nameless. No orders were given; no plan was conceived. I, as one of the more senior patrolmen, asked who was taking what street or escape route. Eastside cars usually watched Main thoroughfares to Paterson and Westside cars would watch Route 21 and routes to Newark. The one thing I hated was when no one coordinated the post cars. As a result, you could have three radio cars on Main Avenue and none on some of the other thorough fares. Car #8 said that he was on Main Avenue, so I volunteered for Lakeview Avenue. I asked Car #1 if he could take Lexington at Randolph and if Car #3 could get Paulison Avenue. All of these streets go to the City of Paterson. After a short time watching for the getaway car, Detective Billy Frank spotted it on Central Avenue, heading north, to Lakeview Avenue and Paterson. Billy, one of our best, stopped the suspect vehicle and drew down on him as back-up officers sped to assist. Detective Frank recovered the gun and a few spent shells inside the vehicle.

And now for the part that involves me. The sergeant, after removing his muzzle, I'm sure, admonished me for "playing" sergeant. Many good cops out there go through this shit all the time. Do me a favor. Don't stop, remain proactive and keep the boys safe when possible. Finally, if it happens to you, have a cold one after work with me in mind.

道

It's funny when you learn about people's perceptions years later; Cops calling me "The Colonel" and such. Road sergeants used to get pissed because many of the rookie's would ask my opinion, over theirs, in many cases. I was recently at Clifton's PBA annual picnic and was conversing with a former chief, Frank LoGioco. He was my sergeant in 1977, when I came on and eventually became chief. My teenage son, Kyle, came over to the chief and me to ask a question. But before he could ask me, I stopped him to introduce him. I said, "Kyle, I'd like you to meet one of my old bosses. Say 'hi' to Chief LoGioco." The chief peered down at my son and said, "Don't let him fool you Kyle. Your father never had any bosses."

"Courage is almost a contradiction in terms.
It means a strong desire to live,
Taking the form of a readiness to die."

GK Chesterton

SEARCH, THEN SEARCH AGAIN

While working narcotics in the City of Paterson, and the rest of the county for that matter, in 1997, I learned in "Top Gun" and DEA (Drug Enforcement Administration) School to always do a double search. Don't ever get insulted if someone wants to search a suspect or a dwelling after you already did. Better to be safe than sorry. This applies to patrol units as well.

In the mid 80's, I was working Car #3, downtown Clifton, while my friend, Richie Lekston, was working Car #1 in Botany Village. Richie and I came on the job together in 77, and worked side-by-side a lot. I always liked having Richie around since he was one of Clifton's toughest and had balls. Botany bar fights always went better with Richie. It was around 1700 hours (5pm), I recall, when Richie and I were dispatched to the Grand Union at Clifton and Lexington Avenues. There was a suspicious white male hanging around out front.

We approached this individual and started asking questions. After a while, he told us that he was parked on the street in back of the store on East Madison and was waiting for a friend. As it turned out, he was from out-of-state and we doubted he had a friend coming anytime soon. I asked him why he would hide his car in the back when there were plenty of parking spaces in the front. He had no groceries and we suspected he might be "casing" the place for a robbery. We told him that we would take him around back because we wanted to see his car. Richie grabbed a hold of the guy by the arm and started putting him in the back of Car #1's cage. The suspect sat in the back seat as

Richie was ready to close the door. I said, "Hold on," and pulled him back out, "you don't mind if I pat you down first, do you?" Before he actually answered, I did a quick pat down of his jacket. Inside his jacket, I found a revolver; I believe it was a .38 inside a shoulder holster. After removing the gun and handing it to Richie, I did a more in-depth search of the actor's person.

Once we handcuffed him and placed him in the back of Car #1, we drove around back where he pointed out his car which had out-of-state southern plates. I think it was Tennessee or Kentucky. He didn't object to us looking in his car, so we checked out a gym bag in the front seat. It contained a .357 Magnum. Now, I agree, we probably should have gotten a search warrant at that point for the trunk, but we didn't. We discovered an AR15 rifle in the trunk. He was charged with several counts of possession of those firearms but we could never prove any evil machinations. There was a suppression hearing in Paterson, where a liberal judge threw out the charges and allowed him to leave. He said that we hadn't shown good cause to bother this man. He even went as far as telling us that we "didn't even have the right to ask him his name." Even though the case got tossed, Richie and I, and who knows who else, got to go home that night. We could have just prevented a "Columbine" type massacre. But today, it was the wisdom of the judge that would prevail.

道

Another story, of which cops have many, comes to mind about searches. One night on the midnight shift, I was working Car #1 in Botany Village, when a call came in at the Tick Tock Diner on Route 3 West. It was about three in the morning when a customer called the police to report two men that had threatened his life. The Tick Tock diner is on the west side of Clifton, while I was on the east side. Westside cars were tied up on other jobs so they had me respond with one west side car and a sergeant. I had to travel a distance to get there, taking Route 21 South, through Passaic and onto Route 3 West. As a result, two cars had arrived before me. As I pulled up with another radio car arriving, I saw two suspects' standing next to their car that was parked in front of the diner, with two police cars blocking them in. The officers were talking to these men and checking out their driver licenses on the computer database for possible hits.

Their names and license plate checks were negative (no wants) and after getting enough information for the report, they were about to let them on their way. The victim was told that he could sign complaints in Clifton municipal court. At this time, it was a "he said, he said." Just when they were getting ready to leave, I asked the sergeant if I could check a little further. When he asked me why, I told him that they looked familiar. I told the sergeant that they looked like a couple of wannabe's that hung out at Martha's Vineyard and Casey's. These were both nice establishments mind you, but sometimes drew undesirables. You know, "Tony Soprano" types. They were standing near the doors of their vehicle, just getting ready to leave as one of the police cars was being moved, allowing them to go. I stopped them just as they were reaching for the door handles and said, "Excuse me fella's, could you both step back here a moment by the sergeant?" They looked at each other, paused, and then complied with my request. As they stood away from their car with three Clifton officers, I opened the passenger side door. I got down on one knee and shined my flashlight under the front seat to discover a small, fully loaded handgun. As I held it up for all to see, I asked, "Does this look familiar?" I handed it off to the sergeant, walked around to the driver door and did the same inspection under the driver seat. Sure as shit, there was a second gun under that seat. I held the second gun and said, "Gee, maybe they were gonna shoot him after all."

Suffice to say they were both placed under arrest. I told Car #7 that he could take them in and write up the job. I wanted to go back down to the Botany, plus, I was getting hungry. Any rookie officer reading this, here's a tip. In this case, because we had a complainant and a "threat to kill," my search stood up. Ironically enough, I cannot, as a seasoned officer with a gut feeling, ask someone their name if I think they are acting suspiciously. But if an untrained citizen calls me to check someone out, then it's okay. WTF!

道

Clifton experienced two vicious mob hits that were highly publicized in the newspapers. One was a hit on Hepburn Road, off Allwood Road, near the Montclair Country Club. It was in the parking lot of the "Hepburn Towers." A shotgun blast ended the victim's flight from the two actors who pursued him as he tried to scale a fence there. Another was in the 90's in the parking lot of the Howard Johnson's motel on Route 3 West, near Passaic Avenue. A bullet to the brain was the mark of a hit.

道

Sometimes the guy who seems very cooperative can be the most dangerous. On the midnight shift (I was off) they brought in a guy for a minor offense. Being minor, the law only called for a complaint summons to be issued. Once these individuals are processed, they're released.

Our AFIS fingerprinting/warrants system was down for a couple of hours, creating a problem between 0400-0600 (4-6am) hours on occasion. The detained individual was very polite from what I was told, as he cooperated throughout every phase of his arrest. Not having any grounds to hold him further, the watch commander authorized his release.

In about an hour or so, his prints kicked back when the system was restored. It immediately became apparent why he played Mr. Nice Guy throughout his processing. The AFIS system verified that he was wanted, I believe in Alabama, for homicide. This was no fault of the officers or watch commander, as they had followed the letter of the law.

道

One day in the late 80's, I was assigned to watch a prisoner at Passaic General Hospital. Relieving the last officer from his post, I found the suspect handcuffed to the bed. While checking the cuffs for tightness, I also noted the IV in his other arm. Sometime later a couple of nurses entered the room and asked me if I could remove the handcuff for a short time so that they could do their job more efficiently. I explained to them that it's better to keep the handcuff on for security purposes.

The nurses told me that he was in a weakened state and in need of a bathroom break; it would be much easier without the handcuffs they insisted. Sizing him up, I decided to remove the handcuff. I asked the nurses to move back while I removed the cuff from his wrist. BTW just a tip, if you ever have to do this, remove the one attached to his wrist, rather than the bed, as it could be used as a weapon if he swings it wildly at your face.

Well, the second the cuff came off, he jumped out of the bed and proceeded to rip the IV out of his arm. Blood squirted out as he started to resemble a dancer from Michael Jackson's Thriller video.

As he came toward me completely enraged, I threw a perfect overhand right. My focus and determination came together, as I could already envision him hitting the floor. Appearing to have some experience in the fight game, he quickly nodded his head toward the floor, causing my fist to strike the top of his skull. It was equivalent to banging two rocks together. A quick left hook to the right side of his head accomplished the desired effect, as he dropped to the floor. As I cuffed him, I glanced over toward the nurses with an "I told you so" look. I told a few of the staff members, including the nurses, to let this be a lesson to them. People can't be trusted and no one can guarantee the actions of another!

It was the first time ever striking a person that my hand began to swell. My knuckle on my middle finger felt like it might be chipped. In demonstrations, I chipped my knuckle once and broke my hand on another occasion. Years ago, I had performed a demo at the Totowa PAL. I had two red house bricks supporting a third as I hit it with a tegatana uchi (karate chop). The brick didn't break, so I hit it again. As I allowed my frustration to get the best of me, I hit it again and again. Finally, my friend, Dennis Buongiorno, pulled me off of it. After the demo was over, we used the sledgehammer, that we used during the bed of nails, to break open the brick. We immediately knew why the brick was so hard; it had a rock inside of it! Guess you never know what could fall into the mix.

So, getting back to the hospital, the ice pack wasn't quite making it. So I called for a relief officer so I could go downstairs for a quick x-ray. Sure enough, the x-ray showed a chipped knuckle. Now that was one hard head! Skulls are very hard which is why I'm a proponent of head-butting when teaching self-defense. It's also unexpected.

道

Getting back to searches, in 1997, I attended "Top Gun" down at the New Jersey State Police Academy in Sea Girt. It was a narcotics/ entry team course for police officers and prosecutors. The group I was assigned to voted me, to be the acting lieutenant during the course. We did a mock raid of a building with cops posing as bad guys inside. Once we secured the building and had everyone handcuffed, we brought them outside. One "suspect" had a small caliber handgun tucked inside his pants, in the small of his back. As I spoke to the officer, who was guarding him in the parking lot, the suspect made his move. Handcuffed behind his back, he managed to pull the gun, turn 90 degrees and fire at me point blank. As I saw him turn and raise his gun, I started to move slightly to my right in order to use a spinning low foot sweep on his forward leg. But just as soon as I wanted to spin, I stopped myself and got "shot." We were standing in a gravel parking lot. Had I swept his foot out with that particular sweep, he really could have been hurt. I was thinking, *duh, he's a cop!* Hitting the back of his head on that gravel, with his hands cuffed behind him, was the last thing I wanted for my brother-in-blue. Point being, that any cop can practice this spinning sweep as you drop to the ground, very quickly, doing the unexpected.

So my friends, if you really feel that you need to check out someone or something further, maybe the hairs on the back of your neck are standing up, and, for safety reasons you feel it's necessary, GO FOR IT! Maybe, just maybe, even if the evidence is thrown out by some liberal judge, you might save a life. Sometimes your own! Search, and then search again.

A rookie I was breaking in asked me if I was getting tired of his questions. I told him, "Kid, you're young and fired up. I'll take that over old and burnt out anytime." I also passed on these words that O'Sensei Brian Frost once related to me...

> *"To ask is to risk a moment of shame,*
> *Not to ask,*
> *Is to risk a lifetime of ignorance."*
>
> *(Author Unknown)*

GUNS, GUNS, EVERYWHERE!

F rom my swearing in on May 10, 1977 to my retirement on May 1, 2008, the amount of guns I saw on the street seemed to multiply. In the 70's, there were a lot of "Saturday Night Specials," or cheap black market .38's. By the time I left, it was mostly semi-automatics and an occasional Mac 10.

Anyone working narcotics in the bigger cities, or working with the DEA, usually see the most guns. How many doors did we kick in only to find some heat lying on the night table in the bedroom? One thing's for sure, when you deal with this many guns, shit happens!

道

It was 1984 when I was working Car #3, downtown Clifton. Dispatch notified all units that Paterson Police were chasing a vehicle south on Route 20/McLean Boulevard South, toward our beautiful city on the Eastside. Knowing that a lot of criminals run between Paterson to Passaic, and often times to Newark, I thought that I would drive east on Clifton Avenue toward the Botany area of town. As I drove that way from Paulison Avenue, dispatch told us that Paterson broke off the chase. I thought, *no, shit, Sherlock, Paterson always breaks it off unless it's a homicide.* I found out later that it was Sgt. McElrath who was ordered to break it off. McElrath was a good cop and later advanced to captain.

The next day, a *rocket scientist* (captain) was quoted, from Paterson PD, that they don't chase cars but write the driver a speeding ticket the next morning. *Are you shittin me?* Somebody steals your car while you're asleep. Some cop chases it on the highway, lets the guy get away, and then adds insult to injury, by mailing *you*, a speeding ticket! How about catching *him* and charging him with 2nd or 3rd degree eluding? You could even write a speeding ticket to the right guy.

Listen up class! When a seemingly desperate individual speeds away from the police at over 100 mph, he's running for a reason. Like the guy I chased with a body in the trunk. It is very rare that the guy accelerates to those speeds when he could have just pulled over at a lower speed when you first saw him, unless, he has something else to hide. In many cases, people steal cars to use them to commit crimes like armed robberies, drive-by's, you name it. Any cop will tell you that many fugacious individuals have warrants out for their arrest. In the case of McElrath's boy, he was wanted for taking the car without owner's consent, aggravated assault and several warrants.

So, like I was saying, I continued down Clifton Avenue in an attempt to guess his destination. I stopped at the light at Lakeview Avenue and here came a rocket ship traveling south from Lakeview onto Central Avenue (street name changes when you cross Clifton Avenue). I put on my overheads, turned right and pursued the vehicle that Paterson let get away. "Car 3 to headquarters," I called out, as I attempted to get close enough to confirm the plate. It was about 4 am with almost no traffic as we accelerated into the City of Passaic. The suspect turned left onto Madison Street and attempted a turn onto Hope Avenue as he jumped the curb, hit a fire hydrant, sideswiped a telephone pole, then ran into a cyclone fence before coming to a stop near the Panasote factory. Two suspects jumped out as I grabbed the one closest to me with my left hand, while holding my Beretta (9mm) in my right. Grabbing the back of his neck I slammed him into the cyclone fence. Knowing I had no immediate back-up and seeing the driver scale the fence, I thought that I'd bluff him. I pointed my gun in his direction and fired a "warning shot" over his head hoping that he would stop dead in his tracks. (Hmmm, maybe that's the wrong word). His friend, who I had pinned against the fence with my left hand, apparently thought that I was trying to shoot him. As a result, he struck my arm down at the crease of my elbow, causing the gun to fire a second time as Passaic officers were arriving on scene. At this point, I holstered my weapon in order to gain better control of the suspect and handcuff him. All of this happened in seconds. Passaic officers immediately began to search for the suspect who got away. Patrolman Anthony Giaconia found him hiding and bleeding under stacks of pallets near the factory on Jefferson Street. As it turned out, he was brought to Beth Israel Hospital, where they removed a bullet just over his heart.

道

A few years later, I was working Car #3, on the day shift. We got a report that a white van was just stolen in Passaic by a black male who may be heading into Clifton. They supplied us with the license plate number, so we all stayed alert on the east side. I was traveling south on Main Avenue in the area of my karate dojo (school) when I spotted a white van with a black male driver, approaching me traveling north. I made a U-turn as I tried to catch the license plate. I could only get a partial because of traffic and cars coming between us. After passing a couple of cars in a calm, calculated manner, I was able to see that the plate did not match the one that Passaic dispatch gave us. The van still looked good, however, as everything else matched. "Car 3 to headquarters," I called out.

"Come in Car 3," Dispatch responded.

"I'll be stopping a white van being driven by a black male on Main Avenue by the White Castle," I continued. "NJ plate number (ABC123)."

"Received; Car 3. Car 1, back car 3, Main and Piaget," said the dispatcher.

The van pulled over right after I flipped on my overheads, so I thought, *this can't be the guy.* I still owed him an explanation as to why I'm stopping him though, so I exited my car. Still in a higher state of alert, I unsnapped my holster and rested my hand on my Beretta. As I reached the vans bumper, I hear over my hand set, "Car 3! That's the van! Passaic gave us the wrong plate!"

Without missing a beat, I drew my gun, slid up alongside the driver window, which was down and put my gun in his left ear. "How are ya?!" I exclaimed. "Step out of the van please." He complied and continued to follow my commands as he found himself cuffed, searched and placed into the back of my car.

As I was cuffing him, a friend of mine, Kenny Dalpos, pulled up in Car #1 and said, "Nice job Pat," as we engaged in conversation. We both agreed that we were surprised he didn't run and kind of glad that we didn't have to deal with a crash. We got back into our cars as I waited for the tow truck, or owner of the van, seeing that it was just stolen. I told him his Miranda rights and wanted to question him about the crime. He said that he understood his rights and began chatting away.

After getting some pedigree questions out of the way, I asked him, "By the way, how come you didn't run? Everybody runs. I'm kinda glad you didn't because there's a lot more traffic out here during the day. My usual overnight pursuits don't usually involve other people. But then again, I do kinda miss the chase."

He sat back in his seat and said, "Shiiiit, I ain't runnin in Clifton! Mutha fuckin Clifton cops shoot niggas! Maan! My mutha fuckin friend, Kevin Jackson (not his real name), was shot by some crazy Clifton cop."

"Was he? I asked.

"Yeah, do you know who shot him?"

"Yeah, it was me.", I answered.

"Oooh, shiiit. I'm glad I didn't run," he lamented.

道

On January 3, 1998, I was back in Clifton after a one year stint with the county narcotics task force. *Oh well,* I thought, *back to patrol work.* It was coming up on a change of shift for the early cars at 2300 hours (11pm). One of our newer guys at that time, Pete Turano, had a motor vehicle stop on Hamilton Avenue at Lexington. The vehicle was facing Lexington at a "T" intersection. Across the street were backyards to the houses on Piaget Avenue. I was working Car #2, Lakeview section on the eastside and not very far from Turano's stop. Pulling up, I called on scene and exited my car, flashlight in hand. Pete was already speaking with the driver, asking for his license and so on. I approached the passenger side of the vehicle, lighting up the interior of the car. The passenger, later identified as Stanley Ray, seemed a little nervous with me getting so close to him. If you watch their abdominal area, sometimes you'll notice a flutter when they're nervous, beyond what would be considered normal. If they are standing, you can put your hand over their heart, if you suspect something is amiss. A rapid, over-the-top heartbeat, when they haven't been running, can also tell you a lot.

I looked down at his feet and thought that I could see something protruding from under the seat. "Please step out of the car, sir," I asked. He stepped out and I asked him to stand up against the rear door. He complied as I thought that I could get a better look at what was under the seat. As I could see Ray with my peripheral vision only, I looked down at the floor using my flashlight to get a better look. Bam! Gone! Ray sprinted away, crossing over Lexington Avenue, heading for some backyards. I turned and quickly sprinted after him as he was about 50 feet in front of me. He jumped over a four foot fence as I tried to close the gap. Ray, now in the middle of the next yard, slowed down, reached in his waistband, pulled a handgun and bang! fired a shot directly at me. Luckily he was spinning around quickly so the bullet missed its mark. Good thing or you wouldn't be reading this book.

Ducking down, I drew my Beretta. Before I could get off a shot, he had already sprinted around the corner of a house, now going out toward Piaget Avenue. Or was he? I jumped the fence and told headquarters, "Shots fired, shots fired!" as I ran to the rear corner of the house. Like most cops who come with a brain, I did a head snap peek around the corner to confirm that he ran up the alley and wasn't lying in wait. My half second peek revealed that he was now about to cross Piaget Avenue, toward the rear parking lot to Lee's Hawaiian Islander Restaurant. I darted down the alley and arrived at the street to see him run into some back yards across Piaget Avenue. Rather than getting blindsided in the yards, I told back-up units to form a perimeter, as I also took a position to help seal the area. Back-up officers arrived on scene and set up a perimeter on this freezing January night. It wasn't long before my hands started to feel numb. We found out from prior incidents that the county dogs don't do so well tracking when it's below 20 degrees. After searching yards for about an hour, we broke it down. Midnight shift units would patrol the area for a while longer but most cars had to respond to other calls by now.

Stanley Ray's friend, the driver, was detained for questioning and charged with motor vehicle violations. It wasn't long before detectives identified Ray and had me view a photo lineup. Once I made a positive ID of the suspect, we had multiple charges typed up, including attempted murder of a police officer. The incident with me occurred on a Sunday night. By Tuesday night, Stanley Ray shot a civilian dead on the streets of Paterson. It was a guy who he had a problem with, and we believed, that it was originally his idea to "cap" this guy Sunday night, until Turano pulled him over. Clifton Detective Doug Miller, also learned that Ray had previously shot at a Paterson police officer. Miller and Paterson detectives learned from a tip line that Stanley had fled to North Carolina and even came up with an address. Paterson PD, wanting Ray for homicide, sent two detectives down to North Carolina, to assist local authorities in Robeson County with his capture.

When police arrived at the residence where he was holed up, Ray barricade himself in the home. It was then that Paterson detectives got his mother to give him a phone call and convince him to surrender. Approximately 45 minutes later, Stanley Ray came out of the house and gave himself up without a struggle. Robeson County Sheriff officers also arrested another local man living in the house. That man was charged with being involved in a shooting on December 3, 1997 in North Carolina and also harboring a fugitive. Two handguns were recovered inside the home.

道

Nowhere, are there more guns, more crime and more drugs than in our urban projects. Clifton has no projects but that didn't stop us from visiting Paterson's and Newark's from time-to-time. When I worked in Paterson with the narcotics task force, I remember a morning where we were going to execute a few arrest warrants with detectives from the Bronx (NYC). I was teamed up with a tough looking African American with long dreadlocks. Best undercover look I ever saw. The Bronx gets crazy, like Newark, which, by the way, confiscated some 703 guns in 2011 alone. Can you imagine how many are left? Man, if I worked in Newark, or the Bronx like my friend Jerry Speziale, this book would be three times as thick!

So, my Rastafarian-looking brother-in-blue was going up in an elevator with me in the CCP (Christopher Columbus Projects) in Paterson, at about 0500 hours (5am). As we were ascending, he looked at me and said, "Man, I'm even nervous in this place!" The projects were the one place that I always wore a vest, but only if I knew ahead of time, that I was going there.

One night, I believe, it was in 1995, I was working Car #2 on patrol when I started chasing a stolen car. We wound up in the Alexander Hamilton projects, also known as the Alabama projects, which were only about a mile from the Clifton border. Most Clifton cars are one man units, so I was as usual, alone. The actor bailed out of the car about 0300 hours and started running for a building to the left. As I chased him on foot, I heard, pop, pop, pop, pop, pop. This made me take cover and try to determine where these gunshots were coming from. Seeing the last couple of flashes, I could see a small group of young men near the building to my right. It seemed that they were creating a diversion so the brother that I was chasing, could get away. He did get away for about 15 minutes until he came across two Paterson Patrol officers who scooped him up for me. They walked over and said, "Hey Pat! You lookin' for this guy?"

So often I got help from Paterson cops, like Vinny Fantone, RIP. It was always good to see them. They knew their turf much better than I and knew places where perps (perpetrators) would hide. Some Passaic County Sheriff's officers also helped me a few times at the Alabama projects. Guys, like Tony Damiano, who appeared a few times on the *Cops* TV show, or Lieutenant, later Captain, "Boo" Selemi, and Ed Shanley, who holds a black belt in goju karate. Ed also trained in Jiu-Jitsu with Michael DePasquale Jr. and his father, who was a Jiu-Jitsu pioneer. Another "movie star" friend I had was Anthony Fasolas. He appeared on the TV show *DEA* and always did a great job! Tony and I cut our narcotics teeth in 1997, where we learned undercover with the county narcotics task force.

Fast forward to 2004, when Tony was working for the prosecutors' office and was on loan to the DEA. He had a dream collar (arrest) on Clifton's Center Street. They locked up five citizens of the Dominican Republic, with 44 pounds of purified heroin, $100,000 in cash and a Mac 10 machine gun with a silencer. The DEA gets the best jobs huh! I was a little jealous. In my next life, I'm working for the DEA.

道

Guns, guns and more guns. The best shoot out Clifton's ever had though, was a jewelry store robbery on Main Avenue where the gunmen shot their way out. It was the Wild West until Patrolman, later Sergeant Harry Van Winkle lit one up in a backyard on Getty Avenue. Harry truly displayed courage and commitment to duty on that day. I was off and missed all the excitement.

Every time we had a suspect waving a gun, I couldn't help but think of what I learned in DEA School. There are sometimes misunderstandings between the public and police. Read on.

One of the instructors picked me to participate in a little demonstration regarding action versus reaction. Both of us would unload our handguns. Handing our 9mm to each other, we both verified that they were unloaded. The instructor played the bad guy and I played the cop. The instructor raised his hands up about shoulder high keeping his gun in his right hand. I took the weaver stance (typical police stance holding gun) and kept my gun pointed at the "bad guys" chest. I ordered him to drop his weapon while he kept his hands up and pled with me not to shoot him. As I repeated my demand for him to drop his gun, he quickly brought his firearm down and "shot me, ostensibly, in the chest!"

We did this three times. Every time we did it, you heard his gun's hammer fall first, in theory killing me, before I could get off a shot. His gun would "click" followed by mine. Only problem is, if this were real, I'd be dead before you'd hear mine click, thus proving that action is faster than reaction.

The instructor then explained to the class, that if someone doesn't drop their weapon, you need to put a couple in his chest, thereby eliminating the threat. If this scenario was real and I shot this individual who refused to drop his gun, there could be witnesses that didn't quite understand what happened. One witness might say, "Hey, this guy was giving up! He even begged the officer not to shoot him! But the cop shot him just the same."

So the moral of the story is; if you're up against a deadly threat, and you want to go home to your wife and kids, you need to stop the threat! Immediately!

道

The last short story of this chapter took place on April 17, 2003. It was a night where both the Clifton and Fairlawn Police Departments would unite and grieve as one.

I was the narcotics commander at the time. My squad and I were in the process of setting up a drug dealer for a "rip." This is where we order up a quantity of drugs to be delivered, in this case the Ramada Inn on Route 3, and we basically jump the dealer when he arrives. The call was made, the location was agreed on, and we waited. While waiting, as usual, we monitored the patrol division's transmissions.

Patrolmen Steve Farrell, one of our more proactive officers, was attempting to stop a vehicle on Route 46, on the other side of the city. The suspect vehicle failed to pull over and initiated a motor vehicle pursuit. I'll now describe what took place that night in general terms. I'll leave the events and any detailed description up to Patrolmen Farrell. He is the only true eye witness of this tragedy that polarized two Police Departments, on this otherwise uneventful evening.

Farrell notified headquarters that he was increasing his speed as he described the pursued vehicle and road conditions. The suspect vehicle entered Route 20 North, from Route 46 East, now entering the City of Paterson. Clifton, of course, assigned a unit to assist Patrolman Farrell but it took a while for the Clifton radio car to catch up. In the meantime, Clifton dispatch got on SPEN (State Police Emergency Network) asking Paterson PD for assistance. In about two or three minutes time, the suspect vehicle turned right, traveled over the Passaic River and into the Town of Fairlawn.

That night on patrol for Fairlawn PD, was a dedicated officer by the name of, Mary Anne Collura. When she heard over the air that a Clifton chase was coming her way, and was in need of assistance, she jumped in as the secondary unit. It wasn't long until the suspect vehicle, containing two actors (suspects), jumped a curb and abandoned their vehicle as they fled on foot near a church in a quiet suburban neighborhood. Steve, being in the lead vehicle, got a little jump on Mary Anne, as they exited their patrol units to run down these fugitives. One actor quickly gave up, throwing his hands up in the air. The second actor was subsequently tackled by Patrolmen Farrell. But suddenly, without warning, as Farrell had only one of the actor's arms wrenched behind his back; the actor managed to pull a handgun out from his waistband, roll to his side and fire several rounds at both officers.

Steve was struck in the right arm and one of his thighs. He was still alive. Mary Anne wouldn't be so lucky. She was struck at least two or three times and died shortly thereafter. Steve's right arm was so ripped up that he had to draw his 9mm Beretta with his left hand. The actor ran over to Mary Anne's patrol car, jumped in and started to flee the scene. Steve, already falling to one knee from his leg wound, managed to empty out his gun at the fleeing felon. Later, I counted the bullet holes in the passenger side of Mary Anne's car, after it was abandoned in Paterson.

It was then that we heard over the radio what no cop ever wants to hear; "Shots fired! Officer down!" I, of course, called off our operation, as we diverted over to the east side of the city. As we were responding, it wasn't long before we heard that the Fairlawn radio car had been abandoned on Broadway, in Paterson, near Barnet Hospital. I responded to Paterson, as I instructed two of my units to respond to Fairlawn, along with other Clifton units to assist at the scene. As I pulled up on Broadway, there were already several Paterson units on scene, as well as the Passaic County Sheriff's Department. Officer Collura's vehicle had been abandoned in the travel portion of the road with its engine running. I gave the interior a cursory look with my flashlight, checking for blood, in the bullet-ridden Fairlawn cruiser. *No such luck* I thought, as the car looked clean. The perpetrators blood would have left multiple clues, not to mention DNA. There must have been at least twelve bullet holes on the passenger side of the radio car. The first bullets striking the front passenger door, as they progressed toward the rear, with the last embedded in the trunk. This was obviously an indication that the vehicle was fleeing the scene, as Officer Farrell emptied his 9mm into the side of the car.

Back in Fairlawn, responding officers from Clifton, Fairlawn and the Bergen County Sheriffs' Department realized the worst. Not only was Officer Mary Anne Collura violently gunned down, but the shooter when fleeing, ran her over with her own police car. Patrolman Steve Farrell, at that point, had dropped to the ground in agony as he awaited the arrival of paramedics.

Back in Paterson, as I protected the scene from contamination, Chief Lawrence Spagnola (Paterson PD) and Sheriff Jerry Speziale (PCSD), responded to the scene. Collectively they had an opulent number of officers assigned to the case. Chief Robert Ferreri (Clifton) responded to the hospital to be with Officer Farrell. Fairlawn's Chief of Police along with Chief of Detectives Michael Mordaga (BCPO) assigned their men to the Fairlawn crime scene. It was an excellent display of inter-agency cooperation.

Most of us pulled an all-nighter, following leads, in an effort to identifying and apprehend the shooter. It wasn't long before Sheriff Speziale, an expert in cell phone and wiretap surveillance, was able to get a fix on our fugitive. Omar Marti, identified as the shooter, was on his way to New York State with a relative, who would later be charged with hindering Omar's apprehension. In an effort to head him off, Clifton Detectives, along with members of the Passaic County and Bergen County Sheriff's Department's, flew up north to await his arrival. Omar's plans changed, however, as we picked up information that they turned around, and headed for a relative's home in Florida.

It was Easter Sunday when I, along with Clifton Detective Sergeant Harry Van Winkle, began preparing to catch a flight to the Sunshine State. We, along with the sheriffs' department and Fairlawn PD, were ready to get our man. Our plans changed again when we learned of a wild morning shootout between Omar Marti and Florida law enforcement officials.

Omar Marti paid for his crimes in a hail of gunfire. This time, he didn't have surprise on his side, shooting officers who didn't even have their guns out. We let the Florida cops know exactly who Omar Marti was, and why he was wanted. No more was he just a punk, low rent, drug dealer from Passaic. In a New Jersey minute, he became the States most wanted. After that Easter Sunday morning, there was no urgency to fly down south. Omar Marti wasn't going anywhere, but into a body bag, to be flown back home.

After about a year, Officer Farrell recovered from his wounds. He returned to work and jumped right back into the career he chose, for better or worse. Today, he is a narcotics detective for the City of Clifton. Now that's dedication!

Today, on average, there's a cop killed in America every 53 hours. Nearly 19,000 officers have made the ultimate sacrifice in our nation's history. Their names are engraved on the marble walls of "The National Law Enforcement Officers Memorial" in Washington, D.C.

"There is no safety in war."

Vergil

CLIFTON NARCOTICS

In June of 2002, Chief Frank Lo Gioco retired. This elevated my Captain, Robert Ferreri, to Chief of Police. Chief Ferreri was looking for someone with narcotics experience to head our narcotics/tactical squad. Working with the Passaic County Narcotics Task Force in 1997, gave me the experience that I needed. The squad used to have a lieutenant and a sergeant supervising, but they wanted to go down to a sergeant alone. The chief also considered my friend, Billy Gibson, who was also a sergeant and quite qualified. Billy, knowing how much I wanted the job and that I had been passed over getting into the squad in the past, told the chief that I should get the job. He truly was a good friend.

Chief Ferreri appointed me commander and replaced two of the detectives in the squad. The captain and lieutenant in charge of the detective bureau and youth services division, respectively, also oversaw my unit. They insisted that there would be manpower changes in the squad because two officers had a "bad attitude." The captain referred to these guys as "Taliban." I personally was just happy to get the position, telling them both that I would work with anybody. I actually got lucky picking up a friend of mine, Thomas Rinaldi, and a young proactive cop, who worked under me in the patrol division, Gary Passenti. The four other detectives in my squad were all seasoned veterans dealing me four aces. Chris Vassoler, Michael McLaughlin, Tommy Burrows and Billy Frank rounded out the squad.

So, here we were, seven of us total, working in a city that could use twice that number. I have to tell you, it felt a little awkward running a squad that didn't seem to want me for years. In retrospect, I guess that it was partially my own fault. I was never politically correct and quite opinionated. Then again, I wouldn't have it any other way.

My first day in the office, I got a call from my friend, Lieutenant Tony Mion, from the City of Passaic Narcotics Unit. Tony said, "Hey Pat, let's do something together." He meant like, yesterday. I said, "Slow down Tony, I don't even know where the white out is yet!" It wouldn't take long, however, as I called my first squad meeting. I told my guys, "I'm not very interested in a lot of user arrests and high numbers, I want the dealers." We started working the guys awaiting trial and told them, like Monty Hall used to say, "Let's make a deal." Working confidential informants much harder than the last commander/lieutenant did was the way to go. This was something I learned at the county.

Detective Billy Frank told me he had a live one. He had a prostitute's phone number and the name of a Passaic drug dealer to go with it. Anyone who calls "Jane" and says "Juice (not his real street name) gave me your number," could make a connection. Jane, Billy was told, was a prostitute who knew a lot of dealers and could provide anything. I decided that because I was new in the squad, I'd like to lead by example. Having experience buying drugs and picking up prostitutes in Paterson, while working for the county, made it a snap.

I took the phone number and office cell phone and went outside to make the call. I sat in my undercover Lexus with the F.M. radio on in the background. "Hello?" a female voice answered.

"Is this Jane?" I asked.

"Maybe, who's this?" she said cautiously.

I replied, "My name is 'Rick' and I got your number from Juice."

She then said, "Yeah, this is Jane."

I smiled and said, "Well, honey, tomorrow is my birthday and I'm lookin' to party."

"Oh yeah?" she asked. "How long?"

I replied, "Well, I am pretty long...Just kiddin. Two or three hours would be good, depending on the price."

"Okay," she agreed, "how about the Windslow?" (The Windslow Motel in Lyndhurst off Route 3 East)

I now had to think fast; The Windslow is in Lyndhurst, but it was important that I got her to meet me in Clifton. "The Windslow! I hate that mother f----- at The Windslow! The last time I was there I wanted to choke the shit out of him (the clerk)! He screwed me out of money. I'll never go back to the Windslow! That asshole! Tell you what, honey, you meet me up the street at the Ramada, I'll show you a good time." The Ramada Inn was only a quarter mile up from the Windslow, but in Clifton on Route 3 East.

Jane said, "Okay, what time?"

"7 o'clock would be cool," I told her. "By the way," I continued, "Can you bring some base?" (crack cocaine).

"How much?" she asked.

"A fifty would be good." After we agreed on the details, I told her that I'd call her the next day with my room number, after checking in.

道

Police departments and local politicians have to realize that the drug problem is a regional one, considering that we are all affected to a different degree. As long as drug dealers are willing to deliver narcotics to your town, you have a drug problem. If dealer's from the urban areas will deliver product to the suburban dealers, who are then supplying your high school and your addicts, that's your problem. We all have to attack this problem together. Some small towns insist that they have no problem, while keeping their head in the sand. If they don't see it, or ignore it, it doesn't exist.

Case in point. In 2003, one of Clifton narcotics detective, Mike McLaughlin's investigation led us to the nice suburban town of West Orange. When we set up on the dealer's house in this pristine neighborhood, we couldn't believe our eyes. After the guy came home from work, cars lined up in front of his house. Drivers would take turns exiting the house with pounds of marijuana. As soon as they got a distance away from the house, we picked them up one at a time. Because West Orange didn't have the manpower to help, we ran out of cars and couldn't keep up. The last car to leave left with a duffle bag. Can you believe the neighbors never called the police? This activity never looked suspicious? WOW! Hear no evil, see no evil, I guess.

道

I'll get back to my "birthday" celebration with Jane, at the Ramada Inn. The manager was great agreeing to let us, "borrow" two adjoining rooms. Chris Vassoler did the surveillance in the parking lot, while the rest of the squad accompanied me upstairs. One of my guys went down to the bar and got me a Heineken, my favorite, of course. I was alone in my room while four of my guys stayed in the adjoining room awaiting my signal. We rigged the adjoining door lock, so they could merely push the door open, giving me immediate back-up. Detective Burrows wired my room so that they could monitor my conversation. I told them I would say, "We're gonna party tonight!" as the signal for them to come busting in. I stole that line from my friend, Nate Butler, who taught me a lot at the county a few years earlier.

I was in the room alone and ready to make the call. "Yo Jane, wassup! I'm ready to go," I said, "come on over, I don't like being alone. Especially on my birthday!"

She replied, "Hey, I'm down in Newark, can you come and pick me up?"

Okay Ciser, think fast, I thought. "Shiiit, I've been drinkin' for two hours honey, and my license is suspended. I ain't drivin' nowhere. I ain't gettin busted on my birthday, I'll call somebody else."

"Wait! Wait!" she answered, "I'll try to get a ride."

I said, "All right, and if you can't, jump in a cab. I'll pay him when you get here. Oh yeah," I continued, don't forget the base!"

Jane then asked, "Hey, can I bring my girlfriend?"

I don't know, man," I answered. "I ain't rich."

Jane said, "No, no, it's the same price; two-for-one."

"Well that's more like it, honey! I got a lot of energy tonight!!"

She said, "Okay, then. See ya soon."

I'm sure that she wanted her friend for security since she had never met me before. I brought the squad up to speed on the plan then did some last minute preparations. I was wearing jeans and a wife-beater tee shirt (you might have to be from NY/NJ to know what that is). I used the Heineken like an after shave lotion to appear to be drinking for a while. There were two full-sized beds in the room. I hid my 9mm under the corner of the mattress, closest to the door.

About 40 minutes later or so, a pearl brand spanking new Cadillac Escalade, pulled into the Ramada parking lot with two black males in the front seat. Detective Vassoler reported that one of these characters, along with two white females, exited the SUV and entered the Hotel. Within about four minutes, there was a knock on my door. I answer the door with my Heineken bottle in my hand. *This may come in handy as a weapon,* I thought. Two females enter the room with the male coming in behind them. I allowed the girls in, but put up my left hand stopping the male. I looked at him and said, "The girls can stay, but you've got to go!" With that, my hand against his chest, I pushed him back, as I closed the door in his face (Gotta keep it real!).

Jane cried, "Wait! He's got the base!"(Crack cocaine).

Re-opening the door I said, "Yo, my man, sorry about that! Whatcha got for me?" We walked past the first bed and stopped near the second one. There was a desk there just past the TV. The girls sat on that bed while I asked him for a $50. He took a good sized rock out of pocket and broke off a chunk.

As I was about to pay him, the girls yelled, "Hey, what about us?" So, I smiled at them and grabbed my crotch.

"Give me another $50, hell, it's my birthday. By the way bro, I said, what's your name if I need more?"

"Black," he said.

Holy shit, I thought, *I recognize him. I locked him up in '97.* I found him in a bodega after he avoided a corner sweep that we executed in Paterson. "Black, huh?" as I gave him my best "brother" handshake. Black began walking toward the door, with me following him out. Just when I was close to the bed where I stored my gun, I yelled, "We are gonna party tonight!" The guys hit the door, as he looked to his left. Using my left arm, I clothes lined him, slamming him down on the bed. As he made impact, I reached with my right hand, pulled my Beretta out from under the mattress and stuck it in his neck. I yelled, "Police! You're busted!" The taller girl that came with Jane came off of her bed lunging at me in defense of Black. Without missing a beat, I hit her with a side kick, flipping her back over the bed. This entire maneuver took about four to five seconds, as the squad secured the room, cuffing all three. I told two detectives to assist Detective Vassoler with arresting the wheelman in the parking lot. "Black," along with his associate downstairs, was charged with possession and distribution. The two females were charged with prostitution and distribution and for playing the middle man, so to speak, in procuring CDS for me.

The girls were separated from the guys at headquarters, for obvious reasons, and to offer them a deal. Lure more dealers to sell to our under- cover detectives and get a reduction of their charges. They were of tremendous help to us, as we would play out similar scenarios again and again, at different locations. The next year and a half would be the most successful time in the squad's history.

道

The first six months of 2002 saw 21 arrests for distribution. The second six months after I arrived, we had 47 dealers behind bars. In 2003, we arrested 92 dealers, in addition to arrests for other crimes/ violations. The squad's most notable jobs were a Montclair Heights home netting 26 kilos of powdered cocaine (we had a little help on this one). Another was Detective Passenti and Rinaldi's 10 kilos of heroin job. Another four kilos of cocaine, along with $86K in cash, delivered to the parking lot of a diner on Route 3. Detective Christian Vassoler played a large role along with Mike McLaughlin and Billy Frank assisting. And lastly; my arrest of a suspect who pulled off seven armed robberies in Passaic and Bergen Counties. I remember feeling such pride and success in ameliorating that squad. It was important to me that we had a reputation like Paterson's narcotics unit or the Passaic County Narcotics Task Force.

Initially, the squad seemed to admire my work ethic. If someone was talking, we were listening, as we climbed the proverbial ladder to the mid-level dealers. Newspapers wrote stories about the squad's remarkable success. The teamwork that was cultivated over the summer of 2002 only grew stronger throughout most of 2003. Then, the worst thing that could happen to any winning team, would rear its ugly head. Misunderstandings, jealousy, and back-stabbing would eventually rue the day. These negative human traits would begin to chip away at all that we built.

Who knows, maybe like a coach that just won the Superbowl, I could've pushed too hard for another successful season. Or maybe some of the guys became prima donnas, as they would complain to the lieutenant and captain, that they were overworked. The reality was, however, that they had the best job in the department. A dozen guys would have replaced them the next day if given the opportunity.

Even worse for me and the City of Clifton, was that one of my bosses became covetous of my position and success. He told me that I pushed the men too hard and that narcotics should be "fun." He apparently wanted the men to like him more than me, as he forgot how to be a boss. It was like a father who wants to be his son's best friend, rather than a responsible dad. It was sad too because when he was a patrolman, he was a real cop. By the time he was a lieutenant, he was the consummate politician. The bureau captain was even worse as he was totally clueless. All of his little suck-ups told him only what he wanted to hear. He did nothing for the department, and worse, destroyed morale. It was his world and department; we just lived and worked in it. So in 2004, I put the squad on automatic pilot to get them off my back. Dealer arrests plummeted as the team I built up, crashed and burned. By the time I made lieutenant in early 2005, I couldn't wait to go back to patrol. Those left in the squad, would never achieve the same level of success again.

$$道$$

In 2004, although the number of dealer arrests took a dive, we enjoyed sporadic success in robbery arrests. In addition to the bounty hunter that I arrested for armed robberies, we had a string of street robberies that we needed to nip in the bud.

In the summer, I took a vacation down to the Jersey shore with my family. This left the juvenile division lieutenant in charge of the squad. Street robberies, in the Botany section, were pervasive late at night by roaming gangs. The lieutenant had one of his juvenile detectives work decoy on Center Street one night. It might have worked, or our decoy might have been stabbed, before help could move in. Regardless, while detectives kept an eye on the cop decoy, an armed robbery came in on Lakeview Avenue. The liquor store robbery was only about a mile or so from Center Street. All units in the Botany broke their surveillance of the decoy to respond to Lakeview Avenue. I certainly hope they picked up the decoy and took him with them. I wasn't there, so I can't say, but they probably did.

When I returned, and discovered that no arrests were made, I developed my own plan. I held a meeting to discuss tactics. First, I told the men, we do not need to jeopardize the lives of our men playing the next victim. There are potential victims all over the Botany late at night. It's an inebriate exiting a bar, or a female parking her car a block away from her home because she can't find a space. We cannot be omnipresent and protect everyone. But if we wait and watch our decoy for hours, someone else on another street will likely get jumped. I instructed the men to set up in the shadows on all the main thoroughfares in the Botany section of town. I wanted two-man surveillance cars on Highland, Lake, Center, Ackerman and Parker Avenues. Watch all potential victims I explained. When you see someone being followed, call out that you're watching a potential victim.

Well, it worked like a charm. The detective bureau, narcotics squad and street crime unit were all out watching. For a few days, it seemed like everyone ran someone down as we caught them in the act. Each night, Gibson, Centurion, McLaughlin, Frank, Vassoler and I, just to name a few, all had arrests. Assailants behaved like a pack of wolves, as they stalked their prey. Now they... were being stalked!

One of the longer foot chases was Billy Frank and I, chasing a suspect into Passaic, through some backyards there. We were neck-and-neck until Billy tripped going over a fence. Seconds later, I tackled the suspect in an alley. Billy helped me cuff him moments later. I joked with Billy (Frank), what's the matter? Can't keep up with the old man?" We both laughed as we walked him out to an awaiting radio car.

Working with the county in 2004, on search warrants, also kept us occupied. One memorable job and a big success, was when we executed eight simultaneous search warrants in the City of Passaic. Our Clifton squad broke up as we were each given different locations to hit. My team consisted of Detectives Juan Clavijo, of Passaic PD, Mike Zaccone, of Wayne PD, and Tony Urena, of the Passaic County Prosecutors Office. On this morning, we were happy to have Clavijo, who, of course, knew Passaic the best. Many times we wouldn't have eight Passaic detectives available for all locations. If Passaic didn't have enough guy's available it was good to have a Clifton detective on the team, as we knew Passaic fairly well ourselves. Wayne PD used to step up by sending Gaeta, Tarpy, Celentano and Hook, in addition to

Zaccone, on various jobs. These guys were always solid back-up and great to have around.

All teams were ready and in radio communication, as we hit our numerous locations. The "player" who we were taking down, thanks to the efforts of Clavijo and Zaccone, was going to do some serious time, if convicted, as it was his "third strike."

I kicked in the door as our team rushed in, even before the roosters were up, startling the actor. After we quickly handcuffed the "alleged" drug dealer, Zaccone flipped the mattress to find a fully-loaded .45 caliber semi-automatic handgun. An additional search produced a .357 magnum with hollow-point bullets in the kitchen drawer. This guy was known to brag that he was ready for anything, except us, I imagine.

All eight search warrants went off without a hitch and without injuries. It's certainly nice to go home at the end of the day!

道

It was January 2005. I was promoted to lieutenant and now had a group of young men in the patrol division, I could mold into real cops. I became known for my motivational speeches. A little levity from time-to-time and a box-of –joe (Coffee), at the start of the midnight shift, went a long way. Some of these guys couldn't wait to save the world, and I was lovin it!

One day, I said to a rookie, "The dead tiger kills the most hunters." Think about it kid. The next night, may be a joke. "Hey kid…" I said as I held up my right index and middle finger. "Why should "all" women masturbate with these two fingers?"

Of course, I got a confused look as he answered, "I don't know lieutenant, why?"

I replied, "Because they're mine!" All the veterans busted out laughing as I slapped the kid on the back, "Welcome to midnights kid, now go out there and lock up some bad guys."

道

I told my men to ignore contracts, good or bad. Don't let bosses who have a "mightier than thou" attitude, bother you. Be a good, proactive cop for all the right reasons; because that's exactly why you became one. Hell, when I came on the job with guys like Gibson, Giardina and Tuzzolino, we would've done the job for free if we could afford it. We didn't give a rat's ass about the contract. Two percent or four percent raise? Shit, we just wanted to be cops. We were making $12,000 a year. I unloaded trucks when I was younger and later worked as a carpenter. Try carrying shingles up a ladder all day and then complain about working too hard manning a radio car. Like Don Henley said, "Folks don't do nothin anymore simply for the love of it!"

Guys and gals try to go off the job on a "two-thirds" pension for the stupidest things. And worse, the unions back them up. Cops go off because they "witnessed" another cop shoot someone. Did you get that! They were not involved in the shooting, they were just there. What punks! When I shot someone, I couldn't wait to go back to work. *Now that's real police work*, I thought. Let me give cops, and would be cops, a tip. If you think it's too hot in the kitchen, stay the hell out! Did you take an oath or what? Things heat up and you're out! WTF is that!

I mentioned my friend, Gary Giardina, a couple of paragraphs back. Now there's a guy with blue running through his veins. After just a couple of years on the job, he was out on Route 3 with a motor vehicle stop. It was late at night when he asked the driver for his license and registration. A car in the right lane, we'll never know if he was drunk or whatever, struck Gary, flipping him up and over, then sped away. Doctors didn't think that he would ever return to work at the PD again. He fought hard through physical therapy and returned to full duty. Having an outstanding career, he rose to become Clifton's

Chief of Police in 2010. Patrolman Steve Farrell's story was even more amazing as he got shot full of holes only to return to full duty. I mention him in another chapter. These men truly have my admiration, what warriors! So, again, don't put yourself in a hole thinking about lousy contracts or shitty work assignments. Go out every day and be prepared to do something amazing. Deliver a baby, save a life, stop a crime in progress. Then my friend, you'll hold your head up high, and know that you signed up for something special.

道

Getting back to the watch commander job, I talked to the rookies with the same broken record advice. Put your palm print on the trunk of the car you stop, just in case you're ambushed and they get away. Keep your hands out of your pockets and stand on a defensive angle when speaking to suspicious individuals. Sometimes I would break my own rule so as to lure someone in. Because of my expertise in foot sweeps, I'd give them the illusion that they could take a swing, while keeping my hands in my pockets. They would step in and go right down. The front foot sweep worked like a charm. Come to think of it, I guess I was the dead tiger.

As a lieutenant on midnights, I took my 0400 lunch break at the Tick Tock Diner, must be one of the best diners in the country. Every time a cop came in there, Clifton or other agency, I'd give advice whether they wanted to hear it or not. "Hey bro," I'd say to the Passaic cop, "I noticed that you pulled your car in to that space out there."

He replied, "Yeah, L T Why?"

"Just a tip, always back in on your lunch break and remember one thing. You're never in a hurry to arrive, but you might be in a hurry to leave! Have a good night!"

After I retired from the PD, my friend George Stampolis, aka G the G, who's the night manager, would follow my tradition. He'd see a cop pull in and tell them, "If Lieutenant Ciser was here, he'd give you some advice." Then he would tell them exactly what I would say. I miss George, so I stop in to see him from time-to-time.

"Example is the best sermon."

Benjamin Franklin

BODIES

It was late April in 1985, when I was working Car #1. We got a call from a Clifton resident, explaining that two teenagers found something suspicious down by the Passaic River. The 13- and 14-year-old boys were fishing, when they spotted a bag by the shoreline. It contained either human or animal flesh. Arriving at the riverbank, near Ackerman Avenue, within a couple of minutes, the boys seemed relieved to see me. After explaining in a little more detail how they came across the macabre package, I took a closer look. After examining the contents of the bag, I determined that it was the lower torso including the pelvis of a female. The torso seemed to have been cut in half near the navel, and the legs were also removed. I did my best to secure the area and not let the boys touch anything else as I summoned the detective bureau. Detective Captain Robert Kelly dispatched his men and notified the Passaic County Prosecutors Office.

After the detectives arrived, and we had the area taped off, I spoke with the lead detective. He originally told me that he thought the remains might be part of a lamb. I said, "Mike, are you kiddin' me? Look here, I've seen enough tush in my day to know what this is. That my friend is a female vagina!" The medical examiner determined that the lower torso was a female, between 40-60 years old, weighing about 130 lbs. She had blond hair and a very interesting condition that helped break the case. She had a colostomy. Part of her intestines were removed and replaced with a pouch that she wore, which collected waste. Detectives checked all area hospitals to gather a list of females with such a condition. It didn't take long to find that a 60-year-old woman who lived on Highland Avenue, not far from the riverbank discovery was missing. Captain Robert Kelly would announce the arrest of the murdered woman's roommate, within days. A knife, believed to be the murder weapon, was found inside his apartment. His bail was set at $750,000. I believe it was about a week later when Patrolman Jeff Reilly responded back to the riverbank where the victim's head was found decomposing in a plastic bag. Eventually, two legs and an arm turned up in Riverside Park in Lyndhurst, which is downriver from Clifton. The live-in boyfriend would later be convicted of this heinous crime.

道

In the late 1970's, we received a report of a vehicle traveling west on Route 3. The caller stated that he saw the trunk of the car lift slightly and a hand was hanging out. The driver was last seen stopping the car on the right shoulder. I was working Car #7, on Clifton's west side, when I spotted the suspect vehicle on Route 3 West, approaching Bloomfield Avenue. I called out the plate and activated my overhead lights. Off to the races we went. My partner that night was Mike Kotora, a rookie cop, who was not involved in too many chases yet. We accelerated as the suspect jumped onto the Garden State Parkway North. We were hitting speeds in excess of 110 mph as we entered Bergen County. New Jersey State Police units joined in the chase. As we approached the toll plaza just before the Passaic Avenue exit, I slowed down to about 60 mph in order to safely (okay, not too safely) navigate through the narrow toll booth. There was no E-Z Pass back then and I think my quarter missed the pouch as I flew by (just kiddin').

As I was gaining on the suspect vehicle, he unexpectedly jerked his car to the left and beat me before the concrete divider. You see, there is no concrete divider at the toll booth, as the booth runs through the northbound and southbound lanes. About 100 feet past the booth, the barrier begins again. So, by him suddenly turning to the left, I overshot the barrier and now could only watch him drive north in the southbound lanes. I slowed down, remaining in the left lane on the northbound side, able to transmit updates to other units and participating agencies. It wasn't long until the driver of the suspect vehicle started to feel the heat as he drove head-on into southbound traffic. The suspect ditched the car on the shoulder and then fled on foot into the wooded area along the Parkway. I transmitted this event as I saw State Police units arriving at the scene on the opposite side of the highway. Making the first U-turn possible, I arrived with my partner within a few minutes.

To our relief, the State Police had the trunk open as they cared for the victim. He had been stabbed several times and locked in the trunk, but fortunately was still alive. An ambulance pulled up relatively soon, as the EMT's took him away. There was more good news, as two troopers emerged from the wooded area with a handcuffed suspect. When we drove back to headquarters, some of the new guys wanted to hear details of the pursuit. "Hey Pat," one said. "How did your car hold up when you drove over 110 mph? Did anything in the car shake?"

"Only Kotora (my partner)," I said.

道

All cops from small towns to large cities deal with death on a diurnal basis. Here in Wayne, where I live, the crime rate is low. However, just the highways alone produce enough carnage to make any rookie puke, never mind the teenagers or occasional hobo struck on the train tracks. Most homicides where a gun is used aren't usually gruesome. It's not like the movies. Many times, bullet holes from a handgun practically seal themselves, so once the heart stops beating there is very little blood. Sometimes it's difficult to find the wound. Stabbings are worse, however, with the use of a machete causing severe trauma, both to the victim and the observer (cop).

道

Motorcycle crashes can be particularly disturbing. Young people seem to love traveling up and down route 21, from Clifton to Newark. The highway has many bends as it follows the Passaic River lying next to it. Rice burners (Japanese racing bikes), as we call them, hit speeds in excess of 120 miles per hour. Bodies are jettisoned from these rocket ships, as these Evel Knievel wannabes test the limits of their machines and themselves.

One motorcyclist I assisted flew off his bike and struck his chest on a jagged guardrail post. When I arrived on the ramp from Route 3 to Route 21 South, I found him sitting up in the grass. His shirt and chest were ripped wide open. He sat there holding his stomach so it wouldn't come out of the hole.

Because he was in severe shock, he, surprisingly, wasn't bleeding all that badly. He looked at me as I squatted down to take a look.

"How does it look?" He asked.

I thought I was looking at open-heart surgery as his heart, in plain sight, was beating at a rapid pace. Pulling large gauze pads from my first aid kit, I could see that they would only fall into this gaping hole. I assured him that he was going to be fine and that I'd seen worse (Not!). A State Trooper pulled up offering assistance. The trooper had a sheet in his trunk so we could wrap it around this guy's chest until the ambulance arrived. He was one of the lucky ones, who lived.

道

Another rice burner came around a bend at "ludicrous speed" (space balls), crashing into the rear of an SUV. The SUV was reportedly doing the speed limit, as the motorcyclist flew through the rear window, like a human cannonball. His head came to rest on the driver's center console (body still attached).

道

Retrieving a motorcyclist boot on Route 3 once, didn't seem to be a problem for one Clifton rookie, until he discovered the man's foot inside.

Imagine seeing "Two Face" from the <u>Batman</u> movie, with one side of his face ripped off. That'll test your first aid skills until the ambulance arrives.

Don Henley's, In a New York Minute, used to come to mind, as we periodically dealt with suicide.

Few jobs were harder than having to ring the doorbell of parents, informing them of the tragic death of their child.

道

Hangings were, from my experience, the most common method used in suicides. Some I remember, while others I've tried to forget. There was one, however, that I'll never forget.

It was a frigid winter night, as the cold penetrated right down to the bone. I was dispatched to Piaget Avenue, just up from Main Avenue, over the railroad tracks. A young woman had thrown herself off the bridge, while snapping her neck with a heavy chain.

The way she killed herself ensured that there would be no coming back. I later learned this was not her first attempt, as she once jumped from a bridge without a rope or chain, never expecting to wake up again. Taking a thick chain, strong enough to easily tow a car, she secured it to the heavy steel fence, along the sidewalk with a heavy duty lock. She then wrapped the other end around her neck and secured that with a second heavy duty lock. Apparently, she didn't want someone to save her with a pocket knife.

Hurling herself over the side, she came to an abrupt stop halfway between the bridge and the railroad tracks below. Finding a path that took me down below, I stopped suddenly while observing her lifeless body. The scene was dark, cold and eerie, reminding me of Black

Sabbath's first album cover. The wind howled only to be outdone by the creaking of the chain as her body moved side-to-side.

I couldn't help but feel deep sympathy for her, as I wondered what could have gone so terribly wrong in her life. My flashlight lit up her face, confirming the worst; her pale cheeks would never appear rosy or see the sun again. I felt sadness before, but for some reason, this surreal setting along with the quiet cold, hit me just a little harder.

It was time to snap out of it and figure out how to get her down. The tracks and gravel below made getting a couple of ladders and bolt cutters difficult, if not next to impossible. So, I walked back-up to Piaget Avenue, where I met the sergeant. We agreed that we would call a tow truck with a winch to pull her up. Vito, from Vito's towing, responded to the scene, along with a couple of firemen. The temperature was well below zero, as we had to take breaks inside our vehicle, so as not to get frostbite on our fingertips.

The cable from the tow truck was ready but we couldn't reach down very far to hook it up to the chain. It seemed like anything we could think of to get her up or down, fell short of success.

Finally, I said, "Look, I'm freezing my nuts off here, and we gotta pull this girl up."

She looked thin enough and being I was a competitive bodybuilder at the time, I could kneel down, reach out over the bridge as low as I could and pull her up with my right arm. If I could pull up two feet of chain at a time, the guys could tighten up the slack. The steel cast iron fence had bars about six inches apart allowing just one arm or cable to be used.

I put my arm through the bars and grabbed the ice cold chain. I yelled as I pulled her up just enough for the others to grab the slack. I pulled again and again as her body rose up to the bridge. Finally she came high enough that two firemen could reach over the four-foot-high fence, grabbing her coat and then upper arms. Once they had her, I released the chain, which, by now, was almost attached to my hand.

Looking into her frozen eyes, I thought, *rest in peace young lady, rest in peace.*

道

Clifton had a triple homicide where the intruder killed the family. It was in the Botany Village section of the city, where we had a husband, wife and one parent, stabbed to death. I wasn't there so Billy Gibson told me the details afterward. I bet he saw those bloody images when he closed his eyes at night for a week. There was one part to this crime that really pulled at the cops' hearts, as well as the communities. The couple had a baby in the apartment with them, who I think was about 18 months old, give or take a couple of months. The good news was that the baby was spared death. The bad news was that the baby had to fend for itself for a few days. When the PD forced entry, they found the baby cuddling up to her cold, bloody mother. It appeared that the baby survived eating spilled cereal from the floor and drinking water from the toilet. This case happened over 20 years ago. I just hope the baby didn't suffer severe psychological damage as a result of this horrific crime.

道

People see cops every day without realizing how difficult it must be. *Hey, there's the cop that gave me a ticket for being on my cell phone. There's the one that stopped my kid for speeding.* These thoughts never go deep enough to realize the day-to-day stress that comes with wearing the uniform. Yeah, I'm sure there are some small town cops who suffer little stress compared to the city cops. I remember one time I read in the local newspaper that a small town chief retired. He said that he was happy or proud, I forget which, that during his career, he never had to draw his gun. Are you kidding me? What the hell did you do for over a quarter century?

But in all fairness, even small towns get domestic violence calls, which can be very unpredictable, as men see their homes as their castle and inviolable. They, many times, don't take well to cops showing up when their spouse dials 911. Statistics on police assaults, including shootings, during DV calls show that it is actually one of the more dangerous encounters for law enforcement officers. I always liked a quote from my brother, Captain Hal Ciser, of the Rutherford, NJ Police Department. "We not only get paid for what happens, we also get paid for what could happen." And it's true; when the shit hit's the fan, there's no, "passing the buck!" In your town, you're it!

Random acts of violence and even mass murder, can find any small town, as well as our urban areas. During my final editing of this book, a seventeen year old in Ohio, open fire inside his small rural high school. On February 27, 2012, this youth shot five innocent classmates inside the school cafeteria, killing three. Chardon, is a small town of about 5,000, according to newspaper reports. You just never know, when violence will strike, regardless of where you're a cop. Lone police officers in rural towns are sometimes in more danger than their larger city counterparts; as their back-ups, are many times, quite a distance away. Large cities can often times dispatch several officers to a location, thereby giving ample back-up to officers in trouble.

Most police work is relative. The City of Clifton has approximately 156 police officers protecting some 85,000 residents. Paterson, who has about five times the amount of crime and about 150,000 residents, has almost five hundred. Because New York City has approximately 40,000 officers, some cops are not as busy as you might think. (Note: These figures were the norm before recent layoffs and cutbacks). You ever drive over to Manhattan and see the guys walking a small beat or directing traffic all night? Then there are cops in certain areas of the city (NYC) that are overworked and totally burnt out, while assigned to an "A" house (high crime precinct). It's no wonder they have 20 (years) and out! The part I'd like to see rectified is the fact that urban cops make so much less than suburban officers. I know, I know, the town or city pays them what they can afford. It just doesn't seem fair that the guys under the most stress are paid the least. My hat is off to those police officers who work in our most violent cities. Their dedication and courage is exemplary.

I'd like to now give a piece of advice to any readers considering becoming a police officer. Many cops across the country are injured, and some are even killed. Most of these men and women were indeed brave modern day warriors, who lived and died to help and protect others. However, a few, unfortunately, were in over their heads and should have been in another line of work. It's a shame really, how in many parts of the country, requirements for police officers have become so watered down due to political correctness. How nice, that we want to include everyone, but at what cost?

Before I was a cop, I was a bouncer in a few different night clubs in North Jersey. You either had to be big, tough or both. To me, being a cop is like being a bouncer for the whole city. Years ago, if you wanted to be a New Jersey State Trooper, you had to be, I believe, 5 feet, 9 inches tall, weigh a certain amount and have a fairly low body fat percentage. This enabled you to pass a really tough physical and box; that's right, box! No one in New Jersey has to box anymore. After all, someone might get hurt! Duh, better to get injured finding out if you have what it takes rather than getting killed later. Ever have a 5 foot, 1 inch female who weighs 105 pounds back you up in a violent street or bar fight? It's like having your little sister with you. So, now you not only have to worry about doing your job, you have to worry about your little sister. I've been in situations, in both Clifton and Paterson, where I was concerned that a small female could have her gun taken away and then the "perp" shoots me! I know officers who have anecdotal accounts of female officers crying hysterically during traumatic events, including riots. There are some larger females, especially if they have some martial arts experience, with whom I have no concerns with. As a matter of fact, we had a female black belt up in our Hazel Park (Koeikan) dojo who was a Michigan State Trooper. I would have worked with her anytime. She was tough. I don't like to paint with a broad brush, but please, let's try to set the bar a little higher. I will say though, that I've seen a few females over the years, make pretty good detectives.

Now, while I'm on a tirade! For this chapter, let's talk about some other "bodies;" like obese, out of shape cops! Paleease! Some of these guys couldn't catch a cold! Who the hell are they going to run down? They'll blow out a knee or worse, trying to run up stairs; and that's only, if their hearts hold out. If I'm chasing down a dangerous felon, and you can't keep up, maybe you should think about giving up! Your job that is! Hey, you're paid to be my back-up, among other things, not just a report writer! I can understand 20 pounds, that's not obese, but when do some of these guys say, "No mas!" Again, the NJ State Police have periodic physicals for their troopers. As a result, most of them look great. Why can't New Jersey's local cops do the same? Fortunately, many of the younger guys' today, especially the military veterans, lift weights, run, or find other ways to stay in shape. Many go to Dunkin Donuts for the coffee only, which, by the way, is healthy for you. Karate-Do training or mixed martial arts, being the flavor of the day is probably the best. If you "resemble" these remarks, I challenge you to do something about it. Don't get complacent, or should I say, fat and happy. And remember this…The life you save, may be your own!

"Your work is going to fill a large part of your life,
And the only way to be truly satisfied
Is to do what you believe is great work.
And the only way to do great work is to love what you do."

Steve Jobs

2007 REUNION

I arrived at LAX (Los Angeles) and boarded the Santa Barbara airbus. I was in town for Sensei Jack Sabat's Tsunami XF (Extreme Fighting) Championship. The show would be held the next night, on Saturday, March 31st. UFC Light Heavyweight Champ and Koeikan Karate-Do black belt, Chuck "The Iceman" Liddell, was there in support of his former Sensei. I hadn't seen Mr. Liddell since he won our championship in Rutherford, New Jersey, in 1993. Mr. Liddell (we're very formal with names and titles in Koeikan) was in his early twenties back then and impressed everyone by beating more experienced black belts. I was the tournament director and congratulated Sensei Sabat on his fine young warrior. Mr. Liddell and I posed for a photo that day, never imagining that this was only the beginning for this future world champion.

Japanese Koeikan, as explained to me by Sensei(s) Edward Kaloudis and Brian Frost (1972 Full Contact Bogu Champion, Japan), was always sort of a "mixed martial art," long before the term became popular. Traditional Japanese Karate-Do systems, many times, include some Judo, Jiu-Jitsu or Aiki-Jitsu techniques in their curriculum. We were always taught reverse joint technique (waza), foot sweeps, throws, strangulation and compliance holds, many of which, I used in my over 28 years in law enforcement. But the main part of our training was, and is, traditional Karate-Do. (kata, kumite and full contact bogu). The term mixed martial arts didn't become en vogue until the 1990's. As a young karate-ka (student) in 1971, the only digression I would make from tournament kumite (free sparring) was kick-boxing/ full-contact karate. My first experience was fighting at Sensei Gary Alexander's Full Contact portion of his Tai-Kai (tournament,) in New Jersey.

Some other events I competed in were the "Jimenez Brothers" of Paterson (EFA) Friday Night Fights and Sensei Jerry Thomson's New Jersey All Stars Karate Team events. Thomson's team, AAU stuff, was comprised of some very quality fighters from various karate clubs throughout North Jersey. I got to train and compete with men like Rich Faustini, Bill Timme and Mike Evangel, to name just a few. My friend Antonio Best was also one of the very "best" at that time (pun intended).

But one of the best fighters I've ever had the honor to spar with, was a man by the name of Gerald Robbins. Robbins was one of the most impressive competitors in any Karate or Tae Kwon Do championships to come around in years. The first time I ever laid eyes on Jerry was in the early 1970's, when I was an up-and-coming brown belt. Jerry was a black belt with superior technique. I wanted to emulate him so badly. I never saw anyone, kick so high and fast, with impeccable balance, until a year or two later when I met Bill "Superfoot" Wallace, in Philadelphia. Jerry had a long and successful run including S. Henry Cho's Championship at Madison Square Garden. The greatest story that I remember, because I was there, was when Jerry competed in the Garden State (NJ) Games in 1986. The Tae Kwon Do Championships were held on Saturday, while the Karate Championship was held on Sunday. Jerry entered both, back-to-back, and of course, won both. We got to know each other better over the years after Jerry started working for the Passaic County Prosecutor's Office. Jerry, back then, was a remarkable man, always remaining humble. I remember when I came back from Athens, Greece in 1987, after winning 1st Place Kumite, Jerry bragged about me. Imagine that, one of the absolute best, bragging about me!

I was now back on Continental heading home to New Jersey, pleased with Sensei Sabat's show and my reunion with Koeikan west coast Yudansha Kai (black belts) including Mr. Liddell. Sensei Sabat, asked me to be one of the three judges for all of the fights Saturday night, which I was honored to oblige. The event began with a wonderful performance of taiko (big drums) by a Santa Barbara based group. These sounds of Japan set the mood perfectly for the traditional Budo (martial arts) demonstration that acted as a warm-up for the MMA matches that would follow. After the drums were silent, Sensei Sabat announced that "The Iceman" arrived. The crowd went wild! Chuck entered from a side door and approached the VIP section, as we spotted each other on the red carpet. As I extended my hand, he shook it and smiled as we gave each other a brief hug. Smiles were rare from the "Ice Man" and I was glad to get one after 14 years. I showed Chuck to his seat at ringside right behind myself and the two other judges.

One of the other judges that night was Mr. Nicholodakis, of San Diego, formally of Detroit, Michigan. Interestingly enough, Mr. Nick was also a DEA agent and a good friend of mine. The other judge was Mr. Beccera, of Santa Barbara. Mr. Beccera trained Koeikan for a number of years with Mr. Liddell at Sensei Sabat's dojo and still trains and teaches there.

Mr. Liddell was not only the current UFC Light Heavyweight Champion of the World, but also a likeable and popular individual, sought out by many to endorse their products. He was, no doubt, the people's champion. Not once did he turn down a request for an autograph or picture from everyone present that night. He could be a man of few words who accepted all of the accolades and remained humble, yet tough as nails. The "Iceman" doesn't smile much, but he certainly did with his Koeikan brothers.

Koeikan, a traditional style of Japanese Karate-Do, was always an austere system. Koeikan uses bogu armor to allow the practitioner to fight full contact while avoiding serious injury. Bogu armor resembles

Kendo armor and was invented by Koeikan's founder, Kancho Sensei Eizo Onishi in 1957. Too many "sport" karate schools employ soft touch or light contact kumite only, never developing the mind for real combat.

In my dojo, I teach the student to enjoy the fight, embrace the punishment and to know that you're not out of the fight until you're unconscious. There were times, on the street or in a bar, when I would merely have to "bitch slap" a loud mouth or punk. If you slap someone hard, really hard, on the side of his head (ear and cheek), you'll often times drop him to one knee. In many cases, that "slap" was done to save a loud mouth from significant harm, like a broken nose or teeth. Remain alert, however, in case your instincts were wrong and he comes back with an attack of his own.

I never liked to take advantage, nor did I take pleasure in taking someone out. I always tried to use just the amount of force necessary, to neutralize the attacker. Even if I had to break someone's nose, I saw it as the "least" that I could do, in order to stop them. Hitting the eye could damage or tear the retina causing blindness; while a punch in the mouth could cause someone to lose their teeth, for life. Permanent scarring could also occur, as their own teeth rip through their skin as a result of a blow. I've had my nose broken five times during my competitive years. Doctor's, sometimes trainers, put it back to normal, however; well, almost normal. Some police officers, with minimal skills, would have to resort to a night stick, which could sometimes result in serious injury. For the guy with "beer muscles," I usually prefer the foot sweep. Sometimes, it only takes one sweep of the leg to get his attention. Sometimes, they'll take another swing and go down again, and then again, before realizing the futility of their actions. As an attacker steps forward, sweep the front leg. If he's up in your face staring you in the eyes, take out his back leg and levitate him, causing him to crash to the ground.

Over the years, many Koeikan black belts developed a really strong knock-out punch. One way to accomplish this is to embrace traditional makiwara training. The makiwara, or striking post, for those who have never been introduced to one, is two pieces of one-by-six pine, perhaps eight feet in length, which are nailed together with a six foot piece between them. One end, the part that goes into the ground, is even. The other end has a two foot gap between the eight foot boards. Now dig a hole in the ground about three feet and bury the even end, with the gap end, sticking straight up. Use some rocks and dirt to backfill the hole. You can also add a bag of ready mix concrete with the rocks for extra stability, if you'd like. The post should now be sticking out about five feet. On one board, the one you're going to strike, you can put an old shin pad or wrap a thick rope around several times from the top, until the rope runs out. I made one of these in my Clifton backyard and then years later in my Wayne yard. I got a real good sound and echo out of the Wayne one, because I set it up at the edge of the woods. As you strike it using a traditional tsuki (twisting punch), one board slaps the other which causes it to "give" when being hit. This "give" reduces strain on your joints.

Depending on how much my knuckles bled, I would strike the makiwara 2-3 times a week but usually every third day. Ten small stones would assist me in my ritual. I would line up the stones near the makiwara, ready to begin. I would perform one thousand punches while standing in migi mae kagami dashi (right side stance). I would then punch the post 50 times counting in Japanese (this would keep me psyched). Then, hantai (change guard to south paw) and perform 50 more. One stone would then be moved, as I would repeat this cadence ten times. It is important to practice a technique at least ten thousand times, in order to understand the proper mechanics.

My brother, Mike, another Koeikan black belt, told me once, that when I punched him in the chest, it felt like he was getting hit with the end of a two-by-four. This, I'm sure, was a direct result of makiwara training. One day, when Mike and I were conversing with Sensei Kaloudis, Mike, who enjoyed austerity training as much as I, asked Sensei how he could punch through more patio blocks, during our demonstrations. Mike could already punch through more blocks than anyone I knew, but wanted even more. Sensei Kaloudis used to punch through five common house bricks stacked one on top of the other to everyone's astonishment. Sensei explained that there were no shortcuts as he walked us over to the cinder block wall where we were chatting. He began to punch the wall, seemingly, as hard as he could. Bam! Bam! Bam! About five punches in all. How he didn't break his hand was a mystery. Sensei looked at Mike and said, "Do that for a couple of years; you'll get it!"

Teaching yourself to hit hard is important but learning to take a hit is equally as important. When you do sit ups, have someone hit you in the stomach with each repetition and have someone kick you every time you do push-ups, alternating sides. Once you get good at this, your partner will be lifting you off the ground with each repetition. Be sure to do knuckle push-ups in order to double the pleasure. O'Sensei Frost used to incorporate medicine ball training into our grueling workouts as well. I encourage you to spar with less experienced students while helping them improve their technique. Have them punch and kick you, full power to the ribs and abdomen, as you work up from green belts, to brown and then black. Fight full contact wearing bogu or other protective gear. Then if you want to kick it up a notch, you can participate in full contact kick-boxing, with Muay Thai being the toughest.

Many Koeikan black belts training under the tutelage of O'Sensei Frost became extremely tough over the years. They are men who enjoyed hitting and getting hit. If you don't like to fight, you'll never make it as a fighter. You have to enjoy the challenge, the raw-combat and the pain, or you'll never last with the best. Chuck Liddell epitomized this concept best when he said in an interview with Men's

Fitness magazine; "There's nobody in the world I wouldn't fight. I'll fight somebody in my backyard for free just to see if I'm better than him." This is the code of the bushi (warrior) Bushido – The way of the warrior (Samurai).

**"The most important part of the battle, takes place
even before you put your hand on your sword."**

Matsura Saizan

THE ART OF FIGHTING,
WITHOUT FIGHTING

Bruce Lee used this chapter's title in the movie <u>Enter the Dragon</u>. This story or concept is taken from the legendary sword master, Tsukuhara Bokuden Takamoto, (1490- 1571) only without the sword. In the movie, an arrogant martial artist is on a boat with Lee. They are on their way to an International Tournament to be held on a somewhat, secluded island. The guy approaches Lee and asks, "What style do you practice?"

Lee replies, "The art of fighting, without fighting!"

So, he looks at Lee as if sizing him up and repeats, "The art of fighting, without fighting? Show me," he demands, challenging Lee to a fight.

Lee tells the challenger that there isn't enough room on the boat but he glances over and says, "How about that small island? We could take a row boat." The challenger agreed as Lee allowed him to step into the rowboat first. Lee let the rope out, causing the rowboat to immediately drift behind the larger boat. This action put an end to any match that might have taken place on the larger boat, had Lee not outsmarted him. As the movie progressed, it became apparent that Bruce Lee could have easily defeated this big mouth. The moral of the story was, of course, it is better to avoid a fight or violence whenever possible.

My best friend at the time, Dennis Buongiorno, and I, got jobs as bouncer's at the Brass Bell in Hackensack, when we were 18 years old.

This was not the only disco/club I would work. It was a good part-time job a couple of nights a week, where I could make some cash and meet some girls. It didn't take long to understand that the owner of the establishment would rather you walk someone out of the bar, rather than having to carry them out. In other words, he'd rather see us use persuasion, than a left hook. Dennis and I were both brown belts and didn't mind mixing it up when the need arose. Trying reason with unruly patrons was a skill that I continuously tried to hone. Dennis, however, usually preferred the rough stuff, manhandling people out the front door. Many times this added fuel to the fire, as the unruly patron would often have friends. I found out that it was better to talk to the sober one in the group, telling them that if they leave peacefully, they could return another night. But if things got ugly, they would be banned from the club. My approach saved the owner from lawsuits, but I have to admit, Buongiorno's approach was sometimes more fun.

I thought being the bouncer, or peacekeeper, in the bars might be similar to keeping the peace in a city. That's why, when Dennis told me that he wanted to be a cop. I thought, *holy shit, that's a great idea.* And so, dealing with people became my specialty. As many fights that I had to end with a good overhand right, there were probably a dozen where I choose the path of least resistance.

Men in uniform are very familiar with the term "command presence." I once told a reporter who was interviewing me for a short story, that people often judge cops on how they look. Certain arrogant individuals test cops and check their reactions when they get loud and in the officer's face. Self-confidence developed through hard rigorous training, over an extended period of time, can give cops a good "poker face." I found that weightlifting also helps.

As an 18 year old bouncer (18 was the drinking age in 1973), I was usually the thinnest one. Even when I boxed in the 1978 golden gloves I competed at 178 pounds, so some loud mouths thought that they could get over on me. But I learned to keep cool and work as a team with the other bouncers. Once I got someone to direct their full attention at me, two other staff members would come up behind him grabbing one arm each. From there he would be "guided" out the door. Yeah, I had to pop a couple of guys but that was the exception rather than the rule.

道

A couple of years later, while bouncing at a club called Krackers, I developed an odd skill that was quite effective in avoiding a fight. It was 3:00 am, as I went around the large, centralized bar and announced, "Motel time! See ya tomorrow! Gotta go!" A male patron sitting alone at the bar, with about half of some mixed drink left in his glass, wasn't moving anytime soon. I walked up to him and said, "Sir, its three o'clock and you have to go."

He replied, "Look, I paid for this drink and I'm gonna finish it."

I looked at him and said, "Oh, the drink. Is that the problem?"

"Yeah!" he replied.

I then reached out, grabbed his glass and proceeded to take a bite out of it. Most of the broken glass fell to the floor as I started chewing on the small pieces that ground between my teeth. I placed the glass in front of him on the bar and said, "I think you're done with your drink!"

He looked at the glass, looked back at me and said, "I think so too!" He stood up and made for the door.

This would not be the last time I'd use this stunt to avoid a confrontation.

道

Being a young bouncer in 1974 and still a senior at Clifton High School, I started to think more like a man and wanted to be built like one. Dennis and I joined the European Health Spa in Wayne and immediately emerged ourselves, becoming addicted to weight lifting.

No more skinny arms, I thought, while I also improved my knock out power. Whenever I visited my Sensei, Brian Frost, up in Detroit, we lifted weights together at Armento's Gym. In later years Sensei got pretty close to the Dabish brothers, who founded "The Powerhouse Gym". These guys were great and they allowed us to train for free. They also occasionally tossed me a tee shirt to bring back to Jersey with me. In the late 1970's, Dennis and I, along with another friend and Clifton officer, Paul Ogden, would fly out to California and visit the original Gold's Gym, in Santa Monica. This gym, founded years earlier by Joe Gold, was where Arnold trained with bodybuilding greats, like Franco Columbo, Dave Draper and so many others. Joe sold Gold's only to turn around and start up World Gym, which also went universal. In 1988, I lifted at Worlds Gym in Glyfada, Greece, which was pretty cool.

道

In 1980, I was big and "cut up" enough to enter my first bodybuilding contest. It was called the "Mr. European Health Spa" and was held at their Paramus (NJ) location. Taking first place was an absolute boost and good start to my amateur career in bodybuilding. As the years progressed, I competed in state and regional contests through 1985. It was in 1985 that I won 2nd place in the "Mr. Colonial America." In 1984, I believe it was, I competed in the Mr. New Jersey or the Mr. Classic New Jersey with none other than Rich Gaspari. Gaspari needed to win this show to qualify for the Nationals, which he also won on his way to the Mr. Universe. Richie blew everyone off the stage this night competing in the open competition. Anyone who follows bodybuilding can attest to the stardom of Gaspari who came in 2nd, only to Lee Haney a couple of times at the Mr. Olympia contest.

Okay, let's get back to cops being judged by their appearance and command presence. It seemed to me that the bigger I got though bodybuilding, the less I had to prove myself to loudmouths. When I weighed 175 at the Brass Bell, guys challenged me much more than when I was 207 pounds. So remember all you young guys, steak and eggs, over donuts and danish.

道

In 1987, Clifton PD had a bench press team comprised of Bill Gibson, Frank Dara, Ross LaCorte, John Sloth and myself. We entered the "All Police" Bench Press Championships down in Little Egg Harbor. Not only did we all win individual trophies, but four team trophies as well. We were really proud of the fact that we beat the Atlantic City Police Department, which is much larger than Clifton's. My bench was never that great pushing 360 in practice. Because I was a bodybuilder and not a power-lifter, I was used to high repetitions. Frank Dara usually out-benched me by about 10 pounds and he always looked great. But it was Ross La Corte who was pound for pound the strongest, winning first place in his weight class. Ross during practice could bench 200% of his bodyweight. At 140, I believe, he could bench 280.

How you carry yourself when you exit the car and talk to people can be especially important. A friend of mine on Passaic (City) PD, Joe Patti (I mentioned him briefly in another chapter) wasn't big at all. But the bad guys in Passaic knew that you don't screw around with Joe Patti. His secret? He never showed fear and had one of the best poker faces and nightsticks in the business. If you work in a township or small city where people know their cops, you can develop a tough reputation early on, so most local guys don't call you out. Joe did it in Passaic, Bobby Challice did it in Paterson, and I'd like to believe I did it in Clifton.

道

One day in the late 90's, I believe it was, I walked into the Getty Grill on the Clifton/Paterson border. The counter girl, who I never met before, looked at my name tag. "You're Pat Ciser" she exclaimed.

"Yeah," I said, "all my life."

She then proceeded to tell me a story that she heard, where I, single-handedly, beat up five guys in the Botany section of Clifton a while back. She commented that I was like Chuck Norris. I told her that I remember a problem with three guys once, but not five. I swept one's feet out from under him, as I brushed by to confront his friend. The third one, not interested in engaging me, fled after seeing what I did to his two friends. So, I would say that he didn't really count; making it two guys rather than five. It's funny how that works sometimes. Someone tells a story that goes from one person to the next and a dozen people later, it changes. I'm not complaining, mind you; it helped me avoid conflict as the years went on.

道

About that poker face, I remember a funny story down on Lake Avenue. We got a call of a vicious Doberman pincher running around scaring the hell out of the area residents. Tim Lyons and I responded in Car #'s 1 and 2. I spotted the dog near a house with a white porch. I thought, *how nice would it be if I could get that dog up the stairs and contain him, until Bobby Boyle* (the animal control officer) *arrived?* It was an overcast day so I looked at Lyons and said, "Hey Tim, do you have your raincoat in your car?"

"Yeah, Pat, I do," he replied.

"Can I borrow it?" I continued.

"Sure! just a sec." Timmy brought me his coat which I wrapped around my left wrist and forearm. K-9 units are trained this way, where the trainer offers his padded arm to the dog, sparring them serious injury. I then opened my pocket knife and held it in my right hand. My plan was to stare down the dog, while keeping my padded arm forward for him to bite if things didn't go well. If he sank his teeth into my arm and I couldn't control him, he would get the knife plunged into his chest from underneath.

So, I'm ready and I lean slightly forward, keeping my left forearm extended and my right knife hand back. Pressing forward with small steps, I lock eyes with the Doberman. The dog, to my delight, ran up onto the porch. There's only one way off of the porch and that's through me. Even with his persistent growling and snapping, I held my ground. I couldn't help but ask myself, *self, is this really a good idea?* But I reminded myself that I had a better chance confronting him than the neighborhood kids.

After about five minutes, Boyle showed up and got out with the snare. Boyle was quite adept with his snare, wasting no time getting the K-9 into his truck. Putting my knife away, I handed Timmy's raincoat back to him. Timmy said, "Good thing I had that coat huh?"

I said, "Ah, it didn't matter, I have mine in the car too. I just didn't want any teeth marks in it." We both laughed as Timmy was always good with a joke.

So, again my friends, like Lady Gaga says, "It's the poker face!"

Stay in shape, keep your uniforms clean and pressed, polish your leather and stay in control. And if all of that doesn't work, use the (foot) sweep.

道

One time we were experiencing a rash of burglaries to vehicles in our Lakeview section near Paterson. A few of us responded to a call of suspicious persons walking around East Fourth Street around 10 pm. We ultimately rounded up four suspects walking around doing some "shopping" or looking into cars. The Eastside sergeant on scene questioned these individuals with no results. The only thing we could do was to take a full report and pass it onto the detective bureau for a follow-up. I asked the sergeant if I could talk to one of them before we cut them loose. I brought one of the suspects over to my car up the street so we could talk. A short time later, I returned him to the sergeant wearing handcuffs. I told the sergeant that they came in that car over there; the one with the Puerto Rican flag hanging from the rearview mirror. The four of them came in from Paterson, pull handles on all the doors they can in about 10 minutes and then go somewhere else. The sergeant looked at me with astonishment and asked, "How'd you get all of that?"

I said, "Sarge… A kind word… and a gun, go a lot further than just a kind word.

**"To win one hundred victories in one hundred battles is not the
highest skill.
To subdue the enemy without fighting is the highest skill."**

**Taken from "Art of War"
Sun Tzu**

11/11/11

It's November 11, 2011 and I'm on a flight out of Newark Liberty Airport to Detroit Metro with Sensei Ikushima. Sensei arrived in New Jersey from Tokyo on November 6th and has been staying at my home in Wayne. Sensei Ikushima, an 8th degree black belt, who has been training with Kancho Sensei Onishi since 1971, has the same amount of years in the dojo as I. Sensei has arrived to fine tune our kata and report, I'm sure, on the state of Koeikan Karate in America since my Sensei, Brian Frost, passed away two years ago. O'Sensei Frost was also an 8th dan and held a full proficiency diploma from Japan.

There was not enough time during this trip to include all East Coast Koeikan Dojo (schools) so I chose Clifton honbu dojo (headquarters), which I own, West Milford (Sensei Mendillo), Wayne "Y" Dojo (Sensei Feinstein) and the West End, Pennsylvania Dojo (Sensei(s) Hildebrant, Scarborough).

We were flying to Detroit, Michigan for a two-day trip to the Hazel Park Dojo (Sensei Brown), the Utica Dojo (Sensei Mason) and the Lake Orion dojo (Sensei Spearing).

My close friend and Koeikan brother, Jim Colo, 4th dan, was kind enough to pick us up at the airport. Sponsoring Sensei's trip from Japan was my pleasure, as I'll never forget how wonderfully I was treated while training in Japan. Sensei Colo, an extremely strong and disciplined individual had been my good friend ever since we met in 1992. He trained relentlessly at the Hazel Park dojo for years under

O'Sensei Frost (Note; Sensei, before death, O'Sensei after). Colo, a true modern day bushi (warrior) who is also a Vietnam veteran, would not only punch the dojo makiwara, (striking post) but would punish it! I remember all too well, the punching power of a few Michigan black belts like Spearing, Alexander and Colo.

Colo and I competed together in 1992 Venezuela. One day, while relaxing by a Caracas hotel pool, Sensei Frost suggested, or demanded, that we spar by the outdoor swimming pool. The surface was either concrete or pavers, I can't remember which; I just knew that I didn't want to hit it.

For us it was an enjoyable battle of kumite (free sparring), as we developed more respect for each other with every blow that was thrown. As I am Sensei Colo's "senior" in the dojo, I had more kumite experience, resulting in my victory. Not without any bruises, however. Pool side observers watched intently, drumming up some interest for the weekend tournament.

Over the years, Kancho Sensei Onishi traveled several times to America including 1971, 1974, 1990 and 2006. Along with keen senses, he demonstrated speed and crispness of techniques not seen on a regular basis.

Sensei Frost, while training in Japan in the early 70's with Kancho, was an uchi deshi (live in student in Kancho's home.) O'Sensei was well versed not only in Koeikan Karate-Do, but also the ways and culture of Japan. He spoke fluent Japanese when I met him in 1973. I used to wonder if he was half Japanese from his excellent kata and mannerisms.

When O'Sensei Frost passed in September 2009, I had to re-evaluate my training and direction. When you lose your Sensei, (teacher) where do you turn? his teacher of course. When I trained in Japan in 2004, I came to know a few of Kancho Sensei's best.

Sensei Gaku Yamamoto was already introduced to me a few years earlier as he visited our Clifton and West Milford schools here in New Jersey. Sensei Yamamoto held the rank of Hachi Dan (8th degree black belt). Another top level senior I came to know was a man who trained longer than I. Sensei Yamazaki (7th Dan), had also been my guest in New Jersey on another occasion (RIP). All of the seniors in Japan, including Sensei Hoshi (8th Dan), were very kind and helpful during my stay in Japan.

One special training session held outside Tokyo, was held on a Sunday. With me being a roku dan (6th degree) I attempted to find my proper place in line when kiotsukete (line up) was called. Naturally, I lined up behind the men who outranked me. To my surprise, however, they insisted that I take the first spot in line as their guest, normally reserved for the most senior seito in the room. Not only did I take the first row position, but Kancho Sensei had me run part of the class. Amazing! We Americans can learn much from them, including humility.

道

Getting back to Sensei Tatsuya Ikushima's visit; it became immediately apparent that he was a perfectionist when teaching kata. For readers without Karate-Do training under their belts, let me explain kata.

When Karate first started out as To De (China hand) in old Okinawa, approximately the 1600's, it was developed to maim or to kill. It was believed that practice fighting would cause too many injuries or even death to their practitioners. They needed to stay healthy to battle their Japanese oppressors.

Kata (forms) were developed over time through both the Naha and Shuri systems. Tomari-te was another system they practiced but it never endured the test of time. Kata is a set pattern of techniques performed while imagining opponents attacking from different angles (eight angles to be more specific). The number eight holds much symbolism in the East (Asia).

Today, scores are given to tournament competitors by judges similar to a gymnastics floor exercise. Speed, timing, balance, hip movement and eye contact are only some of the areas that judges look at. It is said that when you perform kata well, you can see your opponents. If you can get your audience to see your opponents, that is an exceptional kata. As you rise through the belt system, the kata becomes more complex and difficult to master.

Another important aspect is to teach and even research the true or precise movements and meaning in the kata. This, my friends, can become a lifelong journey. Some of the best Koeikan kata that is performed here in the U.S. by Jack Sabat, Jeff Mason, Janelle Mason and Marco Lopez can still be improved by the teachings of Kancho Sensei or his liaison. Hidden bunkai (guarded meanings) of the kata are very important to lifelong students whose thirst for knowledge is endless. We, in traditional Karate-Do systems, have no patience for charlatans not seeking the truth, or "The Way" (Do), when researching these historical movements.

True martial artists perceive training as climbing a mountain that has no summit. It is the journey we embrace and thrive on, rather than the destination.

The original systems of Japan; Shotokan, Goju Ryu, Shito Ryu and Wado Ryu along with Koeikan, Jundokan and Kyokushin to name a few, can all be traced back to Okinawa and To De (changed later in 1936 to Karate). Koeikan's Sensei Eizo Onishi, for instance, was graded to 8th dan by Shuri-te exponent Kanken Toyama. He also trained directly under Sensei Yasutsune Itoso. Not satisfied, Sensei Onishi, with a letter of introduction from Sensei Toyama, would seek out Naha-te Master, Juhatsu Kyoda. After petitioning Sensei Kyoda for a few months, he was finally accepted to his dojo. Dojo translated is, "the place" (jo), where we learn "the way" (do), i.e. Karate-Do, Judo, Aikido and Bushi Do, "The Way" of the warrior.

Eventually, after years of training, Sensei Onishi was awarded 8th dan and a certificate of full proficiency in the Naha-te (De) system, as well. Combining the best of Shuri-te and Naha-te, he later founded Koeikan.

Due to the efforts of Kancho Sensei Onishi, Sensei Kaloudis and O'Sensei Frost, Koeikan is being practiced, to my knowledge, in Japan, United States, Venezuela, Greece and Spain.

One notable facet of Koeikan is our training and competitions utilizing bogu. Bogu gear resembles kendo armor and allows competitors to spar/fight while suffering minor or no injury to themselves. In Japan, bogu is used on a limited contact basis. Here in the United States, we strike and kick full-contact, above the waist, while using the armor.

In the 1990's, while overseeing our International Koeikan Tai Kai (Tournament), I came up with an idea to honor Sensei Frost, introducing the concept of Team Bogu to our event. I named it, The Brian Frost Team Bogu Challenge. Each state and/or country practicing Koeikan could enter a four-man team in the competition. In most cases, teams would consist of four black belts. Brown and even hard hitting green belts could also round out the team. Three fighters would compete, while keeping the fourth one on standby, as an alternate, in the event a team member was injured and could not continue.

As of this writing, Michigan has the most wins since team bogu began. New Jersey has the next highest with California coming in third.

Koeikan's first National tournament was held in 1972 at Montclair State College (now University), here in New Jersey. Sensei Edward Kaloudis was the tournament's founder and director. This championship has run every year since and has always been held in New Jersey. Sensei Kaloudis, and men like him, always dreamed of Karate-Do one day becoming an Olympic sport. It's actually sad to see in 2012 that his wish never materialized.

In 1970, Robin Reilly lamented in his book, <u>The History of American Karate,</u> how it's confusing to see so many different Champions from so many different karate organizations can exist. There is no "one" organization that can claim that their tournament's champion is the one true champion, he continued. Many names reappear, winning a few of the bigger contests, like Chuck Norris, Joe Lewis, Skipper Mullins, Louis Delgado, Victor Moore and Mike Stone, to name a few.

Well here we are, 42 years later and nothing has changed. I guess everyone wants to be in charge, which leaves no one in charge. I always thought that the AAU or USNKF would be the answer to solidify Japanese and Okinawan systems. Everyone seems to want to write and use their own rules. The only thing I ever saw years ago, crowning a true US and World Champion was in full-contact karate/ kickboxing. Benny "The Jet" Urquidez, Lightweight, Bill "Superfoot" Wallace, Middleweight, Jeff Smith, Light Heavyweight and Joe Lewis, the Heavyweight were PKA (Pro Karate Association) Champs in their divisions.

Point competitions have been in existence since the first one was held in 1957 Japan. Many associations have popped up over the years with WUKO (World Union Karate Organization) arguably being the most successful.

The first WUKO World Championship was held in Tokyo, Japan, in 1970. The second was held in Paris, while the third World Championship in 1975 was held in Long Beach, California. I lamented in another chapter how I secured a place on the United States Team but couldn't afford to fly out to the coast.

In 1980, Madrid, Spain, the U.S. Team, which I was not a member, did very well. Tokey Hill won a gold medal in kumite. Billy Blanks won a silver medal and a bronze. Both of these men were very strong competitors who I knew of from the 1979 Nationals held in Virginia Beach. I never competed against them as we were in different weight classes.

Also in 1979, I was a member of Jerry Thomson's AAU New Jersey "All Star" Team and engaged in a "Goodwill" competition with the South African team.

Tokey Hill and I did some training (separately) under the same Sensei for awhile. Sensei Katsumi Nikura was a former Koeikan student in Japan under Kancho Sensei Onishi. He came to the United States in the late 1970's and stayed with me at my Clifton apartment for about two weeks. Sensei Nikura taught some other Koeikan black belts and me Aiki-Jutsu, along with Karate-Do techniques.

Sensei Nikura returned a while later with a group of young students from Japan who trained at our Clifton and West Milford schools.

Getting back to 1980 Spain and WUKO, I always thought that this Tai Kai (Tournament) would open the door to the Olympics. It was not to be, however, as WUKO could run only their world championship every other year, winding up back in Spain in 1992.

In 1990, WUKO became the WKF (World Karate Federation) and seems to be the only association recognized by the IOC (International Olympic Committee). In 2009, the WUKO acronym would surface again by changing one word yet capitalizing on these popular letters. WUKO now stood for World United Karate Organization, thus throwing even more confusion into the mix. (Note: In 1996 the United States Olympic committee recognized the USA-NKF)

Today, Dana White has done a phenomenal job creating legitimate "World Champions" with the UFC. Unfortunately, however, I still don't foresee traditional karate becoming an Olympic sport any time soon.

> *"The ultimate aim of karate lies not in victory or defeat,*
> *but in the perfection of the character of the participants."*
>
> *Gichin Funakoshi*

EARLY YEARS

Growing up on East Second Street, in Clifton, I, like many others, didn't have a clue as to what I wanted to be when I grew up. Never the best student, with a serious case of boredom, I eventually got through Saint Brendan Grammar School. I don't think that I ever impressed anyone during my stay there, especially my parents. And I never, even as I got older, bought into that psychological crap that I was bored because I was really a smart kid. An antsy kid might be a better description, as I was never short on energy. The only thing that I really liked there was basketball.

Attending two years of high school at Passaic County Technical Institute certainly didn't fire up any brain cell activity. The first year I went there, in 1970, was the first year of the new Wayne campus, having moved from the City of Paterson. The school absolutely attracted Passaic County's "biggest losers" (and I don't mean fat people from the TV show). The administration was unprepared as many classrooms didn't even have desks. We used folding chairs and had to keep our book on our lap in most classes. The whole school was in such disarray that a couple of my teachers told us that if we came to class every day, we would get a "C." If we did some work, we could improve the grade from there. But disrupting the class would result in a lower grade. *Man, I thought, I'm college bound now!* Not!

Most of my friends were from Paterson, so we cut class sometimes and hung out downtown. We got into a little mischief but never really went over the line. Passaic County Tech had a lot of tough customers so you always had to be on guard for trouble. Urban black kids would constantly shake down white suburban kids for money. Once in a while, one would target me and say, "Hey, got any spare change?"

So I would put my hand in my pocket and rattle the coins for him to hear. "No," I replied, "I don't," while staring him in the face.

Fraternities were big with some of my friends being members of "Omega." They wanted me to start a Clifton chapter, but I wasn't very interested. Racial tensions really flared one day as a bunch of black kids from Passaic jumped some white ones waiting for the school bus. I remember one time when I was standing in the parking lot, waiting to board the Clifton bus, suddenly, I got punched in the back of the head. As I looked back, I could see about a half dozen kids walking through to the Passaic bus, randomly punching kids in the back of the head. Before we realized what the hell was going on, they jumped on their bus. At that point, because they were behind us, we couldn't tell who hit who!

One black girl pulled out a box cutter right in the school lobby and slashed another sister's stomach. They rushed her to the hospital with a terrible laceration. Some of the sisters used to keep petroleum jelly in their pocketbooks and apply it like a prize fighter, before challenging each other.

So, after two years of this crap, I grew a brain. I told my folks that I wasn't learning shit and wanted to transfer to Clifton High School.

Before moving on, however, I would like to say that, today, Passaic County Technical and Vocational High School is one of Passaic County's best! What a remarkable turnaround. My good friend, Rob Nutile, who also coached my kids with the Panther football team, teaches at PCT. He invited me a couple of times to stop by his criminal justice class and speak to his students about being a cop. Both years I visited the school, I came away very impressed. The kids were absolutely courteous and respectful and a pleasure to speak to and be around.

Getting back to my high school years, I attended Clifton High for two years and graduated in 1974. Going to St. Brendan and PCT, I knew very few kids at Clifton High. I ate lunch by myself every day, possibly feeding into a lone wolf mentality; pretty bad for a graduating class of almost 1,000 kids!

Because of the violence at PCT, I began my Karate-Do training in 1971. By the time I was a senior at CHS, I was a brown belt. Sensei Kaloudis, my friend, Dennis Buongiorno and I, did a demonstration for the school assembly. Clifton High was normally a peaceful school with few troublemakers. After our exhibition, even if there were any tough guys around, I don't think they were interested in "testing" Dennis or me. Many kids signing my yearbook upon graduation would make mention of my "Karate kid" status. The yearbook had me listed as John Ciser. I guess it was just a mix up, as my middle name is John.

Karate-Do training was definitely invaluable to me. It always gave me direction. Sensei Kaloudis, Ron Paliwoda and Bill Kowal always guided me through those early years at the Clifton dojo. Growing up a little rough around the edges, it was my instructors who truly showed me the way. But it was Sensei Brian Frost who I really tried to emulate.

The graduation class of 1974 was 981 strong and had a fairly high number of graduates who became Clifton police officers, including Dennis Buongiorno, Mike Meffen, Jeff Reilly, Barry Feinberg, Nick Donato, George Adelhelm, Joe Klein, Bruce Jubinsky, John Broncatello and Jeff Shom. Dennis Buongiorno and I were absolutely the wildest of the bunch. Training at the dojo together and being nightclub bouncers since we were seniors in high school seemed to prepare us a little more than the average guy.

Sometimes it's that kid who is a little wild who makes the best cop; it's someone who was never afraid to take a chance or jump into an uncertain situation. I went to grammar school with Jimmy Sweeney, from Paterson, who was absolutely a wild kid. No one ever thought that he would become a cop. He retired a Paterson detective sergeant having an illustrious career. John Tori, who I went to Passaic County Tech with, became a Passaic County Sheriff's Officer. Go figure! He was another wild one.

I was a late bloomer, I guess, never letting school interfere with my education. LOL! Whenever I got bad grades, my parents used to tell me that I was going to be a ditch digger. Seeing all the chaos around me at Passaic County Tech, I started to watch people and try to figure them out. I wondered why people did the things they do; like smoke cigarettes, for instance. I sat in the school's lobby each morning waiting for the bell to ring and kids were outside, regardless of the weather, smoking their cigarettes. I thought, look at all those dopey kids, many grabbing a smoke, just to look cool! I didn't believe that they all enjoyed smoking as some were coughing up their lungs. I tried cigarettes, coughed and spit while wondering if it gets better. Most kids probably had the same initial reaction, but felt the need to get over it so they could look cool to their friends.

Weak individuals always give into peer pressure, so they smoke, do drugs and, many times, act like total morons just to fit in with the crowd. How many college kids keep quiet about hazing just to be accepted? I decided to back off on any wild behavior and not worry about fitting in. A year later, I was in Clifton High doing my own thing. Not having many friends, I felt no pressure to go along with the crowd. May 10, 1977, I was sworn in as a Clifton police officer and at age 21, I realized that I had a lot to learn.

道

My first few years on the job, I was a "CETA" cop. Clifton received a government grant to hire more cops. The State of New Jersey paid about a dozen salaries of local boys to beef up the department. It was a lot like the "Safe Streets Act" which became popular years later. We didn't even have to go to the Police Academy, but received on the job training. "Go buy a gun kid and pick up some uniforms at All Cities, in Paterson," I was told.

Mel Hockwit, a Clifton gun dealer sold me a .357, model 19. We were allowed to buy magnums as long as we loaded them on duty with .38 rounds. Shooting at the police range under the guidance of Jim Bolinger was a snap, and fun to boot.

I wasn't sent to the police academy until 1979. Man, have times changed. Clifton did a lot of weird things back then including sending firemen to the police academy. That's right, firemen! Clifton would create the fire-police patrol with firemen driving around in red station wagons. They were supposed to be extra eyes and ears for the police department. They carried guns and worked two-men to a car. They didn't do very much, as I recall, and I couldn't blame them. They were firemen for Christ sake!

So, in 1979, after being on the streets for two years, I was sent to the Essex County Police Academy, in Cedar Grove. Clifton is in Passaic County but sent its' officers wherever there were openings. And besides, Passaic County at the time didn't have much of an academy. Essex County had a relaxed atmosphere, you might say, which was fine with me. Nobody wants to be on the job for two years and then, have some ex-jarhead yelling in your face, telling you how to be a cop. It was an absolute country club, as we didn't even have to run. I was disappointed, however, that we didn't have to box. Competing in the 1978 Golden Gloves, I was certainly ready to box. The first day there, we all were wearing clip-on ties. The director told us that we could remove them and leave them home. Cops from other towns that were brand spanking new, almost seemed disappointed that the place was so lax.

In order to pass the time a little better, I organized the guys to pitch quarters on our breaks. One of the instructors in the amphitheater chose me to remind him when it was break time. Boy, was that a mistake! Not only did I inject more breaks into the day than normal, I also had an unorthodox way of announcing it.

Many of us showed up every day with a pocket full of quarters. When I wanted a break, I would stand up, put my hand in my pocket and jiggle my change (Just like I did in PCT). Another officer would then follow my cue and do the same, followed by another and then another. At that point, the instructor would get the point and give us a break.

One thing they did teach us, however, was the new law. In 1977, we used NJS Title 2A. In the academy, however, we learned Title 2 C.

By far, the best thing that happened to me in the academy, however, would be the cultivating of new friendships. Christopher Trucillo, a Harrison, New Jersey recruit and I, became friends for life. Chris, being highly intelligent and well-grounded, brought me back to my senses, if my pranks and humor went too far. Our class played basketball a lot also and I liked to be on Chris' team. He could hit a three pointer from anywhere on the court. I was the jumper and would feed him the rebounds. If Chris didn't get stuck at 5'11" or so, he probably would have turned pro!

It wasn't his basketball skills that he would be known for, however. A few years later, he switched over to the Port Authority Police Department of New York and New Jersey. It was his integrity and leadership skills that would propel him up the chain of command.

And so on the date of my retirement, May 1, 2008, the Chief of Police for the PAPD, Christopher Trucillo, would honor me with his attendance and a plaque which read, in part:

"I wish to express my personal best wishes and gratitude to you, providing an 'extraordinary' level of service and sacrifice for the well being of others."

I was honored, to say the least.

道

Getting back to 1979 and graduating the police academy, I found myself laid off at the end of the year, from the CETA program. Back on the job as a provisional officer for a year, in 1981, and then finally sworn in as a regular (civil service) in April 1983, I had some further ups and down in my early years.

To me, Post 1, Botany Village, was the best area in Clifton to work, if you were looking for action. I had no interest in working suburban Montclair Heights or other low-crime areas. There's an old saying about putting the round pegs in the round holes and the squares into the square holes. Ancient supervisors, as we called them when I first came on the job, were bosses who either never got that concept, or totally ignored it. Ostensibly, rookie officers would have to earn the right to work a good car or post. Cops who wanted action would ask to work nights. Over the years I could never consider community policing or other mundane assignments. I worked with and for, some real dinosaurs in the late 70's. Many of these relics from the 50's and 60's would walk right into the front door to a bank, no gun drawn or cover position taken and announce, "Hey, your alarm is going off!" Maybe they thought that I was just a snot nosed 21-year-old kid, as I would constantly remonstrate upon observing these blatant safety violations.

Their answer was always the same, "They're always false alarms, kid."

道

It certainly wasn't a false alarm one day back in Little Falls, as we got word that their Chief of Police got shot during a bank robbery. Our neighboring town of Little Falls is a small town to our west. The chief was on duty wearing a suit this day, as an armed assailant walked into the bank. Announcing a hold -up, the actor fired a shot into the ceiling, I was told. The chief drew down on his armed adversary, as they were locked in a bit of a stalemate.

Both men open fired, causing the chief to fall to the ground. It was reported that the chief's gun misfired twice, leaving him at the mercy of the assailant. No mercy would be shown, however, as the gunman shot the chief again before fleeing the bank. The felon was later apprehended and the chief, luckily, recovered from his wounds.

It certainly didn't take me long to point out this story to some of our burnt out, as well as, complacent veterans. Many small towns in North Jersey have had officers who were shot over the years, including Lodi, Fairlawn, Little Falls, Fairfield and Wayne, just to name a few. You don't have to work in an urban area to be at risk.

Policing, in the last 40 years, has dramatically improved. The in-house training (AG Guidelines) and academy training have absolutely professionalized police officers to a high degree. You practically have to be a paralegal today to make lieutenant.

道

Getting back to my early days, I recall asking my captain if I could work our most urban post that bordered the City of Passaic. I explained that I felt I could make a difference down there, with all the rowdy bars and drug dealing. The Captain replied, and I'll never forget this, "Ciser, you're just ink in my pen!" I didn't get the post car and thought he was a jerk. It took a little while for me to realize that he didn't want me to "stir the pot." Having a complacent, old veteran in that car made his job much easier. Fewer arrests meant fewer complaints, and possible lawsuits, against his officers and the department.

Later in my career, I noticed that my best guys with the highest arrest records also had the most complaints against them. Let's face it; no one is happy about getting locked up. Therefore, in many cases, the perpetrator wants to detract from his crime and place the focus on the cop's actions, which I found to be justified 99% of the time.

As a Lieutenant, I told my men, "There's a lot of empty cells back there, make sure you fill 'em up before you go home." A couple of times a day, we brought our prisoners to the County jail thus leaving them empty for the next shift.

Proactive police work was not a term some older commanders wanted to hear. Many were happy to drink coffee and read the paper until we got a call. Clifton was a city where, once many old timers retired, could become one of the most, if not THE most proactive department in North Jersey. There were several reasons for this. The biggest, I believe, was the size of the city and its' crime rate. Major highways, escape routes and being sandwiched between urban areas like Paterson and Passaic, were also determining factors.

Many times, the cops working in small towns, with little crime, like to keep it that way; or maybe I should say their politicians and chiefs want to keep it that way. A low crime rate is good; ignoring crime and the drug trade is not. Many are reactive departments, which only respond to crimes in progress, not stopping many suspicious cars or working the highways in a proactive fashion. Drug dealing many times, exists within their borders, but they fail to assign a couple of men to actively pursue drug leads. They'll ensure their residents, "We don't have a drug problem!" Out of sight, out of mind, I guess.

Larger cities are sometimes overwhelmed with 911 calls giving officers very little "down time" to be proactive. New York City (15 minutes from Clifton) Newark (5 minutes away) and Paterson (our neighbor) cops are under more stress and subject to burn-out more than suburban cops. So here we have Clifton, busy, but not too busy, crime, but not crazy out-of-control crime. Unfortunately for Clifton, its' crime rate continues to climb over the years as other cities stabilize or even show a downward trend.

As of this writing, Clifton has a TO (Table of Organization) of 157 officers. How they do it with anything less than 180 is beyond me.

Clifton is a city of 11.75 square miles and approximately 85-90,000 people (give or take a few thousand) with all of the illegal immigrants, in illegal attic and basement apartments. The police *force* (I'll bet you don't hear that word much anymore), when I got on in 1977 was mostly home-grown boys, who graduated from Clifton High (There were no female officers at that time).

The good part of the residency laws were that most of the cops who grew up in Clifton knew the streets and the people. Cooperation and support from the residents was high as many of the people supported their officers. Later, Clifton would strike a deal with the NAACP (National Association for the Advancement of Colored People) that would open up the Civil Service Test to all state residents. That would later be modified to include all Passaic and Essex County residents, creating a large minority pool. Personally, I always thought that with the abundance of minorities living in Paterson and Passaic, it should've been Passaic County only. Passaic County residents are at least familiar with Clifton.

Some Newark recruits worked out well from a quality perspective, but knew little about Clifton geographically. So, learning the streets and getting to know business owners and residents took some time. It's funny but many towns and even cities have residency laws, as they insist that cops live where they work. Clifton was doing just the opposite as Newark residents and others would leave Clifton after their shift. As a result of this, Clifton could not require veterans to stay. Personally, I lived in Clifton for 40 years and still have my karate school there. Moving to Wayne became necessary as my arrest record continued to climb. You don't want to go to back-to-school night and see fathers that you locked up. You bring your wife and kids to a local diner or restaurant, only to feel uncomfortable, as a customer starts to stare you down (and I hate smacking people in front of the kids).

Let me get back to some problems that we faced years ago and how the department professionalized after 1977. I had a low opinion of half of the workforce, so I tried to hang around the other half, so to speak. We were getting a lot of young rookies at the time, which also helped when looking for a sympathetic ear. It never surprised me that cops back then had a reputation of "donut eaters." There was no such thing as a PBA gym. A few of us like Buongiorno, Gibson, Lanzalotto and I pushed for one. Nothing came together, however, until Officer Ross LaCorte, an energetic newcomer to weightlifting, took the lead. As a result of his efforts over the years, Clifton now has a beautiful, well-equipped PBA gym. Others also helped to a lesser degree.

The first sergeant I had, who impressed me the most, was Frank Lo Gioco. He was a strong, determined, former wild kid who grew up in Clifton and rode a motorcycle. He was always rough around the edges or perhaps a diamond in the rough. Initially we got along as we would talk about diet and weightlifting. It was said that he carried nunchaku(s) and a sawed-off shotgun in his radio car, but I never observed either.

He had only one serious foible, in my mind. He was a stickler for the old ways and protocol of yesteryear. In the 60's and early 70's, cops were still required to wear an eight-point hat on duty at all times, even driving around town. There were other supervisors who felt the same way. Old habits die hard, I'm afraid, but these guys absolutely took it too seriously.

If you're in a bar fight, wear your hat. If you're chasing a suspect through backyards and over fences, wear your hat! I remember as a rookie, Sergeant Pitlivka responded to one of my calls. A man on Newbriar Lane had collapsed in his driveway while cutting the grass. I pulled up in minutes as I found him lying there unconscious and unresponsive. He was purple and I could detect no pulse. I began CPR and mouth-to-mouth as I waited for the ambulance to arrive. Going back and forth with chest compressions and mouth to mouth was draining as I worked up a sweat. The man was no longer purple and, I thought, had a faint heartbeat as the ambulance arrived. Two firemen ran from the ambulance to take over the First Aid/CPR for me as I ran to get the stretcher. Pulling the stretcher out of the ambulance, I rolled it up to the driveway. We then lifted him onto the stretcher and into the back of the rig. "You guys keep working on him," I shouted, "I'll drive!" They were EMT's, I was a good driver; it made sense. We got him to the hospital and into the emergency room so the doctors and nurses took over. At that point, I was sweating like a pig. After cleaning up a bit at Passaic General, the ambulance driver took me back to my radio car. Coming out of the ambulance, satisfied that I did a good job, neighbors still outside began to clap. I waved to them and returned to my car.

Sergeant Pitlivka then called me, "Car 19 to Car 6!"

"Car 6," I replied.

"6. Meet me on Brighton Road with your reports."

"K, Sarge," I answered. (Okay)

Pulling up to the sergeant, I thought he would have something nice say.

But instead, he asked me, "Hey Pat, where's your hat?"

I explained that a hat never would have stayed on my head through all of that running around. He wasn't interested in excuses, only that I adhere to this antiquated rule.

This problem would haunt me for years as I would trivialize the importance of wearing a hat, while concentrating on doing a good job. I would remain intractable, while believed that hats should be for inspections and parades only.

道

Years later, when Sergeant LoGioco was my captain, the hat issue would absolutely tear us apart.

I was working the midnight shift, patrolling in Car #1. A woman on Lexington Avenue called the police to report her husband was being abusive. I had a head cold and it was the winter of 1985, as I drove up to the house. Another officer also arrived but I can't remember who. Back then there were no attorney general guidelines on domestic violence, so we just used our better judgment. After interviewing the woman, she explained that she wasn't injured, didn't want to sign any complaints and just wanted her husband out of the house. The husband agreed to go to a relative's home but wasn't happy about it. After he left, the woman expressed to me that she was really afraid of him, and that she thought he was capable of more violence. She also added that he had beaten her in the past.

I instructed her to call us back if he returns and to, also, if possible, leave the front door unlocked for us without him knowing. Sure as shit, about a half hour later, she calls us back. Knowing the potential danger she was in, I sped back to the house, ran up the front steps and entered the unlocked front door. As I walked into the kitchen, I witnessed him striking her. He quickly hit the floor as a result of my foot sweep, allowing me now, with my knee in the center of his back, to handcuff him. Sergeant John Burke arrived as I was dragging the husband out the front door and into the back seat of my cruiser.

Little did I know, Captain LoGioco, was parked up the street, observing my actions. The sergeant followed me into headquarters with my prisoner where I began the paperwork. LoGioco returned to headquarters and ordered Burke into his office. He asked the sergeant why I wasn't wearing my hat as I ran inside that home. Apparently not satisfied with the sergeant's answer, he ordered my assignment changed. I was to be pulled out of Car #1 and work the front desk for the remainder of the week.

I told the sergeant that I was feeling just a little unappreciated, especially since I came to work with a cold. The next night, instead of taking some cold medicine and coming in, I took a sick day. LoGioco, believing it was an affront to his authority, had my assignment changed to the desk, indefinitely! So, you have this proactive cop, a starter on your team, benched! And all because of something so ridiculous as a hat. He left me on the desk for one solid year. We can only imagine how many guys didn't get locked up that year as a result of the captain's decision.

道

One day on that desk assignment, I became extremely frustrated. Officer Bill Gibson was off duty and was truly a 24/7 cop. Always on the lookout, he spotted a man wanted for several violent rapes of some young women in Hudson County. Bill spotted the suspect vehicle driving around a shopping area near Route 3, possibly cruising for his next victim.

Gibson called for back-up officers who helped box him in, as he was parked at the curb in front of the Allwood Road Grand Union. With guns drawn, they ordered him out of the vehicle. The actor quickly threw his car in reverse and slammed into the police vehicle behind him. He jumped the curb, driving up the sidewalk as officers shot out his tires. He escaped the parking lot and drove out to Allwood Road. Listening to my police radio on the desk, I heard Billy say that the actor was now turning left onto Clifton Avenue toward police headquarters. Billy added that the suspect vehicle was driving on rims only, with sparks flying in every direction.

Hearing this, I jumped out of my seat and grabbed the keys to the armory. The armory was only a few steps away from the front desk as I moved as quickly as possible. Now having a shotgun in my hand, my plan was to run outside into the middle of Clifton Avenue, and intercept that vehicle. I had every intention of firing the shotgun at point blank range into his windshield and then dive out of the way. It kind of reminded me of the time Aaron Norris, Chuck Norris' brother and stunt man, jumping up and kicked through an advancing car's windshield in one of his movies. Only difference was that my plan might actually work. But as I started to load the shotgun and move towards the door, I thought, *I wonder what the captain will think of my idea? You know, standing in the middle of Clifton Avenue without a hat on?* Okay, okay, it had nothing to do with the hat. Thinking better of it though, and wanting to get back on the road, I put the shotgun back in order not to make any more waves.

The wanted felon ultimately crashed his car by Clifton's Elmwood train station and fled on foot. We later learned that he broke into a building nearby and waited out the search.

Passaic police involved in the search for this guy recognized a picture of this fugitive as one of their residents and picked him up at home the next morning. I still think the shotgun blast would've been better though.

道

Labor Day weekend was upon us and I was still pushing pencils on the desk. The daily work schedule was adjusted by just one day. The City of Clifton Annual Picnic was held on that Sunday at our main Memorial Park. The picnic was always a big success, with my dojo (karate school) and me, performing a karate exhibition, before I went to work around noon. The captain heard rumors that some gangs were going to mix it up by the picnic grounds later that day. So he, wanting to play it safe, scheduled me to work a radio car to circumnavigate the picnic grounds for eight hours.

One day! Just one day off of the front desk, to be available for a possible gang fight. I thought, *well I'll be dipped in shit!* My friends on the job couldn't believe it, and some suggested that I call in sick. I said, "No, I'm not going through that again." Plus, I'll get outta here for one day, any day, just to get some fresh air. It was funny, some residents I ran into at the picnic thought I quit or something, not seeing me for months.

As it turned out, all was quiet at the picnic that year except for a couple of minor scuffles. The next day, on the 1500-2300 (3-11pm) shift, there I was, back on the desk. Go figure.

道

Getting back to my original point is the fact that police work continues to improve, with each passing decade. I credit cops from across the country and New Jersey in particular, over the years, with forward-thinking and not being afraid of change. One thing, or should I say one answer, that used to drive me crazy was the following; you ask your boss, "Why do we do it that way?" And the same perfunctory answer was, "Because we always did it that way." Doesn't that drive you nuts! Like we can't use our brain's to come up with a better answer or solution! When I was the Watch Commander on midnights, I always liked to hear positive comments and sometimes "outside the box" solutions. I would tell the patrolman at the line–up, if there are twelve of you here tonight, I want twelve ideas to make things better. I never liked commanders who thought that they were smarter than the rank-and-file. After all, how do you know, who among them will be in charge one day. Tap your resources I always say. Captain John Link, who is younger than I, told me once; Lieutenant, there are no problems, only solutions. He always came to work optimistic and willing to listen to others. That's the new breed that we need!

I'll never forget my conversation with Captain LoGioco one night at the Styertowne Shopping Center, some 20 years or so ago. I explained that back in the 1920's and throughout the 1940's, you could see American men wearing hats. Old pictures would depict men wearing fedoras, while women would sport large, sometimes flowery hats from that era. In the 1980's, however, times have changed and hats fell out of favor, seeing very few anymore. The police wore hats back in the day because everyone did. Today, hats are an impediment to police work, while producing no benefit. Family disputes, bar fights, disorderly person confrontations and running after suspects during the commission of a crime, all become problematic while wearing a hat.

How many cops lose their hats performing their duty only to have them blow away or run over? So please, stop with the hats already and go catch some bad guys!

> *"There are many paths to the mountain,*
> *If we reach the peak,*
> *We will all view the same moon.*
> *However, the wrong path leads nowhere."*
>
> *Taken from the book,*
> *Koeikan Karate-Do, Practice and Precept*
> *O'Sensei Brian Frost*

STATE OF LAW ENFORCEMENT

Working in the City of Paterson, in 97, where the crime rate is at least five times that of Clifton's, I never fully understood the logic, or lack thereof, of the people living in the inner city. When crimes occur in Clifton, especially violent crimes, our switchboard would light up. In Paterson, as well as other major cities, the mantra of "no snitching" and "Warner Brother" (Warn-a-Brother) mentality prevails.

One summer, we chased a stolen car to the Alabama projects in Paterson. It was a hot Friday night, so most people were standing around the parking lot and walkways, playing music or whatever. Heavy drug dealing goes on nightly. The pursued vehicle entered the lot at a high speed. People jumped out of the way in a panic as the stolen vehicle smashed into a few parked cars. The suspect jumped out and started to run as the police exited their vehicles for the foot pursuit. As the suspect ran through the lot, it was like the parting of the Red Sea; everyone purposely stepped back giving him safe passage and quickly stepped forward in front of the pursuing officers, allowing him to escape. Didn't anybody own those cars that were smashed? Isn't anybody pissed that they, or their kids, almost got run over? This scenario, and other similar ones, plays out again and again all over America.

道

In 1997, when I was assigned to work for the county's narcotics task force, we had a similar situation. We were going from one corner in

244

Paterson to the next, making quick arrests of drug dealers selling their wares in plain sight. One of our detectives, working a "scoop" car (to scoop-up arrested persons), had a prisoner handcuffed behind his back in the rear seat cage. On the next block, another detective and I ran into a tenement building chasing a suspected dealer. Things were getting a little hairy so my partner radioed for assistance. The detective in the scoop car responded in seconds, leaving his prisoner, according to him, in the back seat of his locked car. When we all exited the building with our suspect in tow, we found the back door to the unmarked car wide open. The prisoner was nowhere to be found. Paterson Police, Sheriff's Officers and Prosecutors' Office Detectives all converged to assist in the search for our fugacious prisoner. It's still unknown who got him out of that car (Note: There are no handles on our rear door's interior).

Many area residents could be found hanging around outside throughout the neighborhood, affording us many witnesses to this handcuffed male's whereabouts. Someone, surely *someone*, saw where he ran to or was hiding. Of course, no one said a word. Some were purposely protecting him, while others were fearful of snitching. I felt bad for two women who were sitting on a porch in a location where they had to have seen him. When I asked for information, they didn't say a word. I even asked if they could motion with their eyes the direction he ran. All I got was a blank stare.

A Paterson police officer, working a black and white, found the guy lying in some high weeds near an abandoned property and turned him over to us. The detective charged with watching him was clearly relieved.

Had this incident happened in Clifton, the switchboard at headquarters would have lit up like Christmas; shame on us as a people, to allow, our once-great cities, to deteriorate so rapidly. These abject neighborhoods look more like third-world countries than once proud America. They all fall here in New Jersey, as well as the rest of the Nation, one at a time. Newark was once a beautiful city, as was Paterson, or Silk City, as it was known. Sure enough, Clifton will be next, if we don't stand up to drug dealers, gangs and feckless, head in the sand, politicians.

Guns are everywhere in our large cities. Cops are constantly caught in the crossfire, as are innocent bystanders. Cops don't wake up every morning thinking, *I wonder who I could kill today.* But there are gang members who do. Cops have to make split second decisions in a world gone crazy as their detractors lie in wait. The media shouts, "Why did he fire?" while the family at a cop's funeral asks, "Why didn't he fire?" Cops today are more concerned about public lynching of officers, rather than the violent adversaries they confront.

If men, like Al Sharpton and Jesse Jackson, would concentrate more on saving the lives of inner city youth from each other, instead of seeking headlines going after cops who made a mistake, maybe we would finally see some results. With their national notoriety they could start with the countries five most violent cities, or should I say war zones. These would be St. Louis, Camden (New Jersey) Detroit and Flint (Michigan) and Oakland (California). Maybe it wouldn't kill them to listen to men like Bill Cosby, J.C. Watts or Alan West, for real solutions to the problem.

Police officers in our major cities take guns off of suspects at an alarming rate. If cops really wanted to shoot anyone, don't you think half of these guys would've been shot? Most police officers in America are good family men who want to go home to their wife and kids. But many in the media looking for ratings, at our expense, give credence to many charlatans and their stories of police conspiracies. No doubt, we have a few bad cops in America, but it's minor with the vetting process that we all go through to get on the job.

Good folks in our major cities are scared to death of the gangs and drug dealers in their midst. Sympathizers of these miscreants need to wake up and smell the coffee. Lawlessness has become the "norm" as gangs roam the streets in our urban areas. Committing crime alone isn't enough anymore as they play "Knock-out King" when they're really bored.

For those of you not familiar with the Knock-out King "game", I'll bring you up to speed. Gangs roam the city streets looking for a victim. It could be anyone vulnerable; older folks or the homeless usually being good targets. In most cases, it's someone who likely is unable to fight back. The group chooses a lead attacker who walks up to the victim and out of nowhere, starts to pummel him. If the victim goes right down, the lead attacker can punch and kick the victim into submission as he is left to bleed. If the victim puts up a fight, then the rest of the gang jumps in to ensure victory for the lead attacker. These attacks have been reported in New Jersey, Massachusetts, Chicago and St. Louis. Many victims have been hospitalized from this brutal act and at least one death has occurred as of this writing.

Speaking of Chicago; in March 2012, over St. Patrick's Day weekend, 49 people were shot on the city's Southside. You read that right; 49 in one weekend. Ten of which died, including a six year old little girl. Where was Al "Tawana Brawley" Sharpton after this fiasco? He certainly flew down to Florida fast enough a week or so later, to protest the killing of a 17 year old. While that teenager's death was tragic; do we know why he would protest the death of one in Florida, and not the death of ten in Chicago? The answer is simple; there were many more cameras rolling in Florida. Even in our small city of Paterson (pop. 150,000) here in NJ saw over 100 people shot in 2011. At least they have a real Reverend, like Allan Boyer from the Bethel African Methodist Episcopal Church, who collaborates with the Paterson Police through "Cease-Fire". Cease-Fire is a partnership between activists and police to end, or at least curtail these shootings.

Good folks living in that Chicago neighborhood, should demand, that the police go after these gangs like the marines go after al-Qaeda. If the community doesn't trust white cops to crack down in that area, then make up a squad of African American officers to do the job; but do something already! Residents have to take a stand and call the "tip lines" that are set up and support "stop and frisk". If the police suspect that many street thugs carry guns, check them out already. We can't be worried about hurt feelings when our children are being slaughtered. Yes, I understand that we'll be giving up some of our freedoms, but when you live in a "war zone" like this poor little six year old, all bets are off.

There are 244 known gangs operating in New Jersey, with the Bloods, Crips and Latin Kings boasting the most members. Approximately 1,575 sets roam the streets at night causing law abiding citizens to wonder if they'll be the next victim of a violent crime. In 2010, New Jersey recorded 364 homicides with Newark coming in with 85 alone. In 2011, Newark saw 91. Can you imagine how many people got shot, and lived?

Community activist cry that the prison population in 2008 had reached an astounding 1.5 million inmates. Truth be told, this is the only positive statistic to report. As high as crime is today, and still totally unacceptable, crime has actually fallen over the last 20 years. You want to know why? Because 1.5 million felons were not at liberty to break into your house, jump you in a parking lot or steal your car when you leave it running outside the coffee shop.

The "Pew center" stats of 1.5 million people incarcerated cost the taxpayers billions; but could you imagine the cost if we let them out? Homicides, rapes, violent crime and property damage would go through the roof. You know what I say? Build more prisons. When we lock them up, the police that is, keep them for a while. You'll never know how many potential victims you saved. With tougher sentencing and "Three Strikes" laws being enacted, we've even seen homicide rates decrease, from 9.8 per 100,000 residents in 1991, to 4.8 in 2010. (Note: Police officer deaths are on the rise, however.)

California's broke! So some rocket scientist out there announced recently that they needed to release a flood of prisoners to make ends meet. They feel that they can't afford to keep them. Truth be told, they can't afford to let them go. So again the politicians who we elect to make the right decisions, and to keep our families safe, sell us out.

In 2011, according to the National Law Enforcement Officers Memorial Fund, 177 police officers lost their lives battling crime in

America. This is just another statistic, for those who don't feel the pain of a loved one lost. Hey, cops are vilified today, accused of making too much money, while dealing with the worst our society has to offer on a diurnal basis. Cops aren't called upon to enjoy pleasantries with socialites. If you're calling a cop, there's a real problem, which usually includes a drunk, a drug addict, a criminal or any combination of these.

And the more we let the media and activists go after cops, the less work you're going to get out of them. Why do your job, if you're going to be hammered in the press?

Remember the Navy SEAL who was brought up on charges because he punched a terrorist in the stomach? You gotta be shittin me! We want these guys to be Rambo one minute, then Mr. Rodgers the next! And this goes for the cops as well!

No wonder our cities are under siege! No one has any balls to do anything about it! For every cop who is charged with some BS excessive force complaint, there are 100 more who lie down and say; I'm not getting involved, as a result. And if the cops don't want to get involved, who will?

One time, my son, Ryan, who wants to become a police officer, heard me talking about police morale going way down. He asked me why I thought it was so important that morale remained high. I explained that we give a cop a set of car keys and tell him to go out on patrol for 8-12 hours. There is little supervision as each officer decides how much he wants to work on any given night. All cops, respond to a radio call or assignment, but what about the times when there are no calls in their sector? This goes for walking, "beat" cops, as well. If we don't encourage our officers to be proactive and look for violators, and we let the media beat them up, when they do, we're done! Every time a major city puts out a specialized street crime unit, they eventually get "hammered" in the press, for being too heavy handed. And you don't think that the criminals are too heavy handed? What's your follow up act going to be? Stick up for al Qaeda?

As a result, supervisors sometimes want their men to do the bare minimum, just to avoid a shellacking in the press. Shame on them! As a lieutenant, if I never got a complaint against one of my men, it probably meant that he wasn't working!

As a rookie in the late 70's, I remember an old timer who was working dispatch. He used to read the paper and smoke cigars as he manned his post. A young officer and friend of mine who was in police headquarters told me a story of when I was working Car #1. I spotted a suspicious looking car in the Botany section of Clifton.

"Car 1 to headquarters," I said, as I followed the vehicle.

"Come in Car 1," said the cigar-smoking burn-out.

"Headquarters, run 123-ABC NJ plates for stolen."

"K, (Okay) Car 1," he answered. Without even attempting to run the plate, this poor excuse for a cop, turned the page to his newspaper. After about 60 seconds, he said, "Car 1, come in."

"Car 1," I said with anticipation.

"Computer's down Car 1."

That was the bullshit we had to put up with back then. Finally, those old dinosaurs retired and things got much better.

But today, some departments are going back to those days, as their bosses fear litigation. Do me and your department a favor. If you're old and can't, or won't lead, then get the hell out of the way and retire already. I've seen too many burn-outs in my time, who take up space, preventing younger officers an opportunity to move up, just so they can continue wearing their uniform. And, if you're afraid of the press, then you're really in the wrong line of work.

These internal problems are mild compared with the external ones we face as a society.

Our culture is in the gutter. Our teens use words like "bitches and ho's," while emulating rap artists, some of which are dead or recovering from bullet wounds. We make celebrities out of a bunch of losers at the Jersey shore. When I travel overseas, friends of mine can't believe some of the stuff coming out of Hollywood. We want autographs from people that can't stay out of rehab.

Why don't we admire strength, courage and people of integrity? (This would probably leave out a lot of politicians). Altruistic people from all walks of society, who help others every single day, are nobody. Better to admire a recovering Hollywood alcoholic, drug addict or the winner of The Biggest Loser. I'd rather admire people who don't smoke, over-drink, take drugs, or binge until they're 400 pounds.

It's time to teach strength and accountability? Now there's a novel idea! Looking for a free ride is just a ride to failure. A toddler who takes his first step becomes proud of himself after his parents make a big deal of it. He then seeks more attention and praise as he grows, becoming more independent and proud of himself. Something soon goes wrong in many kids' lives, however, as they follow the bad habits of poor role models around them. Making matters worse, if someone constantly tells a child that he or she will be a loser when they grow up, they, many times, will become just that.

道

One time I stopped a car for a motor vehicle violation. The driver, a black male, was asked to exit the vehicle because he was lacking documents that I asked to see. I engaged him in conversation as he seemed to be a likeable guy. He displayed a positive attitude and a sense of humor.

As he was fumbling with his wallet, I could see a picture of a little boy. I asked, "Who's the cute kid?"

"Yo Yo," he replied, "das my little nigga!"

"What did you just say?" I exclaimed

"Das my nigga!"

I decided at this point that he needed a little talking to. I raised my voice a little and said, "I don't want you to EVER, call that cute little boy your *nigga* again." Don't you realize that you're putting your son at an extreme disadvantage calling him that unacceptable slang word? And don't give me that crap that you're saying 'nigga' instead of 'nigger' so that makes it okay. You are, I see it in your face, apparently very proud of your son. I'm sure that you want nothing but success for him. But you have to start him off on the right foot. By calling him that awful name, you're telling him that he's less than what he actually is. From now on," I continued, "I want you to tell him, as much as possible, that he is going to be someone special when he grows up. Tell him always, that nothing can ever stop him from succeeding if he puts his mind to it. And most of all, tell him to stay away from negative people, that don't have his best interests in mind."

By the time I finished my little lecture, this guy was thanking me and said that he never gave it much thought. That word was, and is, engrained in our culture. It's used just as much as "bitches" and "ho's." When I was young, we would never call a pretty young girl, either of those names. We had too much respect for them. This crap has been going around for so long now, that it's accepted behavior in certain circles.

Many young people today demand respect, yet give little in return to those around them. You read in the newspaper of widespread violence in the inner city, with black-on-black violence off the charts. How often we learn, in the police world, that someone got shot only because they disrespected someone. Did you get that?! Some young person, who had their entire life still in front of them, got killed, because they "dissed" someone.

These hoodlums are, in most cases, too far gone and set in their ways to reform. But the young one's not yet poisoned by gangs and drug dealers, can be taught to respect themselves, while also respecting others. All children, regardless of economic class or condition, need to hear encouragement from a very early age. Magic Johnson was right when he said, "All kids need a little help, a little hope and someone who believes in them."

We need a grass roots movement, especially in the black community, to abolish that kind of language. Maybe some well-respected celebrities like Jay Z, Beyoncé, Usher and Will Smith could push a movement like this. Why don't African American sports icons get involved to get people in the inner cities to show respect toward one another? We, as a nation, should abolish the "N" word, and all other abject jargon that continues to hold people down; no matter who says it! And NO ONE! Should be afraid to talk about and tackle these issues!

Another thing I'd like to see, although I'll probably never see it in my time, is the elimination of race divisions. Wouldn't it be nice if African Americans could one day just be Americans? When I competed in karate competitions overseas, we weren't divided. We were all Americans. If you're a cop of any race and you're getting shot at, you don't care what color or race the cop is that comes to your aid. Our troops overseas fight as Americans, not European, African, or Hispanic-Americans. I was part of a multi-racial narcotics squad in Paterson that worked extremely well together.

But if many of us in society see everything as black and white, instead of good and bad or right and wrong, we'll never climb up together out of this morass. We as individuals need to admit to our own shortcomings and encourage personal responsibility for our actions. Listen to what Michael used to say about the man in the mirror.

BTW, one side note to police officers. Stop describing black suspects as African American. Black folks come from more than one continent other than just Africa. Someone is African American when they tell you they are, or when you have prior knowledge of the fact. Stop saying, I've seen it done, that an African American just robbed the bank. You wouldn't say an Italian American, or a European American just robbed the bank. We all say; a white guy! So please, stop falling all over yourselves trying to be politically correct.

There is no more honorable calling than that of our modern day warriors of all races. The concept of good over evil, must never be darkened, must never become gray and must never be tainted. We should measure what is in a man's, or woman's heart, when they sacrifice themselves to protect our citizens and not allow political correctness to interfere. The nobility and character of the police officer should be a paramount concern when vetting them. The willingness to take risks, yet consider the ramifications while protecting others, is a desirable trait that should be encouraged and even lauded.

Our true warriors, SEALs, Rangers, Marines, SWAT members in our urban areas, and even the righteous lone wolf cop, think not of their own safety, or how much is in their paycheck. It is the pride they feel from doing a job that most people could never dream of doing. People in the United States cry that too many lives are lost in Iraq and Afghanistan, yet people forget that we have a volunteer military. Men volunteer to be police officers and SWAT members, as well. The real "warrior" (i.e. Special Forces) wants no sympathy while lying in his coffin. It is the life, and death, that he chose. Rambo said it best, "Better to die for something, than live for nothing!" This, of course, is a difficult concept for most people.

One of the worst things for a member of our Special Forces is, to never see battle. The years of training, the absolute torture that these warriors endure and even embrace; the family lives and loved ones missed; the solitude. These men are indeed special and should be held in highest esteem.

America--- such a violent nation. Our "60's Hippie" generation became its college professors and politicians. These "Baby Boomers" were going to teach "tolerance," or is it weakness; as our society and culture continues to crumble. Many ex-military men became our police and fireman, and know much, about strength and self-reliance.

It was never the intention of this book to become overly political, but we MUST STOP encouraging weakness. Stop telling people that are drunks and drug addicts, that it's not their fault. Sorry to break the news to you; it IS their fault. What if tomorrow we no longer had strong men and women volunteering to do the right thing, day-after-day, while holding the line against anarchy?

In closing, America will always need their modern day warriors. For this book I'd like to stay on point and speak of our officers in blue, who spend upward of a quarter of a century or more, putting their lives on the line to protect us all. The optimistic rookie needs only encouragement while dealing with the worst our society has to offer. We need to give our police whether local, state, or federal, the tools and support they need to fight the good fight. Let us together, keep them strong and committed for years to come! Samurai - one who serves; Police - to serve and protect.

Watch *their* hands, watch *your* back
And go home at the end of your tour.

Lieutenant Pat Ciser (Ret.)
City of Clifton, NJ PD

THE STATE OF BUDO (MARTIAL ARTS) TODAY

Martial arts in America today are so much different than in the 70's. Back then, it was Bruce Lee movies and the <u>Kung Fu</u> series on network television. Today, of course, everyone wants mixed martial arts.

If you studied any of the "original" four systems of Shotokan, Goju-Ryu, Wado Ryu, or Shito- Ryu you also engaged in basic Judo, Jiu-Jitsu and Aikido. In Koeikan, which also came from Shuri-te and Naha-te, we always did a lot of Aiki-Jitsu. Today, however, it's all about Brazilian or "Gracie" Jiu-Jitsu (original spelling). Over the decades, I've seen the flavor of the day change like the direction of the wind. In the 70's, many of the eclectic systems with no ties to Japan or the orient in general, changed their systems for marketing purposes. I say, shame on them for selling themselves out. Many local karate schools would suddenly hang out signs advertising, that they are "magically" kung fu masters, after David Carradine's show became so popular. Franchise schools come and go like "Jerome Mackeys." These "McDonald's" type operations, including today's Tiger schools, couldn't perform a traditional kata (form) to Japan's standards if their lives depended on it. Once you put the almighty dollar before your morals and convictions, you get lost.

About 15 years ago, a friend of mine from an Okinawan system used to criticize Tae Kwon Do schools. He used to call them "Take My Dough" schools for their numerous colored belts and promotion fees. We also laughed about their eight-year-old black belts. But sadly, today, his dojo and Sensei do all the things that used to make us laugh back then.

Karate-Do (The Way of the Empty Hand) should always be about character building and self-defense; it shouldn't be a race to the top! In Koeikan, we have a saying, "Koeikan, more than just fighting, but never less." We, Koeikan in America, would like to think that for every tough guy we've trained, like Liddell, Spearing, Beccera, Skawinski or Colo and every technician we developed like Sabat, Mason, Hernandez or Lopez, to name a few, we've trained hundreds to be men and women of good character and integrity. We also do not believe our system to be superior to others. We do believe in exceptional individuals however. Men like Chuck Norris and Joe Lewis, for instance, would have been world champions regardless, of the karate –do system they studied. (Note: Norris – Tang So Do)

In staying true to our roots, as Sensei(s) Kaloudis and Frost taught us, would be the key to our survival. My ties with Kancho Sensei Onishi in Machida City, Japan, are as strong today as they were 40 years ago by those who came before me. How many karate studios today hang out signs, just like the Kung Fu signs years ago, advertising that they now teach Brazilian, or Gracie Jiu-Jitsu? Most of these guys never even met a member of the esteemed Gracie family.

Mixed martial arts, you know, UFC (Ultimate Fighting Championships) type training should be left for the big boys, or tough guys. Personally, I like it, but was born too early. I think kids today should follow a route similar to Chuck Liddell. Mr. Liddell began Koeikan Karate-Do training at age 12. He would rise through the ranks to Shodan, first degree black belt, and become our best full-contact Bogu fighter.

When you start out in the martial arts, you should begin with a good foundation. When learning about balance you should also encompass learning about balancing your life and priorities. Learning to give respect is even more important than getting respect. Concepts like earning respect, rather than demanding it, also have merit.

Battling and defeating your inner fears, or "demons," including your insecurities, must be accomplished before you can defeat others. Teach kids to keep a cool head and a warm heart.

Most black belt instructors in a traditional dojo, teach values and ethics to kids who might not otherwise be exposed to these valuable concepts. Single mothers should absolutely take advantage of disciplined martial arts for their sons, if there rarely is a male role model around. Daughters can also of course benefit, from the study of a traditional system.

I'm not a fan of schools that take three- or four-year-olds. I could never do it. This is only a high-priced babysitting service. My own kids had to be six to get on the floor at my dojo; although I have, on occasion, taken some five year olds that seemed mature enough. Let babies be babies I say. Get them into kindergarten to learn some social skills and shake their nerves off first. Some little ones get hurt or frightened early on and quit. Unfortunately many times, they never return, doing an injustice to themselves. Had these kid's parents only waited until they were ready, both physically and mentally, they might have become decent black belts one day.

Speaking of black belts, what's up with all of these eight- and nine-year-old black belts? If your father can still put you over his knee and give you a spanking, I'm sorry, but you're not a black belt. Even the term "Shodan" translates, first man! Why do instructors lie to these kids? I can see it now, some sheltered kid from the suburbs, with his "controlled environment" black belt, gets jumped and pummeled by a street-wise city kid. The youngster later cries to his parents and asks what happened, as he believed he was a black belt! "We're sorry son," reply the well-meaning parents, "You're not *really* a black belt; only within the walls of your karate school, where they protect you like we do." When you can fight the men and hold your own, then you can be a "first man." Giving out rank too quickly only feeds the ego and causes students to want more, creating a never ending cycle.

We have a saying in Koeikan, "Shut up and sweat!" Don't be overly concerned about the color belt around your waist. And if you're a black belt, don't worry about your degree. Most people can't tell the difference between a 3rd, 4th or 5th dan anyway. If you ever get jumped, the assailant doesn't care what number black belt you received at your last promotion. In UFC competition, your opponent doesn't give a rat's ass about what degree you possess. People who rise to the top too fast are often only kidding themselves.

I used to tell my Sensei, Brian Frost, that I had no interest in my last couple of promotions. He insisted, however, that I need the appropriate rank to have a voice in National Koeikan affairs. As of this writing, I am celebrating my 40-year anniversary studying Koeikan (Co-A-Con) Karate-Do and hold the rank of roku dan, 6th degree black belt. In my system, as well as others, the 8th degree (hachi dan) is given to someone who has achieved full proficiency in their art. I could never, in good conscience, accept such a rank. In my mind with my foibles, I could never live up to such a grade. There are those people, however, who devote themselves in such a way, as to deserve this prestigious rank. This thought process holds true for me today, as I have too many things going on in my life to emerge myself completely, in the full study of my art. If the day comes when my children are all grown and I have the time to gather the knowledge that I need, I could one day change my mind. I think not, however, as I could never master the art to the same degree as my Sensei, Brian Frost, (1953-2009). The man was a walking encyclopedia, on both sides of the Pacific.

Many black belts train to 5th or 6th dan, only to become complacent and satisfied with themselves. They no longer need instruction, as they feel no need or desire to accumulate additional knowledge. Some will elevate themselves through some fictitious organization comprised of, like-minded, narcissistic individuals. Then even worse, they ordain themselves "god," or, 10th degree black belt.

道

The JKA (Japan Karate Association) examination guide written by, Hidetake Nishiyama, begins with this paragraph:

"The martial art of karate-do has no limitations to offer its practitioners. Karate-do is the unlimited development of the individual's physical and mental powers. Each day presents a new opportunity to improve over the day before. Indeed, the training of karate-do can be likened to a staircase that has no end. Every step brings one closer to the goal. But the ultimate goal is very high. The true karateka (student) counts each step as a substantive measure of his progress. These measures are referred to as ranking levels. Each individual will find himself at his own particular level of training achievement. Some will be higher than others. And yet, it is all relative, for the final goal cannot be reduced to the mere attainment of one level. The objective is rather to progress, to advance, and to achieve in the context of continual training and seeing of karate-do."

Much of this mindset has been lost, as we delve deeper into sport karate and western weakness. Americans are not a patient people, as we constantly strive to outdo one another with a title, or rank.

The concept of self-improvement should have no limits, as our thoughts mature with our aging bodies. This ensures wisdom over foolhardiness.

As we age, we can no longer kick as high, punch as hard, or move with the same speed as we once did. So it is only right then to achieve up to Go dan, (5th degree black belt) through physical training, while seeking perfection in our technique. Roku dan (6th degree) and higher, can be accomplished through altruism and the continued propagation of your art. Give to your students all that was given to you and more.

Turning out dozens of qualified black belts to continue the journey and even branch out to start up new dojo (schools) on their own, can only be a feather, so to speak, in their Sensei(s) cap.

How many hundreds of kids, or even over a thousand, in a forty or fifty year span does the Sensei/Shihan guide through the years? Many of us get handwritten missives from appreciative moms about how we've influenced their child to do his or her best!

My Clifton dojo has been in existence since Sensei Kaloudis opened the doors in 1965. We have parents and even grandparents, who trained with us years ago bringing in their youngsters. Many instructors, I'm sure, can attest to this.

Roy White, of the New York Yankees, trained with us in the 70's, only to encourage Willy Randolph (Yankees/Mets manager) to train with us in the 80's. These were both fine athletes and gentlemen, by the way, and we were honored to have them both.

道

Getting back to Sensei Nishiyama and the JKA examination guide, let me point out the following excerpt.

"In order to test for second degree black belt, one should train for a minimum of two years after grading to first. Three additional years of study should precede grading to third degree, followed by four more years for fourth degree and five more after that for fifth degree." This suggestion, to Karate-Do practitioners, continues this progression all the way up to 10th dan. The guide also suggests a minimum age of 40 for 7th dan, 50 for 8th dan, 60 for 9th dan and 70 for 10th. (Meijin)

My guide was written decades ago and is, no doubt, followed anymore by few. My point is that high grades should be reserved for the most senior men of good character rather than the brash youngster under 40. Young people, including myself years ago, sometimes find it difficult to leave their egos at the door.

If your karate training is still about you, you are not ready to be referred to as Kyoshi. (A title generally equated with 6th or 7th Dan).

I'm certain there are many systems that exist today that do not follow this philosophy or protocol. I condescendingly smile at the 18-year-old 4th degree black belt, who says he's been training, a whole eight years. Or the 8th degree black belt at a Tai Kai (tournament) who is not known to anyone. Where'd *he* come from? How about the Korean who must have gotten promoted on the flight from Seoul to JFK? Some are 3rd degree black belts when they depart, but arrive in New York as a 6th dan. Some guys don't even have to train anymore, yet come around tournaments and promotions wearing their black belts, to prove to themselves that they are still relevant.

Anyone reading this, that is interested in training, or has a child interested in training. Be sure to scrutinize your local martial arts schools and watch a couple of classes before jumping in. If they don't let you watch, walk out! Good instructors have nothing to hide. I don't believe in "black belt" programs either. I have no idea if you have what it takes!

道

Now, a note to police officers; I like mixed martial arts, I like Jiu-Jitsu. However, there are problems for cops who go to the ground. Police officers are not supposed to be rolling around with someone. Suspects should go over the hood, against the wall, or lie on the ground to be cuffed. If you take someone down on the tatami (mat), you're fine. If you go down to the pavement or concrete with someone, you have a problem. Not only can you damage your uniform, leather and firearm, but also your elbows, knees and shoulders. Falling on a mace canister or ASP (retractable baton) can really be a problem, especially if the mace sprays on contact.

I know several police officers who took up MMA type fighting only to give it up as the injuries mounted. I recall one story from a local night club. Not being there, I can't swear to its veracity. But whether it happened just like this or not, doesn't take away from the lesson learned.

A local bouncer was a Jiu-Jitsu player, who took a loud mouth in a bar, down to the ground. His technique was good as he had this trouble maker all locked up. Unfortunately, for the bouncer, the loud mouth had a friend, who easily kicked the bouncer in the head. Now don't get me wrong, shit happens all the time, as fights are many times violent and unpredictable. I just feel that when you're on the ground, arms tied up, you leave yourself in a very vulnerable position. Personally, I'd rather stand and fight.

Jiu-Jitsu using gyaku-te techniques, such as arm locks and choke (strangulation) holds, are very effective in addition to Karate-Jitsu techniques. Foot sweeps, as I mentioned in other chapters, work particularly well. Just remember, keep it simple. Every new adversary didn't see what you did to the last guy, so do it again!

What bothers me about some police academies is the fact that some instructors teach like they're trying to prove themselves every day. Some try to impress recruits with things that they'll never be able to do, unless they train for five years first. Instructors must realize that most of their recruits are "white belts," or tyros, with no balance. I heard a story of a guy once who showed some recruits how he could take the slide off of a perpetrators pistol. Are you kiddin' me? That's tough enough in a "controlled" environment; can you imagine trying to pull that stunt on a desperate criminal? Even if he could pull it off, does he expect a white belt to do it? Was this show off trying to get these guys killed? Keep it basic, and maybe the rookie cop will actually learn something he can use, and, live to tell about it.

道

Years ago, Clifton's Chief Frank Lo Gioco, sent me to PR-24 school. It was a two day course for advanced officers who wanted to become instructors. The PR-24, also known by martial artists as a tonfa, was starting to replace the basic baton. The first day I arrived, I realized that I could do more things with the instrument than the instructor could. For anyone still in the dark as to what a PR-24 looks like, I'll describe it. Imagine a police baton or nightstick, with a six inch piece of wood coming out of the side, about a quarter of the way up the cylinder. It could be an excellent tool for blocking and jabbing. It was flawed, in my opinion, for serious striking (like riots). The reason was that you held it by the handle that jetted out, leaving you with a poor grip. If you had to strike hard, the handle could and usually would, slip inside your hand on impact. Even the "come-a-longs" were complicated, as students had to give too much thought, as to how to wrench someone's arm behind their back with it. There's no time for analytical thoughts when subduing someone, keep it simple. Even guys who performed fairly well in class undoubtedly lost most of their skills six months out.

When the course was over, I went back to my chief and thanked him for sending me and gave him my evaluation. I said, "Chief, the PR-24 would be a good weapon if you let me get a saw and cut off that stupid handle. Then, you'll have a really efficient night stick that gets the job done."

Someone, somewhere, encouraged politicians and law enforcement groups to support this new, modern nightstick in order to make a lot of money. They "sold" a new idea, making millions in the process. Wouldn't you know that we switched back to the (retractable) baton or ASP, proving, that you can't fool all of the people, all of the time.

While I'm still up on my soap box, let's look at the other side of training, preparing for that violent attack. As you've probably realized by now, I've never been just a kata and ippon kumite (point sparring) kind of guy. I'm battle tested after 30 years, in bars, and on the street. Let me tell you one overlooked area of training in many traditional styles of Budo. Punishment! If you're training like they do in some areas of Japan, for the cultural aspect of the art only, then there is no need to read the next few pages. (Japan has very little crime, so they may never need their training for self-defense).

Black belts sometimes get into street battles that are extremely violent; so violent in fact that they sometimes lose. They don't lose because they don't know how to fight. They lose because there is no fight inside of them. Have you ever heard the saying, "It is not the size of the dog in the fight, it's the size of the fight in the dog"? If you don't fight full-contact, if you don't have other seito (students) strike you during sanchin (deep breathing exercises), or other drills, you're only getting half of the training. Developing toughness of both mind and body should be a paramount concern when preparing for battle. I even make my sniffling kids say after they get hit, "That hurt! But it didn't hurt that bad."

Then I say, "Now get back in there."

One time, I slapped a loud mouth in a neighborhood bar when I was off-duty. The slap, mind you, was a heavy hand across the left side of his head. I'm sure that it had a nice "sting" to it. He went down on one knee as this one technique, designed to not cause serious injury, took all the fight out of him. His mouth was prepared for battle but his heart was not!

Have someone punch you in the abdominal region with each sit up, kick you while in the up position of your push-ups and use medicine ball training and punch the makiwara (striking post) until your knuckles bleed. Put your mind into your training until you convince yourself that you are invincible! Do not lie back too long when sizing up your opponent. Train, train, train; this is the only way to achieve success. Good luck Bushi, (Warrior) may all of your battles be brief.

"Each day is the journey, and the journey itself is home."

Basho Matsuo (1689)

TIPS ON SELF DEFENSE

This final chapter will address self-defense tactics that are basic yet effective, when done properly. My motto is "keep it simple." And again, as I mentioned in previous chapters, each adversary is different. You can use the simplest techniques again and again, perfecting them as you go along.

One caveat, however, is to remember what Dirty Harry (Clint Eastwood) said, "A man's gotta know his limitations." Unless you train for years, you may not feel comfortable taking a knife or a gun off an assailant. In many cases, you may have to stun, mace, or even shoot someone to survive. Make sure that you go home to your loved ones at the end of your shift, or if you're not a cop, at the end of your day.

The most important advice to remember is, never, never, never give up. If you read the newspapers and see that there were numerous homicides one year, do you also know how many people got shot or stabbed, yet lived to tell about it? If you do get shot, and you aren't dead, get the hell up and fight back. Like Jesse Ventura said in Predator, "I don't have time to bleed!" One media personality, I have truly come to admire, is Curtis Sliwa, of the Guardian Angels. Here's a guy that was viciously attacked, shot several times, dove out of a moving cab and lived to tell about it! What courage. What determination.

There is a saying in Japan, "Nana Karobi Ya Okii (Seven times down, eight times up, or, never give up)." Sometimes, people get a flesh wound and curl up, feeling sorry for themselves. I call this "the fallen baby syndrome." Let's say that a toddler falls down. If you turn quickly and gasp, while making a big deal about it, the kid starts to cry. They sense from your actions that they must be hurt and know they can get some sympathy. But if you make light of it, and tell them to get back-up, many times they will, while not shedding a tear.

Here's another tip. If you go to the firing range and shoot still targets, you'll immediately realize that it's not all that hard to do. Have you ever fired at moving targets? Pretty big difference, huh? If you're getting shot at, keep moving, dive for cover. I, like most cops, like to face the door when I'm eating in a diner or restaurant. Many times, I survey the place as I wait for the waiting staff. Maybe I'm a little nutty, or just like to play it safe. I wonder, where can I dive to as I reach for my 9mm; if someone comes in to do a robbery? If I can't draw fast enough, can I throw this table over? Is there a bottle of ketchup or other item on the table I could use to buy a second or two? Remember, a gun in your holster is worthless, if someone gets the drop on you!

I remember once there was a Paterson cop in a bank on Crooks Avenue, on the Clifton boarder, who was off duty. When a robber announced a "stick up," the Paterson cop put his gun in the guy's ribs, stopping him cold in his tracks. Always be prepared.

Many martial arts schools practice techniques that they'll never use effectively on the street. I especially like guys that can kick a knife out of someone's hand. Listen carefully; many assailants are extremely dangerous. To be successful, you need to control the knife or gun. Some self-defense is fine for Hollywood; but if you get shot or stabbed, a director doesn't yell, "Cut!"

If you don't carry a gun, always be cognizant of potential weapons around you. Females especially should use keys protruding from between their fingers when making a fist. A pen hidden in your hand is perfect for stabbing motions to the face and eyes. An umbrella, also for stabbing, a picture on a wall, a vase or any other available object, might be just what you need to buy a little time.

Conditioning is also very important when deciding if you're up for a battle. Fighting someone, tooth and nail, can be exhausting, and lead to defeat, if you are terribly out of shape.

Some black belts train for a good part of their lives, yet were never in even one street, or bar fight, in order to test themselves. Rocky (Stallone) said, "Things get rough in the ring." While I can attest to that statement, things get even rougher on the street! I can tell you this! If a dojo technique looks weak and flashy, it is probably weak and useless.

Always remember, attack the attack! Don't step back; step in. You can't head butt or use other strikes and sweeps if you back-up. If someone pulls a gun, it's often better to attack. If you can maintain a short burst of violence the assailant may never get the chance to fire his weapon. If you retreat, he can empty the gun into you in seconds. Also remember, wounded isn't dead. Also, many street thugs glean much of their perceived power, through their gun. If you can knock it down, or away, they momentarily feel the need to retrieve it. This causes them to drop their guard, if only for a second; and that my friend, is when you get a good shot (punch) at their face. Stun them once, then hit again, and again, and again. Be relentless and create the most violent assault, you are capable of.

When confronted with a gun, also consider who is holding it. A teenager, who doesn't consider the ramifications of taking a life, can be more dangerous than an older felon who comes with a brain. Teenagers today in our urban area's pop off rounds like it's a video game. Most have little or no experience shooting, as they have limited ammunition to practice. Recent studies also show that holding a handgun sideways is the least accurate way to shoot. (Duh! Big surprise there) Poor aim is sometimes good for the targeted individual, but bad for innocent bystanders.

If someone is holding a gun on you, and you feel confident that you can disarm them, then go for it. If someone is aiming at your wife or kids, you might want to give him your money and jewelry.

Each situation is different, as you'll need to weigh all options. If an attacker is going to do something to your wife or daughter, and it would be difficult, if not impossible, for all of you to live with that memory, then you need to take action.

Knives are different. What would you rather have in a fight, a knife or a club? I'll take the club and beat you senseless with it. You have a better reach with the club, and can create an extremely violent attack, if you're motivated.

You might also be able to outrun the assailant and his knife as an option. Use anything available to fight back. Years ago, you could snap an antenna off of a car and whip him with it, not anymore, however.

If you're in a confrontation with an unarmed adversary, I tell my students to be Italian. The joke is that many older Italian, used to talk with their hands. Keep your hands at chest height and forward while you talk. This way, you can lash out with any number of techniques while defending yourself better than if your hands were at your sides.

A quick head butt, palm heel strike to the bridge of the nose or a "Y" of the hand strike to the throat can usually set the tone early. And remember, after you "stun" your opponent, you need to follow up with a quick barrage of attacks until the threat is eliminated.

I've included some basic self-defense moves in this chapter with illustrations. It's difficult to imagine, the speed and timing of these techniques, in still pictures. Therefore, I always suggest that you seek out a qualified, no-nonsense instructor, in your area for further instruction.

I'm partial to Japanese forms of self-defense, using basic Karate and Jiu-Jitsu moves. Don't forget, Brazilian Jiu-Jitsu comes from Japan. They, like Americans, simply "tweaked" it. Good luck!

Attacker comes up behind female victim.

Female already has keys protruding out of her clenched fist.

Female punches at the eyes of her attacker.

Up close depiction of strike.

Attacker grabs defender by the neck.

Defender reaches up and slams down over attacker's arms while
rotating torso to her left.

Grabbing wrist of attacker, the defender uses an elbow smash to the face.

Defender then follows up with a rising front kick to the groin.

273

Defender slams his head into attacker's face.

Defender stomps his heel into attacker's instep.

Defender breaks hold of a weakened attacker.

Defender strikes using his elbow.

Defender hip throws attacker over right shoulder.

Follow through.

The kicker prepares for a high side kick.

As the defender (L) attempts to slip the kick while moving in, the kicker kicks downward to the hip crease.

Attacker puts defender in a "full nelson".

Defender, as quickly as possible, lifts his arms overhead, then drops out of hold.

Defender, while continuing to drop to the floor, grabs attacker's clothing while kicking him in the face.

Attacker throws overhand right.

Defender slams attacker with head butt.

Defender swings arm over the top of attacker's right arm locking same.

Defender slams attacker to the ground.

Officer (R) reaching out as quickly as possible, (technique used in Hope Avenue chapter) placing right hand over top right head and left hand to chin.

Spin head to his right. (Where the head goes, the body follows.).

To control suspect, only slow down speed at this point.

If the desired effect is to snap the neck, continue quick rotation
and slam head forward as his head faces to his right.

With speed and determination, slip both hands between the suspect's right arm. Your right hand should appear to be grabbing the bicep.

Taking a step to the right side and rear, use your right hand to grab the back of the suspect's arm, while your left hand pulls his arm up behind his back.

Grab high near the back of the collar or even higher,
grabbing the hair, locking his arm.

Assailant attempts to slash the defender.

The defender uses both hands to create a wide "butterfly", trapping the attacker's wrist.

Using a circular motion, the defender moves closer while swinging the attacker's arm up.

284

Now shoulder to shoulder with the attacker,
the defender pulls the assailant to the ground.

Defender then employs an arm lock.

Stab (thrust)

Defender moves left while trapping knife hand.
(Must be around the hand, not the wrist.)

Moving very quickly the defender steps forward while swinging the attacker's arm up and over. This aiki jutsu move causes the attacker to fall hard to his right side.

Finish or step left foot over the attacker's arm for additional arm lock/pain.

Overhead Stab

Defender uses cross block.

Defender swings attacker's arm down to his right.

Defender ducks under the attacker's arm and begins to throw the attacker.

Attacker flips over and hits the ground.

Assailant announces, "Give me your money!"

Defender knocks gun up with right
hand causing possible bullet to miss.

In the same immediate motion, the
defender slams his left arm over the
top of the assailant's right arm,
at his elbow.

Locking up the assailant's arm, the defendant slams
the assailant to the ground.

Inflicting pain.

Assailant puts gun to defender's back

Defender quickly spins into the assailant as
the gun may discharge.

Reaching under, then slams over the assailant's right arm,
the arm is further locked in place.

Defender then immediately slams the assailant to the ground.

Assailant points gun at your chest demanding money.

Quickly twist to your left grabbing the gun with your right hand.

Put your left hand on the base of the handle and rotate gun now twisting the assailant's arm over. This is done while taking a step around slightly to the assailant's right. Push up on the barrel of the gun, ripping it out of the assailant's hand.

Finish.

"In looking back over the events of my life,
I can see now,
that I began to understand the way of the warrior,
when first,
I began to feel compassion."

Miyamoto Musashi (1584-1645)

Patrick J. Ciser, a former international karate champion and three-time gold medalist, is a highly decorated retired police lieutenant for the city of Clifton, New Jersey. Ciser lives in Wayne, New Jersey, with his wife, Lisa, and their children. He continues to teach Koeikan karate at his Clifton studio.

CPSIA information can be obtained at www.ICGtesting.com
Printed in the USA
LVOW050536230612

287351LV00002B/23/P